The Czechoslovak Crisis 1968

The Czechoslovak Crisis 1968

Edited by

Robert Rhodes James

Institute for the Study of
International Organization
University of Sussex

Weidenfeld and Nicolson

5 Winsley Street London W1

© 1969 Institute for the Study of International Organization,
University of Sussex

All rights reserved. No part of this publication may be
reproduced, stored in a retrieval system, or transmitted,
in any form or by any means, electronic, mechanical,
photocopying, recording or otherwise, without the prior
permission of the copyright owner.

SBN 297 17866 0
Printed in Great Britain by Cox and Wyman Ltd,
London, Reading and Fakenham

Contents

	Preface	vii
1	The Czechoslovak Background	1
2	The Soviet Dilemma	12
3	The Role of the Warsaw Pact	31
4	NATO and the Crisis	56
5	The United Nations and the Crisis	92
6	Interpretations and Conclusions	110
	Selected Chronology, January–December 1968	127
	Appendix 1: The Warsaw Pact	161
	Appendix 2: The Warsaw Letter and the Czechoslovak Reply	168
	Appendix 3: Security Council Resolutions, 22 and 23 August	181
	Appendix 4: The Moscow Agreement, 27 August	183
	Appendix 5: Legal aspects of the Invasion of Czechoslovakia	185
	Select Bibliography	189
	Index	191

Preface

The Institute for the Study of International Organization was formally established by the University of Sussex in the summer of 1968 for the purpose of encouraging interest in, and promoting knowledge of, the work of international organizations, by means of research and the promotion of conferences, courses, and seminars. The Institute has received grants from the Rockefeller Foundation, the Carnegie Endowment for International Peace, and the Joseph Rowntree Memorial Trust; accommodation and other assistance is provided by the University of Sussex.

The particular interest of the Czechoslovak crisis to the Institute lay in the fact that three major international organizations – the Warsaw Pact, NATO and the United Nations – were closely involved. The wise observation of the late Lord Norwich (Duff Cooper) may be recalled: 'Storms produce lightning, and by those flashes in the dark we can see men, if only for a moment, as they really are.'[1] The same truth applies to nations and to organizations.

It was accordingly considered that the Institute could make a useful contribution if it undertook an analysis of the crisis and its implications for the international organizations involved. A conference was held on 14–16 October at Stanmer House, at which a number of speakers initiated a series of discussions before an invited and participating audience. The contributors included Mr Faustio Bacchetti (NATO), Colonel G. Draper

[1] Duff Cooper, *Old Men Forget* (Hart-Davis, 1953), p. 253.

THE CZECHOSLOVAK CRISIS 1968

(University of Sussex), Sir Geoffrey Harrison (former Ambassador to the Soviet Union), Dr Rosalyn Higgins (Chatham House), Brigadier Kenneth Hunt (Institute for Strategic Studies), Professor Ivo Lederer (Stanford University, California), Mr Malcolm Mackintosh, Mr D. Pesic (London correspondent of the Yugoslav periodical *Politika*), Professor Leonard Schapiro (London School of Economics), and Mr Kamil Winter (former head of current affairs, Czechoslovak Television). The decision was subsequently taken that the Institute should develop the background paper which it had prepared into a more detailed analysis of the crisis itself and its context and implications.

The events of 1968 in Czechoslovakia are so recent, and the situation remains so uncertain, that the value of such an analysis may be questioned. Certainly, no commentator on contemporary events can be unaware of the formidable difficulties and dangers involved in such an enterprise. The most obvious difficulty is the fact that his information is at best fragmentary, and even evidence that seems authentic at the time may subsequently turn out to have been spurious. Many of his conclusions, although in themselves valid, may be swiftly overtaken by the rush of events. The detailed information that the historian expects as his right and his intellectual capital is denied to the contemporary historian. Few – if any – witnesses and participants are devoid of bias to some degree, and even the most objective can have only a partial account to render. And, as often in the case of the military historian, it is often impossible to check such versions against proven facts. Even if the historian is granted access to national archives these can only present, at the best, half of the story.

Perhaps the most important peril in the writing of contemporary history lies in the fact that the historian himself is to some extent a participant. Historical objectivity becomes progressively easier with time, but although the years may soften emotions and sharpen judgements, the fact that the historian has been personally involved as a contemporary of the events he is describing hinders the cool analysis that comes from the personal and emotional detachment that a later student can provide. The task of the historian seeking the truth is always difficult; that of the contemporary historian, following swiftly on the heel of events, is incomparably more difficult.

But although these and other dangers and difficulties must be acknowledged and recognized, the commentator on contemporary events can play a significant and constructive role, even if it is limited to provoking informed discussion about current events. He has the advantage, denied to his successors, of following events from day to day as they develop and of discussing them with individuals intimately involved; although his sources of documentary information are few, documents do not always give the full story. The principal contribution that the contemporary historian can make is to draw together what facts are obtainable and to initiate the process of assessment and analysis that must be undertaken if nations and organizations are to survive. Unlike most of his contemporaries, the historian has the time and the opportunity and the independence to undertake this work. This independence, of course, carries with it further dangers. The historian is, literally, irresponsible. No decisions can stem directly from his conclusions. He is not exposed to immediate challenge in public debate. He may, as in the cases of J. M. Keynes in 1919 or Dr Kissinger in 1957, see his work quickly attain acceptance by others in positions of authority or influence, but it is the responsibility of others to seize upon or reject his interpretations, to act upon or ignore his proposals. But the example of Keynes and *The Economic Consequences of the Peace* emphasizes the harm that can be done by the independent commentator who bears no responsibility for his arguments.

Thus, when recent events of the importance and complexity of the Czechoslovak Crisis of 1968 are examined and analysed, the historian of his own times must begin by recognizing the disadvantages under which he must operate. But he must also acknowledge the fact that his work cannot be regarded merely as an academic exercise. For, as countless examples prove, the historian, the economist, or the political scientist, although in the literal sense irresponsible, may come to bear responsibility for the contribution that he makes.

THE CZECHOSLOVAK CRISIS 1968

I wish to express my warm appreciation of the most generous assistance and advice given to my colleagues and myself by many individuals and representatives of organizations whom we have consulted. I hope that they will accept this general public acknowledgement of their most valuable advice and guidance. I should particularly like to thank the principal contributors to the Institute's Conference on the crisis for the admirable papers they presented and for their generous assistance. None, of course, is in any way responsible for this study or its conclusions. And I should like to make another exception in the case of the Institute's solitary secretary, Miss Rees, who has borne the burden of the considerable secretarial work involved.

University of Sussex   Robert Rhodes James
11 February 1969

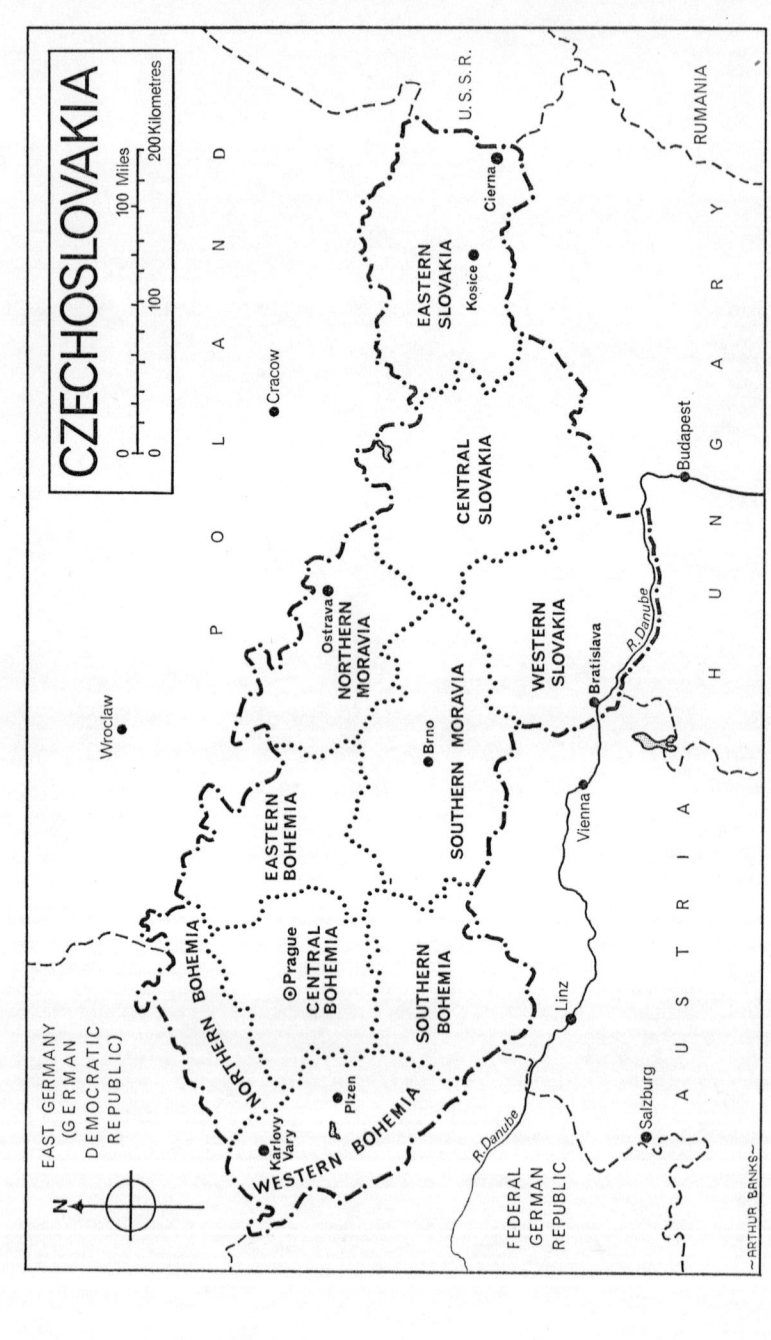

1
The Czechoslovak Background

ANY contemplation of the startling events in Czechoslovakia in the winter of 1967–8 provokes recollection of the words with which James Stephens opened his personal narrative of the Easter Rising in Dublin in April 1916: 'This has taken everyone by surprise.' The immediate beginning of the crisis in Czechoslovak–Soviet relations may be conveniently placed on 5 January 1968, at the time of the removal of Antonin Novotny from the post of First Secretary of the Czechoslovak Communist Party that he had held since September 1953, and his replacement by Alexander Dubcek, since April 1963 First Secretary of the Slovak Communist Party. But although this event may be marked as the beginning of one crisis, it also marked the end of another, which must be briefly related.

One of the most conspicuous dangers of hindsight is to discern patterns where none existed and to endeavour to describe with felicitous and impressive clarity situations which were in fact of extreme complexity. In addition, the historian is always exposed to the danger of starting with the results of events, and imparting the aura of inevitability to previous circumstances. It should accordingly be recalled at the outset that the fact of the downfall of Novotny came as a considerable surprise to most observers of the Czechoslovak scene, and should be stated that this surprise was justified.

It would be unwise to describe the crisis within Czechoslovakia between 1963 and 1967 wholly in economic terms, yet the economic element was of crucial importance in the development of the movement against the Novotny régime. Czechoslovakia has, in comparison with the countries of Eastern Europe, a developed industry on a Western pattern comparable only to that of East Germany in the communist bloc. But the imposition of centralized and detailed Party planning and control upon this system resulted in inefficient operation, the retention of out-of-date methods and machinery, and the consequent frustration among those who had the ability and experience to see these defects but had no power to introduce improvements. Czechoslovakia's position in COMECON[1] required that the main emphasis was placed upon the production of heavy engineering goods; deprived of contacts with Western technological developments and not receiving the advantages of expanding Soviet skills and experience, the standards of Czechoslovak technology remorselessly declined. Though her relatively advanced industrial base made the specialization implied by membership of COMECON less unwelcome than for other less developed members (e.g., Rumania), Czechoslovakia's contribution to COMECON was out of proportion to the advantages that she received.

The only serious attempt at economic reform was initiated in April 1958 when, copying the Polish measures of 1956–7, the Czechoslovak Government introduced several rather radical changes in industrial management. Enterprises were allotted goals for the surrender of their profits to the State for a five-year period, thereby in principle allowing them to retain the balance for their own investment. The decentralization of authority over investible funds was, however, accompanied neither by a devolution of the rationing of materials nor by any willingness of the central authorities substantially to curtail their plans for capital formation. The reforms in favour of enterprise decision-making were thus only partial, and conduced to an inflationary crisis for capital goods which was a major factor in the shortfalls towards attainment of the goals of the Five Year Plan for 1960–65, and which was the subject of a Government announcement in July 1962 abandoning the Plan. By this stage the measures of devolution had been

---

[1] See M. Kaser, *COMECON – Integration Problems of the Planned Economies* (Oxford University Press, Second Edition, 1967).

THE CZECHOSLOVAK BACKGROUND

withdrawn and the former centralized mechanism had been fully re-established.

The Report that accompanied the announcement of the abandonment of the Five Year Plan[1] and its replacement by a one-year plan for 1963, which was to be followed by a seven-year plan to cover the period from the beginning of 1964 until the end of 1970,[2] showed that underfulfilment was particularly serious in heavy engineering and capital construction, in which in some areas production had fallen in comparison with the same period in 1961. Steel and rolling material were underfulfilled, which affected in quantity and quality metallurgical supplies for the economy as a whole. (Total industrial production in 1963 was 0·4% lower than in 1962, while fixed capital investment declined by 11·4%.)[3] It was evident that the almost total failure of the 1958 economic reforms was principally the consequence of the lack of enthusiasm by the Czechoslovak Ministers, and the chances of their success had been destroyed by the deliberate limitations imposed by the central authorities. The experiment, half-heartedly undertaken and thankfully abandoned by the Government, had served to emphasize the fundamental impediment to economic expansion. It was in 1962 that the proposals of Dr Ota Sik, the Director of the Economic Institute of the Czechoslovak Academy of Sciences and a member of the Central Committee of the Communist Party, which had previously been foreshadowed in certain technical journals, first began to appear in the Czechoslovak daily press.

Central control of the economy and its self-evident inadequacies was not the only factor causing frustration and discontent. The hopes raised after Stalin's death and denunciation were muted by the reaction of older Party members to the events in Poland and Hungary in 1956. The Novotny régime was less repressive than its predecessor, and there were no repetitions of the staged Slansky and Clementis trials of the early 1950s. But Party control extended deep into cultural and social affairs, even affecting such apparently harmless organizations as anglers'

[1] *Report of the Czechoslovak Central Authority State of Control and Statistics on the Development of the Czechoslovak National Economy for the First Half of 1962* (*Rude Pravo*, 28 July 1962). See also the *Financial Times*, 23 August 1962.
[2] In fact the economy was run on a series of one-year plans from 1963 to 1965.
[3] J. F. Brown, *The New Eastern Europe* (Pall Mall Press, 1966), p. 64.

clubs.[1] The press was prevented from discussing controversial matters, and rehabilitation of the victims of the Stalinist purges was not begun even half-heartedly until 1963. The rehabilitation question, affecting as it did a number of leading Slovak figures, was bound up with Slovak national feeling and resentment at the erosion of the few remaining vestiges of Slovak autonomy during the Stalinist period. Novotny himself was identified with the failure to take account of Slovak susceptibilities, and not without cause.

It was this canalization of the various streams of discontent and frustration at the dead and interfering hand of the Party, so well typified by Novotny himself and virtually all his colleagues, that provoked the first serious stirrings of resentment and impatience with the national leadership. The first unsuccessful attempt to displace Novotny as First Secretary (he had also become President of the Republic in November 1957) occurred in 1962; another attempt was made in April 1963, at the time of the meeting of the Central Committee which approved the rehabilitation of a number of leading Czech and Slovak victims of the purges initiated at the 12th Party Congress in December 1962. Although Novotny himself survived, the gradual process of the removal of his support began,[2] although there was not, as yet, any serious challenge to the régime. This challenge developed slowly, almost surreptitiously, over the following three years. But already, early in 1963, there were indications of the latent strength of this movement. The election of Dubcek in April 1963 as First Secretary of the Slovak Party and a member of the Czechoslovak Party Praesidium, in spite of Novotny's objections,[3] was one indication. This event was of significance not only in the light of Dubcek's subsequent career.

[1] See 'Turning-Point in Czechoslovakia', *World Today*, September 1968, p. 360.
[2] It may be noted that only one member of the Czechoslovak Politburo, Alexei Cepicka, was removed in the de-Stalinization moves in 1956. Kohler and Balicek were removed in April 1963, and Siroky in September 1963.
[3] 'Slovak comrades were not completely rehabilitated and did not take up those places in political life which they had held before. . . . Later there was a political campaign against not only the partially rehabilitated but also the new leadership of the Slovak Communist Party. Before the 13th Party Congress attempts were made to replace Dubcek with Chudik. The conflict culminated with a charge of nationalism at the October plenum in 1967 against the Central Committee of the Slovak Party and Dubcek personally.' (*Pravda* (Bratislava), 14 April 1968.)

THE CZECHOSLOVAK BACKGROUND

The centralization of Czechoslovak government had been particularly resented in Slovakia, where the movement towards reform and economic autonomy had caused concern to the régime. Although the 1960 constitution establishing the Czechoslovak Socialist Republic had further diminished Slovak autonomy, the decision of the 12th Party Congress to examine the legality of the political trials in the period 1949-54 – thus including the trials of leading Slovaks, including Novomesky and Husak – had been one indication of the potential strength of Slovak resentment. Novotny's removal of Balicek as First Secretary of the Slovak Party and the subsequent election of Dubcek was the first important success achieved by the Slovaks. Throughout 1963 criticism of the régime was most apparent in Slovakia, and the Bratislava cultural weekly *Kulturny Zivot* was conspicuously outspoken. The removal of Siroky and his replacement as Prime Minister by Lenart, taken with Dubcek's election, considerably improved the positions of the Slovak Communist Party in the Czechoslovak Party's central organization. Novotny attacked the 'separatist tendencies' of Slovakia, and particularly the claim for economic autonomy, in June 1963; in the following March these claims were curtly rejected; in June 1966 Brezhnev himself visited Bratislava to give warnings of the evils of 'nationalism'. The presence of these Slovak claims and the mounting resentment in Slovakia against the central government presented, as it were, a crisis within a crisis, although it must be emphasized that, as later events demonstrated, the Slovaks wanted reform rather than secession.

The three-year period before the 13th Party Congress in June 1966 saw what was in effect a gradually developing public struggle within the Party between the conservatives and the reformers. Such general terms are always dangerous in the description of complex political events, and they become progressively less satisfactory when the roles of individuals on specific issues are closely examined; but in this case there is justification in describing the opposing groups in such terms, while at the same time recognizing that the differentiation cannot be comprehensive or precise. The development of the contest between the two groups was illustrated by the publication of proposals pointing towards decentralization and autonomy in economic management and to the reduction of the role of the Party in cultural matters.[1] In September 1963, Dr Sik published his proposals for economic reform in an article entitled 'The Remnants of Dogmatism in Political Economy must be overcome' in the party monthly *Nova Mysl*. The debate on Sik's reforms occupied a year, and it was not until October 1964 that a new programme based largely on Sik's proposals was published. In January 1965 the Central Committee approved the reforms, which were strongly criticized by the conservative elements still in control. Novotny's own equivocal attitude showed his realization of the wider political implications of introducing a comprehensive scheme of economic decentralization.[2]

These political implications were already apparent. In a speech to the 13th Party Congress in June 1966, Sik said that:

Conditions must be created in which, if somebody comes up with an idea ... that differs from the views of the top official, his initiative will not be doomed from the outset. It is not enough to say that such initiatives are allowed and that nobody can be victimized. So far, people's experience has been different, and it is experience that counts, not words.

Sik went on to say that his proposed new management system would be 'a great step forward in the democratization of our society', and he pointed to the necessity to make a deep study of 'the entire problem of democratization of relations within the Party and in the whole political and administrative sphere to prepare for genuine institutional and legislative changes'.[3] The acceptance of the Sik reforms by the 13th Party Congress marked a very substantial victory for the reformers, but the reforms themselves were not applied on a nation-wide scale until the beginning of 1967, and their application by an unenthusiastic leadership compromised their chance of success from the outset. The government had to intervene in order to deal with inflation resulting from price increases with no

[1] See the article already cited in *World Today*, September 1968, p. 361–2.
[2] See Novotny's report to the Central Committee in December 1966, when he warned against 'rush, and half thought-out conclusions and measures in the development of socialist society' (Bratislava Radio, 20 December 1966).
[3] *Rude Pravo*, 5 June 1966. For a description of the Sik reforms, see J. F. Brown, op. cit., 96–100.

THE CZECHOSLOVAK BACKGROUND

corresponding improvement in production, and wage controls were reintroduced at the Party plenum in September 1967. These events did not demonstrate the impracticability of Sik's reforms. They did demonstrate the results of the years of inefficient centralized control, and the inability of the régime to deal with a situation now so far out of control that only the most drastic measures, with which the Czechoslovak leaders had no sympathy, could suffice. The failure to go through with economic reform merely emphasized the impossibility of effective measures being taken by the Novotny régime, and this fact, linked with the effects of the further decline in the Czechoslovak economy, further undermined its position.

Although the 13th Party Congress had provided a victory for the reformers in the economic field, in others it was apparent that the Government was determined to maintain its authority. The Congress was followed by the promulgation of a new Press Law which came into force on 1 January 1967. The new law placed the press under the control of the Ministry of Education and Culture and established a Central Administration for Publications, whose function was in effect censorship. Furthermore, the directives given to the officials of the new Administration went beyond even the provisions of the Press Law itself.[1] This constituted a very real setback to the process of the increasing degree of freedom enjoyed, and utilized, by the writers since 1963, and provoked a revolt at the 4th Writers' Congress in June 1967, when a resolution was passed against censorship and interference by the Party despite the warnings and protests of the Party's chief ideologist, Hendrych.[2] The Party reaction at the September plenum was to place the Writers' Union weekly *Literarni Noviny* under the control of the Ministry of Culture and Information and to replace its editorial board by Novotny nominees. It was significant, however, that the Government got its way only after considerable opposition. An effective national boycott of the restructured journal followed these actions, and emphasized that the writers enjoyed a wide support.

Further strands in the web of disaffection were provided by

[1] See the broadcast of the Chairman of the Writers' Union, Professor Goldstücker, on Prague Radio on 21 February 1968, when he announced the rescindment of the directives and the abrogation of the Press Law.
[2] For the text of the resolution, see *Literarni Noviny*, 8 July 1967.

the resentment in lower Party organs at the excessively rigid system which entailed the reference of every decision to a higher authority, and the disillusion of the youth with the apparent failure of the bureaucracy to take any real interest in their affairs.[1]

It must be emphasized again that the seriousness of the situation for the Novotny régime lay in the universality of the disillusionment with its conduct of affairs. The dilemma facing the régime had been the classic one for all authoritarian governments operating in a country with recent experience of democratic government. Between the extremes of tight control coupled with repression on the one hand and abdication of authority on the other, there lies a vast middle ground in which the balance is delicate and difficult. The purpose is to maintain authority and control without adopting measures of restriction that could provoke a violent counter-movement. Like all principles of government, it is easy to describe the objective; the attainment is always difficult. In the context of communist concepts of government, it becomes incomparably more difficult.

It is perhaps important to stress, even at this stage, that the successors to the Novotny régime remained, at least in their own eyes, loyal to Marxist-Leninist principles and were accordingly confronted with what was in effect the same fundamental dilemma. It may also be emphasized that Novotny succeeded reasonably effectively in maintaining his position, and that there was justification for the comment of an observer in 1966 that 'Novotny now seems inclined to make concessions – albeit concessions granted from above, and at a pace that he himself sets.'[2]

But the factor that made the position in Czechoslovakia so exceptional was the growing strength and confidence of the critics of the Novotny régime within the Party structure. By themselves, the protests of writers and students were of relative unimportance; coupled with the economic difficulties throughout the country, the resentment of the Slovaks, and the sympathy within the Party for these criticisms, the situation slipped out

---

[1] The student demonstration in October 1967 against the failure of the University to provide a working lighting system was symptomatic of this.
[2] J. F. Brown, op. cit., p. 33.

THE CZECHOSLOVAK BACKGROUND

of the control of the régime. It could be argued that this loss of control demonstrated the perils for a communist régime of making any relaxation in its authority, but this conclusion overlooks the extent and complexity of the problem facing the régime in the later 1950s and early 1960s. The increased contacts with western culture permitted after the 12th Party Congress in 1962 contained dangers which were recognized by the régime; but even by this stage the process of liberalization had reached a stage in the Party which was extremely difficult for the leaders to check or control. Throughout the period 1960–67, the régime was in fact fighting a series of rearguard actions against its critics within the Party, and the degree of popular support for those critics was steadily increasing. The gradual infiltration of moderates into some of the key positions in radio, television and the Party itself moved the balance further against the government. Dr Cestmir Cisar's tenure – albeit relatively brief – of office as a Secretary of the Central Committee in 1963 and the appointment of Mr Jiri Pelikan as Director General of Czechoslovak Television in June 1964 were two significant examples.

A brief reference must be made to the importance of television and radio in the process of undermining the Novotny régime. The government was surprisingly indifferent to the possibilities of television in particular until it awoke to the belated realization that it was being skilfully exploited against itself. The subsequent appearance of members of the government, wholly unversed in television techniques and uninterested in acquiring them, reading turgid lectures at great length did nothing to improve its stature. An experiment in permitting question and answer sessions was hurriedly abandoned after the inability of ministers to perform adequately had been manifestly demonstrated. In contrast, the medium of television brought to popular attention hitherto unknown men, some of whom were adept in the techniques of television, and whose sincerity and ability were impressive. It would be unwise to over-emphasize this aspect of the crisis in Czechoslovakia, but the contribution of television to the general loss of confidence in the Novotny régime must be regarded as a significant one.

By the autumn of 1967 the opponents of the régime within

the Party had reached a position when they judged that another attempt to displace Novotny contained a strong possibility of success. The proposal that the offices of First Secretary and President should be separated was the tactic whereby Novotny's authority was to be challenged. It appears that the first serious clash occurred at a meeting of the Central Committee on 30–31 October. After it was apparent that there was deadlock in the 11-member Praesidium, the fateful decision was taken to refer the matter to the Central Committee, consisting of 110 voting and 46 non-voting candidate members, on 19 December. There was no quick decision, and it was not until after an adjournment of a few days that the result was announced on 5 January 1968. The official communiqué stated that the Committee had criticized failings in the 'methods and style of work in the internal administration of the party and in the practical application of the principle of democratic centralism and internal party democracy'. Novotny was removed from the post of First Secretary, and Dubcek elected in his place; his downfall was completed by his resignation of the Presidency and replacement by Svoboda on 22 March, and by his dismissal from the Central Committee and suspension from Party membership on 30 May.

This was in effect a *coup d'état* achieved within the Party structure by a group hostile to the régime, an event in itself that was remarkable. The deadlock in the Praesidium and the reference to the Central Committee showed how the result was even then in the balance, but in the event the machine was used against Novotny, and nothing occurred in the process of his downfall to which any legitimate protest could be made.

The fact that the critics of the régime had taken care to operate within the Party structure, and adopted public attitudes which at first sight seemed virtually identical with the deposed leaders, misled some outside observers as to the deep significance of what had occurred. Dubcek's first statement after his election was to emphasize 'the fundamental Leninist principle of our party, its unity and loyalty to Marxism-Leninism ... the Socialist principles of internationalism, of the development of Socialism, which are the foundation of our integral State of Czechs and Slovaks, the basis of the safety and international security of our country, which is an inseparable part of the world Socialist system, firmly linked with the Soviet Union'. There was no reason to question the sincerity of this statement. Brezhnev himself paid a brief visit to Prague early in December, from which he apparently concluded that Novotny's support in the Central Committee was not sufficient to warrant any attempt to sway the decision, and he subsequently sent Dubcek the customary message of congratulation on his appointment. Dubcek was, after all, a Moscow-trained communist. His personal credentials would presumably have seemed reassuring to the Soviet leadership. It would be wholly incorrect to make the assumption that Dubcek and his associates saw themselves as anything but loyal to the true principles of Marxism-Leninism which had, in their view, been distorted under Novotny. What was not appreciated, even by the new Czechoslovak leaders, was the strength and unity of the movement which had overthrown Novotny, and, consequently, the full implications of the decision of the Central Committee.

2
The Soviet Dilemma

AT a time when Soviet policies had been undergoing a prolonged period of dilemma and difficulty the unexpected emergence of a crisis within the European bloc was unwelcome. The foreign policies of all nations tend to fluctuate, affected as they are by a myriad of changing considerations and new factors. But Russian foreign policy has demonstrated a consistency of attitude that is none the less difficult to categorize succinctly. Perhaps the nearest approximation would be provided by the phrase 'cautious expansionism', and yet even this term is not really comprehensive. But it may suffice in a brief analysis. Methods and even objectives have changed; there have been periods of relative withdrawal and quiescence; but the central theme has returned after such intervals.

The opportunism which is an integral part of the attitudes of cautious expansionism, and which is closely coupled with usually realistic assessments of the possibilities of situations to further Russian interests, has given Russian policy a consistent basis of objective on the one hand and a flexibility and resource on the other which together provide its greatest strength. It also renders any forecast of Russian actions peculiarly difficult to make. But, for all its fluctuations of tactics and techniques, there is in Russian foreign policy a genuine discernible orthodoxy. *Plus ça change; plus c'est la même chose.*

Orthodox foreign policy has been conducted by the Brezhnev–Kosygin régime within the framework of Marxist-Leninist doctrine as interpreted and reinterpreted by Stalin, Khruschev and

THE SOVIET DILEMMA

themselves. This policy is based upon two cardinal principles: to strengthen the Soviet Union and maintain cohesion of the communist camp; and to provide general support for national liberation movements. In the pursuit of these objectives they have chosen to operate within the carefully developed concept of coexistence with states of different social systems. Coexistence should not be misinterpreted. It does not mean the acceptance of international co-operation through mutual goodwill; it means competition with capitalist and hostile states in all possible forms short of mutually destructive war. The difference between the Western concept of détente[1] and the Soviet view of peaceful coexistence is quite fundamental. Détente has as its principal assumption a full development of relations between communist and non-communist states, leading to further settlements. Peaceful coexistence has as its principal assumption the maintenance of the rivalry between the two systems short of war. Détente assumes the diminution and, hopefully, the ending of the contest between the two systems; peaceful coexistence means the successful continuance of that struggle by other means.

Nevertheless, the acceptance of the policy of coexistence by the Soviet Union has been of very considerable significance. In practical terms, the need to avoid a military confrontation with the United States – particularly after 1962 – has come to mean the acceptance of fairly clearly defined spheres of influence and interest based upon a balance of forces and weapons. The second principle and the concept of coexistence underlying Soviet policies are accordingly bound to come into conflict from time to time, and pose in acute form the Soviet dilemma in attempting either to accommodate their actions to orthodox ideology or to adapt or modify ideology to lend authenticity to their actions. Their support of the Arab cause, with the resultant loss of Soviet prestige after the defeat of their protégées in 1967, appears to have owed a good deal to the former attitude.

The successors of Khruschev have displayed a caution in foreign policy which at times, and particularly in 1965–6, has been interpreted as uncertainty. Initially, the Vietnam War presented the Soviet leaders with a particular dilemma, and it would appear that they only gradually came to appreciate the

[1] See page 126 for the development of this point.

many potentialities of the situation. The war strained American relations with virtually every European nation, thus provoking discord in the western alliance and assisting communist unity in Eastern Europe; it gravely compromised American influence in South-East Asia; it provided an invaluable opportunity for the reduction of Sino-Soviet tension by engaging Chinese resources and by diverting Chinese hostility towards the United States; and it inflicted additional pressures on the internal difficulties in the United States. Soviet policy accordingly moved towards exploitation of the war while taking care to limit its possible expansion. The policy was developed with greater confidence in the context of the studied moderation of the US Government in its relations with the USSR and the rapid development of Soviet strategic weapons to the point where virtual parity has been achieved. What appeared to some observers to be contradictory policies – exploitation of the war and extensive material support for North Vietnam on the one hand and limited bilateral co-operation with the United States on the other – in fact developed into two elements of the same policy.

In the Middle East, where the dangers of the situation getting out of control have been infinitely greater than in Vietnam, Soviet support for the Arabs has been pragmatic and opportunistic, but considerably more cautious. The increase in Soviet naval power in the Mediterranean may be thought to dispute this interpretation, but the Russians have always sought to establish a naval presence in this area, and their activities can certainly be partly attributed to the necessity to demonstrate visible support for the Arab cause after the disaster of the June War in 1967. The exploitation of the Middle East situation demonstrates both the opportunistic and the expansionist aspects of Russian policy, but it also demonstrates the caution of the Soviet leaders in an area in which there is a real danger of being drawn into a major confrontation with the United States.

In Europe there have been no signs of an 'adventurous' Soviet policy since the new régime took power in October 1964, and the emphasis of statements and actions has been heavily on the preservation of the *status quo*. The Soviet interpretation of European Security is in effect a term to describe the permanent

THE SOVIET DILEMMA

acceptance of present frontiers and spheres of influence, the removal of American forces from Europe, and the division of Germany. It was significant that the proposal for the disbanding of NATO and the Warsaw Pact and their replacement by a European Security System to guarantee the perpetual preservation of the European *status quo*, put forward in the Bucharest Declaration in the summer of 1966 and repeated at Karlovy Vary in the spring of 1967,[1] was subsequently shelved when the West German Government launched its initiative to restore normal diplomatic relations with Eastern European governments. The Soviets now found it more convenient to put the emphasis on the preservation of hostility towards West Germany by the combatants in the war. The Soviet support for Ulbricht and Gomulka in their attempts to prevent the rot spreading further after Rumania's exchange of diplomatic relations with Bonn in January 1967 marked the effective burial – at least for the time being – of the much-vaunted European Security System.

But the episode was of importance in the context of the Soviet interest in the strains within NATO, which were evidenced not only by the attitudes of the French Government, and which were now of particular relevance and importance in view of the approach of 1969 and the possibility of at least one member of the Alliance giving notice of its intention to withdraw from it. The erosion of NATO unity has been a consistent element in Soviet strategy since the signing of the original Treaty, but the methods employed since 1964 had been more subtle and considerably more effective than those of Khruschev; the Bucharest Declaration was an intelligent development of that policy, and its tactical abandonment demonstrated the realization of the Soviet leaders that internal strains were not confined to NATO.

The record of the Brezhnev–Kosygin leadership does not lend itself to interpretations of the adoption of an actively expansionist policy, particularly in Europe. Outside Europe, Soviet policy has been expansionist in the sense that specific opportunities for causing embarrassment to the Western powers, or sowing discord among them, or for exploiting local situations with an eye to their possible future advantage, have been readily

[1] The bilateral treaties enabling Soviet forces to remain in central Europe were specifically excluded from the proposal. See also pages 33–34 below.

and often skilfully taken. But in Europe, the Soviet leaders have become preoccupied with preventing changes which might operate to their disadvantage, rather than with working out an overall plan for expansion.[1] As one experienced commentator has recently remarked, 'one discerns in the Soviet behaviour (rather in contrast to Khruschev's) the absence of a grand pattern, though a quick willingness to exploit specific opportunities. Soviet policy in Europe thus seems in abeyance.'[2]

Any expectations that the Soviet leaders may have had of their capability to contain developments in Czechoslovakia had been severely undermined by the events of the first three months of 1968. The basic Soviet dilemma was to be confronted by a situation in which not to intervene at all in Czechoslovak affairs could lead to a position in which the leading role of the Communist Party was in serious jeopardy, with all the obvious implications for the other members of the European bloc and also possibly for the Soviet Union itself. There were also important military considerations, which put Czechoslovakia in a very particular position in Soviet strategy. If the Czechoslovak army, holding a vital defensive area in Central Europe, could no longer be regarded as completely reliable, the military implications were extremely serious, and the apparent reluctance of the new Czechoslovak Government to hold joint manoeuvres on Czechoslovak territory would be bound to reinforce such suspicions.

The geographical and political implications were even graver. The possibility of a power vacuum existing in such a sensitive area in Europe could only have alarmed the Soviet leaders profoundly. Fear of German expansion and influence in Eastern Europe, always present in Soviet calculations, had been increased by the events of 1967. This important factor had to be taken into account together with the implications of the possible

[1] It may be noted that, in one respect, the preparations for the re-establishment of something resembling a united world communist movement, the Soviet leaders pursued a traditionalist policy which had been in abeyance. This policy was persisted with, even though the preparatory Conference, held in March 1965, had registered disunity rather than unity.
[2] B. Z. Brzezinski, 'Peace and Power', *Encounter*, November 1968.

destruction of the control of the Communist Party in Czechoslovakia, and the immediate military consequences if Czechoslovakia in effect if not in name drifted into a position of neutrality. It is accordingly not difficult to appreciate the causes for serious concern felt by the Soviet leaders concerning the Czechoslovak situation by the early spring of 1968. It is also not difficult to deduce why it was that the decision was made to warn the Czechoslovak leaders of the dangers of the course they were pursuing and, subsequently, to initiate a policy of gradually mounting pressure upon them.

It is important to differentiate between a decision to intervene in Czechoslovak affairs and one to invade Czechoslovakia, and it is a differentiation which many distinguished commentators on the crisis have failed to make.[1] There seems little doubt that military advice in Moscow would tend to favour effective, and if necessary drastic, action to check a worsening situation. But these considerations were of secondary importance to the political ones. The consequences of invasion were bound to be serious, and not least on the possibilities for the World Communist Conference. At a time when the Soviet Union was extracting the maximum benefit from the Vietnam War, particularly from its reactions among the non-aligned nations, the possibility of launching an invasion upon Czechoslovakia was politically highly unwelcome. There is no evidence that a military invasion was seriously considered at this early stage; all that can be said with definiteness is that the decision was taken by the middle of April that the risks of non-intervention were greater than those of intervention. Intervention was to include the threat – at first implicit and then explicit – of the use of force. It is perhaps doubtful, bearing in mind the characteristics of the Soviet leadership, that a clear policy was decided upon, beyond the recognition of the fact that the Czechoslovak situation could not be permitted to develop in the manner shown since 5 January. Thus, and with probably no clear objectives or full understanding of the potentialities of the situation, was hesitantly inaugurated the policy of pressure upon the Czechoslovak Government and Party.

[1] See, for example, Herman Kahn, 'How to think about the Russians', *Fortune*, November 1968.

Viewed from the Soviet standpoint there appear to have been a number of key features in the development of the situation in Czechoslovakia between 5 January and mid-April that made intervention essential. The first was the easing of restrictions on the press and radio, which permitted free discussion of the 'democratization' of the Party very shortly after Dubcek's election, and which sometimes came very close to the advocating of a formal Opposition party.[1] The second was the changes in personnel in the Party and Government. The third was the publication of the Action Programme on 9 April.

The personnel changes were in themselves startling enough. Cisar replaced Hendrych as Party Secretary in charge of ideology. Eight of the eleven members of the Praesidium were replaced. Only four of the members of the previous Praesidium and Party Secretariat remained, while only five of the twelve Heads of Central Committee Departments and two of the eleven Regional Leading Secretaries survived. This clean sweep of Party appointments was accompanied by the removal of Novotny from the Presidency on 22 March and the appointment of Svoboda in his place. Early in April the appointment of the new government was announced. Cernik replaced Lenart as Prime Minister, and only four members of the previous government were included. The Minister of Defence had resigned before the new cabinet was announced, and there was also another change at the other key Ministry from the point of view of the Soviet interest in security and Party control, that of the Interior. Sik was one of the new Deputy Prime Ministers, as was Mr Hamouz, the previous Minister of Foreign Trade, who had also recognized the need for increased trade and technological exchanges with the West.

These changes could only be interpreted as the first stage in a complete transformation of the personnel of the Party throughout its structure, an interpretation that was given greater strength by a careful reading of the Action Programme. This

[1] See, for example, Vaclac Havel, 'On the Subject of Opposition' in *Literarni Listy*, 4 April, who appeared to argue for the establishment of an alternative party, as compared with Zora Jesenica in 'The Rights of the Citizen' (*Kulturny Zivot*, 5 April), who agreed that all groups should express their views through the National Front, but that the Communist Party need not possess the dominant influence.

THE SOVIET DILEMMA

in fact provided the first clear picture of the upheaval that had occurred.

The main points of the Programme were as follows: (i) the need to reform the whole political system, so as to combine 'broad democracy with scientific, highly qualified management', and a guarantee against a concentration of power in few hands; (ii) the need for a new Press Law to exclude the possibility of factual censorship; (iii) the need for personal safeguards, including the right – subject to preventing a brain drain – to travel abroad, and freedom from political victimization; (iv) the rehabilitation of political victims; (v) the need for a new constitutional law defining the status of Slovak national bodies, on the basis of some kind of federal system; (vi) alliance with the Soviet Union and the Socialist countries would continue to be the cornerstone of foreign policy, but friendly relations were to be developed with all countries, and the possibility was mentioned of specifically Czechoslovak views being formulated on international issues; (vii) decentralization of industrial decision-making; (viii) the need for new legislation to define electoral procedures and the position of minority parties in the National Front; (ix) the importance of opening the economy to world markets, whose ultimate aim would be to create conditions for the convertibility of the Czechoslovak currency.

The language of the Action Programme was as remarkable as its proposals. The party, while continuing to rely upon the working classes, would also 'support the growing unity between the intelligentsia and the workers'; the 'dogmatism and subjectiveness' of the past would be abandoned; there would be equality of rights for Czechs and Slovaks; the Communist Party would rely upon 'the voluntary support of the people', and 'cannot just assume authority, but must continuously earn it by deeds'; the National Assembly must 'really make laws and decide important political questions, not just approve drafts submitted to it', while divergent opinions were described as 'a necessary manifestation of responsible efforts to seek the best solution'; although the Party was to remain supreme, restriction on the membership of other parties was to be removed. And, although the Programme reiterated loyalty to the Warsaw Pact and COMECON, it was significant that in relation to the latter organization it was stated that 'we shall strive to see to it that economic calculation and mutual profitability of exchange are more fully emphasized'.

The Action Programme consisted, significantly, of recommendations and not directives. Despite the obvious haste with which it had been put together and the imprecision of much of its phrasing, the Programme made it quite clear that even if the new leaders did not envisage the surrender by the Party of its dominant role, it interpreted this very differently from the Stalinist form of 'democratic centralism', amounting to autocratic control by the top Party organs. In view of the central importance of this question for the Soviet leaders it is worth quoting in full the relevant passage. The Programme was stated to be based on the present stage of development in Czechoslovakia, in which a *rapprochement* of all social groups is possible because 'there no longer exist antagonistic classes'. Appeals for unity run through the Programme, which called for co-operation between the workers and the intelligentsia to bring methods of economic management up to date. On the Party's role the Programme said that:

> This leading role was ... often comprehended as a concentration, a monopoly of power in the hands of party organs, which corresponded to the false thesis that the party is the instrument of dictatorship of the proletariat. This harmful concept weakened the initiative and responsibility of the State, economic and social institutions, damaged the authority of the Party, and made it impossible for it to exercise its own function. The aim of the Party is not to become the universal administrator of society, to rule over all organizations and every step in life with its directives. Its mission lies above all in arousing Socialist initiative, in showing ways and real possibilities of Communist perspectives and, through systematic persuasion and through the personal example of Communists, in winning over all working people.

The Programme also called for a new Constitution aimed towards 'the unfolding of a Socialist democracy and a new system of political direction of society', which must be thoroughly discussed and the conclusion formulated by all the elements constituting the National Front. Other features of the Programme were consistent with this basic attitude, including the

THE SOVIET DILEMMA

recommendation of a new Press Law 'to exclude the possibility of preliminary censorship of the press.'[1] The declarations of loyalty to the Warsaw Pact, the Soviet Union, and COMECON in the Programme were emphasized by Dubcek and other Czechoslovak leaders.[2] The immediate Soviet reaction to the passages concerning the position of the Party was to ignore them in *Pravda*'s short summary on 17 April; the sections on preliminary press censorship and ending of restrictions to travel abroad were also not mentioned. The Polish and East German press did not summarize the Programme at all, while that in Rumania and Bulgaria followed *Pravda*'s line in omitting reference to the sections relating to increased individual liberty and the role of the Party. Not altogether surprisingly, the most complete and accurate account was given by the Yugoslavs.[3]

At this point it is convenient to summarize the development of Soviet reactions to events in Czechoslovakia up to mid-April. Dubcek had apparently reassured the Soviet leaders during his first visit to Moscow as First Secretary at the end of January, and the communique referred to 'full identity of views'; but Prague Radio made it clear that the meeting at Dresden on 23 March attended by Soviet, Bulgarian, Hungarian, Polish, East German and Czechoslovak party leaders was in fact a 'confrontation'.[4] Dubcek himself admitted that the other leaders had expressed 'understandable concern' over developments in Czechoslovakia, and on 29 March Brezhnev warned in a public statement in Moscow against the dangers of imperialist subversion in communist countries. There was no direct reference to Czechoslovakia, but the inference was clear. In addition to the significant reaction of *Pravda* to the Action Programme, there was a reference to fears expressed by speakers at Czechoslovak provincial party meetings of the consequences of lifting press censorship and 'subversive attacks' against the Action Programme.[5] French sources reported Brezhnev expressing, on 23 April, his concern at Czechoslovak developments and his

[1] The new law was passed by the National Assembly on 26 June.
[2] e.g. Dubcek in a speech at Brno on 16 March and Cernik in announcing the Government's plans to the National Assembly on 25 April.
[3] *Borba*, 11 April.
[4] Prague Radio Home Service, 26 March 1968.
[5] *Pravda*, 30 April.

belief that Dubcek was becoming the prisoner of 'reactionary and anti-Communist elements'.[1] On 4–5 May, Dubcek, accompanied by Cernik, Smrkovsky (the new chairman of the National Assembly) and Bilak, visited Moscow for what was described by *Tass* as a 'brief friendly meeting', a marked contrast to the account of the January meeting. When the new Czechoslovak Ambassador to the Soviet Union, Vladimir Kouchy, presented his credentials on 6 May, President Podgorny made a marked reference to the presence of 'anti-socialist' elements active in Czechoslovakia. On 8 May there was a meeting of the party leaders of the Soviet Union, East Germany, Poland, Hungary and Bulgaria in Moscow, with little publicity and no communiqué. As in the Dresden meeting, Rumania was not invited.[2] On the following day an East German newspaper alleged the presence of United States and West German military units in Czechoslovakia. The Soviet Defence Minister, Marshal Grechko, accompanied by General Epishev (the head of the department dealing with political control of the Soviet armed forces) visited Czechoslovakia on 17–22 May; this visit coincided with one by Kosygin himself from the 17th until the 25th. On 24 May it was announced in Prague that Warsaw Pact command staff exercises would be held in Czechoslovakia in June.

These indications of increased pressure demonstrate the significance that was now being attached to developments in Czechoslovakia, and the realization of the potentialities of the Action Programme. In addition to the personnel changes in the Party, the free debate in the Czechoslovak press on the structure of the Party and the appearance of groups such as the Club K-231 of former political prisoners and the 'Committed Non-Party Persons' (KAN) had strengthened Soviet concern at the presence of a potential threat to the absolute supremacy of the Party. But the process was not checked by these actions, and there were strong indications – to Western observers as well as others – that the momentum of the movement was becoming stronger than the Czechoslovak leaders could contain. At the May plenum of the Party (29 May–1 June) Dubcek emphasized

---

[1] *Le Monde*, 6 May.
[2] The Rumanian Party Central Committee passed a resolution on 26 April noting that it had not been represented at the Dresden meeting.

the dangers of what he called 'anti-socialist tendencies' for the process of democratization, and his attitude towards the conservative elements remaining in the Central Committee was noticeably more moderate than his speech a month earlier, at which he had spoken of the necessity to elect a new Committee before the 14th Party Congress in the spring of 1969.[1] Novotny was expelled, but attempts to persuade other conservatives to resign were unsuccessful. Dubcek and his colleagues stressed the leading roles of the Party and the essential condition that any organizations aspiring to a share of political power must be members of the National Front and not work in opposition to its programmes. Although he was not very critical of the press, he remarked that the Party expected that it would not 'spontaneously and without participation of the appropriate organs' accelerate the process of development. All this, combined with Dubcek's emphasis upon the Party as 'the guarantee of good relations with the other socialist countries', demonstrated the fact that the Soviet criticisms and warnings had not been without effect. Subsequent Czechoslovak press comment saw the plenum as an unsatisfactory compromise between the conservative and liberal elements in the Central Committee. This was a fair comment. The position of the Czechoslovak leadership was now becoming difficult. The liberal members of the Party, conscious of strong popular support, and exhilarated by their remarkable success over the past six months, were pressing for further reforms and the speedy implementation of the Action Programme. The conservatives, acutely aware of the precariousness of their position in the current mood and now also aware of the increasing concern of the Soviet leadership at developments, were attempting to check the pace. Dubcek's task at the plenum was necessarily to placate both sides, as the realization of the alarm of the Warsaw Pact allies compelled at least some nominal concessions to the conservatives.

On one point he was forced to bow to liberal pressure to bring forward the date of the 14th Party Congress to 9 September 1968. It would be at this Congress that a new Central Committee would be elected and the Action Programme

[1] See the Czechoslovak News Agency report of his speech on 26 April at the Prague City Conference.

endorsed as official Party policy. The indications are strong that Dubcek only accepted this change with considerable reluctance, although it is doubtful whether he appreciated the momentousness of the decision. All calculations of timing were changed by it. In short, if the process of democratization were to be checked, it must be achieved by 9 September, and not by the spring of 1969.

On 27 June the '2,000 words' manifesto written by Ludvik Vaculik was published in four Prague newspapers. This in effect called for quicker progress in the democratization of the Party and the departure of those who had abused their power. Some commentators have seen considerable significance in this remarkable document; others doubt whether it had, of itself, very great influence upon the Soviet leadership. It can at least be said that the manifesto, taken in its context, must have had some effect upon Soviet estimates of the situation within Czechoslovakia. The prompt disavowals of the manifesto by Dubcek himself and the Praesidium as a whole[1] were not in the circumstances likely to carry ultimate conviction or to increase Soviet confidence in his ability to control the situation. It is from this time that the attacks on 'imperialist' and 'counter-revolutionary' activities in Czechoslovakia by the Soviet and especially the East German and Polish press and radio greatly increased in quantity and stridency. *Pravda*, in criticizing the '2,000 words', ominously drew comparisons with the situation in Hungary in 1956.[2] The East German press attacked the manifesto under the title 'The Strategy of Imperialism and the Czechoslovak Socialist Republic.'[3] There had been in the previous weeks emphasis upon the importance of the leading role of the Party in a Communist society,[4] but the sharp reaction to the '2,000 words' marked a significant change in the fierceness of the criticisms of the Czechoslovak movement in Eastern Europe.

The pressure upon the Czechoslovak leaders was now greatly increased. The first stage was the menacing build-up of the Warsaw Pact manoeuvres from staff exercises to full-scale army

[1] Prague Radio Home Service, 28 June.
[2] *Pravda*, 11 July.
[3] *Neues Deutschland*, 13 July.
[4] See, for example, the broadcast in Slovak on Moscow Radio on 25 June, on the subject of 'the leading role of the Communist Party in a Socialist Society'.

THE SOVIET DILEMMA

exercises which included the use of Soviet tanks,[1] followed by an equally ominous delay in the withdrawal of these forces after the exercises. Soviet forces were still on Czechoslovak territory at the time of the second major stage, the Warsaw meeting in mid-July of leaders of the Soviet Union, East Germany, Poland, Hungary and Bulgaria. The Czechoslovak refusal to attend was predictable, since they had taken the line that they would not take part in a multilateral meeting but would be prepared to discuss the situation bilaterally with their allies;[2] it therefore seems clear that the Soviet intention was to hold the meeting without Czechoslovak participation. The Warsaw Letter of 15 July sent to the Czechoslovak Central Committee provides the clearest evidence of the depth and extent of the Pact leaders' lack of confidence in the capacity of the Czechoslovak Government and Party to prevent a threat to the 'foundation of socialism in Czechoslovakia' constituted by the unhindered activities of right-wing and anti-socialist organizations outside the Party. In short, Party control – and there was a specific reference to democratic centralism – was at stake, and the reference to the existence of forces capable of ensuring compliance with the demands of the signatories underlined the seriousness of the situation. The Warsaw Letter is so remarkable a document that it is included in full as an appendix to this study,[3] as is the Czechoslovak reply of 18 July. This reply again stressed loyalty to the Pact and to COMECON, but although it admitted the existence of some anti-socialist forces, ascribed this primarily to the shortcomings of the Novotny régime. Furthermore, the reply made it plain that the Party proposed to proceed on the lines of the Action Programme. This reply may be regarded as a very courageous or a very foolish action. It resulted in the demand by the Soviet leaders for a meeting with the Czechoslovak leaders in Moscow. The meeting eventually took place

[1] See page 53 below (note 3).
[2] See *Rude Pravo*, 9 July 1968, a report on the 8 July Party Praesidium meeting which emphasized that bilateral talks between fraternal parties 'acting as partners and held at a suitable time' are necessary; and Prague Radio, 17 July 1968, reporting on the Praesidium meeting on 16 July, stating that the Warsaw meetings had taken place without Czechoslovak participation, the Czechoslovak Party being in this case 'in favour of preliminary bilateral talks', and not having the opportunity of participating in the preparation of the Warsaw meeting.
[3] See Appendix 2.

on 29 July at Cierna-nad-Tisou, on the Czechoslovak–Soviet frontier.

In the interval between 18 and 29 July the tension between the two sides was further increased by the public criticism of the Warsaw meeting by General Prchlik, the head of the Party Central Committee department for Military and Security Affairs, who also claimed that the Warsaw Pact did not permit the stationing of troops of one party to the Treaty on the territory of another without the latter's consent.[1] His return to army duty on 25 July may be interpreted as another attempt by the Czechoslovak leaders to improve relations with their Pact allies, but the gesture was accompanied by the abolition of his department – hardly likely to be viewed by the Soviet leaders as a reassuring indication. On 19 July there came the revelation of the 'discovery' of a secret cache of American arms in Czechoslovakia near the West German border.[2]

Between the middle of July and the meeting of the Czechoslovak and Soviet leaders at Cierna-nad-Tisou on 29–31 July, the charges against the Czechoslovak Government reached such a height of virulence in the Soviet and East German press that the possibility of Soviet military action became seriously considered by outside observers,[3] in some cases for the first time. This tension lasted until after the Cierna meeting, at which, after an initial period of harsh accusations levelled at the Czechoslovak Praesidium by the members of the Soviet Politburo, an accommodation of some kind appeared to have been reached. The brief joint communiqué spoke of an atmosphere of 'frankness, sincerity and mutual understanding'. *Pravda*'s attacks on the Czechoslovak leaders stopped abruptly on 1 August. These hopeful indications were confirmed when a meeting took place on 3 August at Bratislava between the

---

[1] See Appendix 1 for the text of the Warsaw Pact. It has been set out in full because it is not often given in Western studies of Eastern Europe and Soviet foreign policy, a fact that became most evident at the time of the invasion when the significance of the details of the treaty was realized.

[2] *Pravda*, 19 July.

[3] Although the evidence is not conclusive, the indications are to the effect that at least Dubcek, and probably many of his colleagues, never seriously considered that a Soviet invasion was likely. This confidence, which was very evident in Prague in July, goes some way to explain what appeared to many observers to be defiance of Soviet threats.

THE SOVIET DILEMMA

Czechoslovak leaders and the signatories of the Warsaw Letter in effect to ratify what had been agreed at Cierna. The communiqué issued after the meeting was of interest in that there was no reference whatever to the situation in Czechoslovakia. The lull in the press campaign against the Czechoslovak leaders after Cierna and Bratislava, and the warm welcome given to their results, indicated that Soviet leaders believed that they had succeeded in turning the Czechoslovaks back from their fatal course. The announcement of the completion of the withdrawal of Pact forces from Czechoslovak Territory was another indication. It has been suggested that this was all part of a calculated plan to relax tension and lull both the Czechs and the West into a false security, but the available indications point strongly to the conclusion that such assurances as may have been given at Cierna had been regarded as satisfactory by the Soviet leaders – or, more probably, by a majority among them. If, in retrospect, it appears surprising that the assurances were accepted in view of the attitude of the Czechoslovak leaders since April or their failure to control the situation, the consequences of a decision to invade must have appeared daunting to an essentially cautious and possibly divided Soviet leadership.

The importance of the time factor must be emphasized again. The decisive date was 9 September, when the 14th Party Congress was due to meet. On 14 August the press assault on the Czechoslovak leadership in the East European press was renewed, and in the next week became even more denunciatory than in July. On the same day, Marshal Grechko met the East German Defence Minister, General Hoffmann, 'to exchange views on general political questions and co-operation between the fraternal armies'.

In the ten days' lull between the apparent concord at Bratislava and the violent renewal of the propaganda offensive on 14 August there had been certain events that appear, in retrospect, of significance. On 4 August the appointment of the new Chief of Staff of the Warsaw Pact forces, General Shtemenko, was announced, an event that has led some observers to assume that plans for the invasion of Czechoslovakia were completed.[1]

---

[1] Even if this assumption is correct, it does not mean that a decision to invade had been taken. ·

On 8 August *Literarni Listy* contained an attack on the Russians for their interference in Czechoslovak affairs by Josef Valka; on the following day *Pravda* published an article on democratic centralism and the perils of permitting factions in communist parties, although the Valka article was not replied to until 14 August. On 9–11 August President Tito visited Czechoslovakia, and President Ceausescu followed him on 15–17 August, to sign the new Twenty-Year Treaty of Friendship, Co-operation and Mutual Aid. Neither of these events would be viewed favourably by Moscow, but it is difficult to believe that either by itself would have justified invasion. Nevertheless, they may have substantially added to Soviet fears that in preparation for further resistance the Czechoslovak leaders were attempting to re-insure their position. It is possible that a more significant factor was the publication, on 10 August, of the new Draft Party Statutes to be put before the 14th Party Congress on 9 September[1].

The content of the Statutes could be said to follow logically from the Action Programme, and this was their principal offence. The Preamble to the Statutes stated that the Party 'is aware that its strength lies in its close ties with the people, their life and needs. That is why it constantly strives to win the people's confidence and voluntary support and why it subjects itself to the people's control'. The chapter on the fundamental principles of 'the Party's inner life and activity' stated that democratic centralism would guide the Party and majority decisions would be binding, but 'minority views can be formulated and entered into the minutes. The minority is entitled to stick to its views and demand their renewed examination on the basis of new knowledge or practical experience. Holders of minority views can be exposed to ideological influence alone'. The Statutes also called for an information system permitting the unhampered flow of information in both directions as a condition of 'ideological unification' and 'intra-Party democracy'. As a safeguard against the accumulation of too much power in individuals, there was to be a limit of tenure of Party posts. Election to these posts, moreover, was to be by secret ballot. There would appear to have been two alternative Soviet

---

[1] The text was set out in *Rude Pravo*, 10 August.

interpretations of the publication of the Draft Statutes. Either the Czechoslovak leaders had gone back on any assurances which had been extracted from them on Party reforms, or they had lost control of the situation.

It is impossible to state with any precision when the decision to invade Czechoslovakia was taken. It can reasonably be assumed that the emergency session of the Central Committee of the Soviet Communist Party on 20 August was for the purposes of information only. It may also be reasonably assumed that the abrupt ending of the hostile press campaign against the Czechoslovak leaders after Cierna and its resumption on 14 August was deliberate. It can be argued that the only significant public Czechoslovak action taken between these two dates was the publication of the Draft Statutes on 10 August, and that this was the vital event, and accordingly the decision to invade was taken some time between 10 August and 14 August. This argument has as its basis the need to prepare and co-ordinate the renewed press onslaught on 14 August, and which further reduces the period to the three days after the publication of the Statutes – 11–13 August. On 12–13 August Ulbricht visited Dubcek at Karlovy Vary, and it is possible that his report to Moscow was of decisive importance and that the actual final decision was taken on 13 August. It is perhaps not necessary to look for one single event in the period 3–14 August. It may well be that a combination of events, of which the publication of the Statutes and the visits of Tito and Ceausescu were major component parts, was decisive. But it should also be emphasized that it is possible that the decisive factor could have been a failure by the Czechoslovak leaders to carry out undertakings given to Warsaw Pact allies about which no firm evidence exists at present. It cannot be ruled out that a conservative faction in the Praesidium considered that the moment for a successful challenge to Dubcek's leadership could now only be mounted with direct Soviet support. It is also possible that the causes are to be found in a wider East European framework. In the absence of decisive evidence, it can only be stated that the inherent probability of the matter is that the decision to invade was taken at some time between 10 August and 13 August.

At the time the significance of the sudden resumption of the press campaign against Czechoslovakia was not appreciated. The first intervention of the Red Army journal *Red Star* into the controversy must be noted; in its issue of 14 August it referred at length to the growth of hostile and dangerous trends in Czechoslovakia, declared Soviet willingness to assist the Czechoslovak Party and people against such challenges, and asserted the indivisibility of the defence of Eastern Europe.[1] On 20 August the East German press emphasized that socialist internationalism included a readiness to enlist help from fraternal countries.[2] But the invasion of Czechoslovakia on the night of 20–21 August by Soviet forces, assisted by units from their East German, Polish, Hungarian and Bulgarian Warsaw Pact allies, achieved total military and political surprise. At the reiterated urgings of the Czechoslovak Party and Government there was no organized resistance. By the morning of 21 August all key centres, including Prague, were firmly in the control of the invading forces and many of the Czechoslovak leaders were in Soviet hands. Subsequent events were to demonstrate that the central dilemma that had faced the Soviet leadership since April had not been resolved by this devastatingly swift and complete occupation. The crisis in Czechoslovak–Soviet relations entered a new and no less complex period.

[1] *Red Star*, 14 August.
[2] *Neues Deutschland*, 20 August.

3

The Role of the Warsaw Pact

ALTHOUGH the invading force that occupied Czechoslovakia on 20–21 August was predominantly Soviet and the control of the operation was in the hands of the Soviet commanders, the presence of Warsaw Pact forces constitutes one major difference with the invasion of Hungary in 1956, and it is a feature of the crisis that merits examination. It must be emphasized that the scarcity of evidence precludes firm judgements being made about detailed military developments within the Warsaw Pact, but there is sufficient evidence to justify an attempt to assess whether the Soviet leaders have viewed the Pact primarily in political or in military terms, and whether it can be said to merit the description of an international organization with its own decision-making and decision-influencing machinery. Such an examination necessitates an account of the development of the Pact between 1955 and 1968.

It will be recalled that a meeting of the Political Consultative Committee of the Warsaw Pact had been held in Sofia on 6–7 March, at the outset of the crisis in Czechoslovakia–Soviet relations, to be followed by the Dresden meeting on 23 March at which the Czechoslovak leaders had been confronted by the five Pact allies who took part in the August invasion. It will also be recalled that the Czechoslovak leaders had consistently pledged their allegiance to the Pact, and that the manoeuvres held near and on Czechoslovak territory in June and July were held under Pact auspices. These and other elements in the crisis necessarily provoke the question as to what was the role of the Pact in the crisis, to what extent the policy of pressure and the invasion was a genuinely co-operative venture, and accordingly whether factors other than only direct Soviet national interest were involved.

The text[1] of the Warsaw 'Treaty of Friendship, Co-operation and Mutual Assistance' itself provides evidence for the motives for the conclusion of the Treaty and also pointers for the directions in which it might be expected to develop. The second paragraph of the preamble underlines the importance of the Treaty's role as a counter to the inclusion of West Germany in the Western Alliance. It was at the end of a series of unsuccessful Soviet attempts to prevent this that the Warsaw Pact was concluded. At the Berlin Conference of Foreign Ministers in February 1954 Molotov repeated the Soviet proposal for the neutralization of Germany while at the same time proposing an all-European Treaty of Collective Security based on a neutralized Germany divided into two states. Subsequent Soviet moves to prevent the ratification of the Paris Agreements led to a proposal for an all-European Conference on Collective Security in November 1954, which was attended only by East European representatives and a Chinese observer. This conference decided to take 'common measures for the organization of armed forces and their commands' if the Paris Agreements were ratified. Ratification was completed on 5 May 1955; the Federal German Republic joined NATO on 9 May and on 11 May a 'Conference of European Countries for the Protection of Peace and the Security of Europe' opened in Warsaw. This was attended by Prime Ministers and Ministers of Defence and Foreign Affairs from the Soviet Union and the seven East European countries together with the Chinese Minister of Defence (also a Deputy Prime Minister) as an observer. On 14 May the Warsaw Pact was concluded. The incorporation of East German forces in the joint Pact forces was decided at the first meeting of the Political Consultative Committee in Prague in January 1956.[2]

[1] See Appendix 1.
[2] No Chinese observers or Albanian representatives attended Warsaw Pact meetings after 1961. The Albanians protested in 1962 at not being invited to a meeting of Pact Defence Ministers. Albania formally withdrew from the Pact on 13 September 1968.

THE ROLE OF THE WARSAW PACT

The Warsaw Pact was seen by the Soviet leaders as a political counter to the North Atlantic Alliance. The text of the Treaty as a whole[1] shows signs of being modelled on the North Atlantic Treaty, the main differences being that it ceases to be valid if an all-European Treaty of Collective Security is concluded (Article 11), the area in which armed attack on one party involves the others in its defence is limited to Europe (Article 4), and the Treaty is stated to be open to accession to 'peace loving states' (Article 9). Bulganin, in a speech to the Indian Parliament on 21 November 1955, said that 'the conclusion of the Warsaw Treaty was ... made necessary by the behaviour of the Western Powers and we are ready to abandon it as soon as a system of European security is fashioned and the Western Powers separate themselves from the NATO Pact and the Paris Treaties.'[2] At the Geneva Conference of Heads of Government in July 1955, the proposal for a non-aggression pact between NATO and the Warsaw Pact was made for the first time, a proposal often to be repeated (e.g. at the May 1958 meeting of the Political Consultative Committee). Subsequently public statements by the Pact members have urged the abolition of both Alliances (e.g. the Bucharest Declaration of July 1966).[3] The conclusion of the Pact was therefore a move to secure the Soviet aims of neutralizing the North Atlantic Alliance and working towards a European settlement on their own terms including in particular the continued division of Germany.

The third main political aim was to provide a multilateral institution to reinforce the cohesion of the communist camp after Stalin's death had removed his personal unifying influence. Under Article 7 Pact members undertook not to join any coalition or alliance and not to conclude any agreements whose objects would conflict with those of the Treaty. Under Article 6 the Political Consultative Committee was set up as the supreme body 'for the purpose of the consultations among the Parties envisaged in the present Treaty and ... for the purpose of examining questions which may arise in the operation of the Treaty'. This in its turn was entitled to set up additional bodies

---

[1] See Appendix 1.
[2] Quoted in *Neues Deutschland*, 23 November 1955.
[3] See also page 15 above.

and at the first meeting of the Committee a standing commission was formed to draft foreign policy proposals together with a unified secretariat composed of representatives of the member states. Both of these have their seats in Moscow, as does the unified command whose establishment was decided on the same date as the conclusion of the Treaty. The first and subsequent commanders-in-chief of the joint armed forces have been Soviet officers as have the chiefs of staff who have always acted as Secretary General of the joint secretariat.[1] The political significance of these military arrangements is obvious.

The evidence thus suggests that the Pact was seen by the Soviet leaders at the time of its conclusion as having a primarily political role, but it would be misleading to suggest that military considerations were not without importance. It is true that the existing network of bilateral treaties of Friendship, Co-operation and Mutual Assistance provided as effective mutual defence obligations as did the Warsaw Pact itself.[2] (It was not until June 1964 that the agreement between East Germany and the Soviet Union was transformed into a Treaty similar to the others but this did not effect the defence position.) Soviet strategic thinking was advancing towards a more realistic assessment of the implications of a fast moving nuclear war which would require better co-ordination of the use of East European manpower and military resources than had existed under Stalin. The joint command provided the structure for intensification of Soviet methods and training. It is moreover clear that the Pact was seen as providing a basis for stationing Soviet troops in member countries even if this could not be read explicitly into its text. The decision on the formation of the unified command published on the day of the conclusion of the Pact refers to the distribution of the joint armed forces on the territories of the Parties to be arranged 'in accordance with the requirements of mutual defence, in agreement among these States.'[3] The

---

[1] The commanders-in-chief have combined that post with the office of First Deputy Minister of Defence of the Soviet Union; the chiefs of staff have also been members of the Soviet General Staff with the title of Deputy Chief of General Staff.

[2] See Appendix 1, page 166, for details of the bilateral treaties and their renewal dates.

[3] Text in *Pravda*, 15 May 1955.

Austrian State Treaty was signed on 15 May 1955, so superseding the Soviet right to maintain troops in Hungary and Rumania to protect supply lines to Austria. As is shown by later statements, it was no coincidence that the Warsaw Treaty was concluded before this situation arose. The Soviet Declaration of 30 October 1956 setting out the relationship with her allies in the light of events in Hungary and Poland stated that 'in accordance with the Warsaw Pact and the Governmental agreements, there are . . . Soviet troops in the Hungarian and Rumanian Republics. Soviet units are in the Republic of Poland in keeping with the Potsdam Four-Power Agreement and the Warsaw Treaty'. The Soviet Treaties with Rumania and Hungary on stationing troops (15 April 1957 and 27 May 1957 respectively)[1] do not mention the Warsaw Treaty as a basis for the presence of Soviet troops, but joint declarations preceding the treaties describe the stay of Soviet troops as in accordance with the Warsaw Pact. The preamble of the Soviet-Hungarian Agreement expressly mentions the joint declaration.

The years following the conclusion of the Pact were dominated within the Soviet Bloc by the Soviet 20th Party Congress, the Polish 'October' and the Hungarian Revolution. The Soviet leaders were concerned to contain the consequences in Eastern Europe of de-Stalinization and the Warsaw Pact was mainly significant during this period as an institutional link and a framework for the stationing of Soviet troops in countries of Eastern Europe where their presence, apart from any wider strategic considerations, was vital in support of unpopular régimes. The importance of this aspect of the Pact was underlined by the Soviet reaction to Imre Nagy's attempt to withdraw from the Pact and his declaration of Hungarian neutrality on 1 November 1956, which clearly played a key role in precipitating the second and decisive Soviet military intervention. It is also significant that in defending the Soviet action in Hungary Russian lawyers argued that the Soviet Union was under an obligation to maintain troops in Hungary by the terms of

[1] UN Treaty Series, Vol. 274, No. 3964, pp. 144–171, and Vol. 407, No. 5864, pp. 158–183.

Article 5 of the Warsaw Treaty which provided that the parties should adopt agreed measures 'to protect the peaceful labours of their peoples, guarantee the inviolability of their frontiers ... and provide defence against possible aggression.'[1] As foreshadowed in the Declaration of 14 May 1955 on the joint command, bilateral agreements regulating the stationing of Soviet troops in member countries' territories were concluded between December 1956 and May 1957.

Before 1960 there is no evidence to suggest that any far-reaching military development took place within the Pact. Despite the announcement in the communiqué issued after the first meeting of the Political Consultative Committee that this body would meet 'whenever necessary, but at least twice a year' the next meeting was not until May 1958. There were no more than three meetings announced between 1955 and 1960. On each occasion the primary purpose, at least on the evidence of the published communiqués and declarations,[2] was to provide a forum for public endorsement of Soviet policy on major international issues. For example the 1958 meeting endorsed the Rapacki plan for an atom-free zone in Central Europe and the East German proposal for a German Confederation. On the military side reductions in the strength of Soviet and East European armed forces were endorsed and approval was given to the withdrawal in the near future of troops stationed in Rumania and the reduction of Soviet troops in Hungary by one division. Otherwise the only information published was that 'decisions were also taken on certain organizational questions concerning the joint armed forces'. The first Committee meeting in 1956 had discussed and adopted the decision on the unified command, agreed to incorporate the East German contingents in the joint forces and appointed the East German Minister of Defence as one of the Deputy Commanders-in-Chief provided by all members except the Soviet Union. On the organization of the Pact no more was stated than that 'organizational problems concerning activities of the joint armed forces ... were solved'.

The documents issued after the Committee meeting in

[1] Meissner, *Dokumente zum Ostrecht*, Chapter IX, part 2 (Verlag Wissenschaft und Politik, Cologne, 1962).
[2] Texts in Meissner, op. cit.

THE ROLE OF THE WARSAW PACT

February 1960 were wholly designed to set out the communist position on relations with the West and seemed intended to establish the negotiating position for the planned Paris Summit Meeting to follow the visit which Khruschev had paid to the United States. The declaration stated that, since the signature of the Pact, its members had reduced their forces by 2·6 million; the Soviet demobilization announced by Khruschev in January 1960,[1] would bring this figure to 3·6. There was no further indication of any specifically military measures. An additional sign of the relatively minor role played at this time by the Political Consultative Committee in military matters was the fact that the appointment of Marshal Grechko in place of the first Pact Commander-in-Chief, Marshal Konev, was apparently approved without a meeting of the Committee. This change was announced in Moscow on 25 July as having been approved by the Committee. The way in which this was handled may also be a pointer to the relatively far-reaching powers of the Pact Secretariat under its Soviet Secretary General.[2]

During this period there was certainly some progress towards a degree of military integration including the standardization of weapons and arms production. There is also evidence of Soviet improvement of air defences in Eastern Europe by the provision of more modern and effective equipment.[3] But the joint command as such appears to have remained largely dormant.[4] Many reasons probably contributed to this situation. It is doubtful that the Soviet leaders would have felt inclined to place great trust in local East European forces soon after 1956. This was a period of major debate on military strategy in the Soviet Union. Khruschev himself played a leading part in this and his January speech set out his view on the changes resulting from the development of modern nuclear weapons. In this he stressed the paramount importance of these new weapons and said that some types of traditional forces were obsolescent. He

[1] *Pravda*, 15 January 1960, speech to the Supreme Soviet.
[2] *Neue Zurcher Zeitung*, 29 July 1960.
[3] Raymond L. Garthoff, 'The Military Establishment', *Eastern Europe*, Sept. 1965, p. 14.
[4] T. Wolfe, *The Evolving Nature of the Warsaw Pact* (Rand Corporation, December, 1965), p. 5, where he refers to *Spy in the US* by Pavel Monat with John Dille (Harper and Row, New York, 1962).

concluded by announcing the force reduction noted above, adding that the fire-power provided by new equipment would mean that the reduction would not impair the fighting capability of Soviet forces. The Soviet development of ICBMs by the end of the 1950s could also be interpreted as reducing Soviet dependence on their East European allies.

All this, combined with a political climate in which Khruschev was pursuing a policy at least ostensibly designed to relax international tension, provides some explanation of the apparent failure to give the Warsaw Pact any effective military cohesion. It was not until 1961, when the political climate had greatly changed and the Sino-Soviet dispute was coming into the open and assuming greatly increased bitterness, that the first joint military manoeuvres were conducted in the name of the Warsaw Pact.

The U-2 incident in May 1960, followed by the collapse of the Paris Summit, no doubt reinforced the opposition of Soviet military leaders to Khruschev's proposed force reductions. At the same time the first public confrontation between the Soviet and Chinese Parties took place at the Rumanian Party Congress in June. This was followed in November by the 81-Party meeting in Moscow which was also dominated by the dispute. The political and ideological argument was reflected in Sino-Soviet military relations. It is clear from subsequent Chinese accusations that the Soviet leaders were reducing military co-operation with the Chinese in the late fifties, culminating with a refusal to provide information on atomic weapons under a technical agreement of 1957.[1] It is possible that Khruschev in any case intended to make his proposed troop reductions more palatable to military circles by moving towards greater reliance on Warsaw Pact forces. There is evidence to suggest that the new commander-in-chief, Marshal Grechko, was more favourably disposed to an important role for the Pact than his predecessor.[2] Whatever Khruschev intended, the communiqué of the

---

[1] See T. Wolfe, *Soviet Strategy at the Crossroads* (Harvard University Press, 1964), pp. 216–224 for a detailed discussion of Sino-Soviet military relations.

[2] Wolfe, *The Evolving Nature of the Warsaw Pact*, pp. 12–13 and note 4.

March 1961 meeting of the Political Consultative Committee reflected the worsening of the international situation and stated that the Pact members had 'agreed on measures which they consider it necessary to carry out in the interests of further strengthening their capacity and consolidating peace throughout the world'.[1] It is not clear whether this was a reference to specifically Soviet or overall Pact military measures. In any event Khruschev, in July, speaking to graduates of the Soviet Military Academy announced the postponement of the planned Soviet troop reductions and also an increase in Soviet defence expenditure.[2]

On 8 and 9 September a meeting of defence ministers of the Warsaw Pact took place in Warsaw after which it was announced that the chiefs of staff had been instructed to work out practical measures for further strengthening defence in view of NATO military preparations. On 25 September it was announced in Moscow that joint manoeuvres would be held in October and November. This was the first such announcement and at about the same time it became known that the Warsaw Pact states were deferring the discharge of conscripts and advancing the date of their new intake.

All this was closely related to Soviet moves over Germany and Berlin. First Party Secretaries from the Pact member states had met in August in Moscow to issue a statement on 6 August expressing their determination to bring about a peace treaty with Germany by the end of 1961.[3] It was added that if this could not be done by agreement with the Western powers the Pact members would be forced to conclude a treaty with East Germany regulating among other things the situation in West Berlin. On the day the Berlin Wall was constructed a further statement was issued in Moscow on behalf of the Governments of the Warsaw Pact states calling on the East German authorities to 'establish such an order on the borders of West Berlin as to block the way for subversive activity against the Socialist countries'.[4] The political background and reasons for the Soviet

[1] *Izvestia*, 31 March 1961.
[2] *Pravda*, 9 July 1961.
[3] *Pravda*, 6 August 1961.
[4] *Pravda*, 14 August 1961.

decisions should therefore be given full weight, but the relevance of the continuing Soviet debate on strategy, in which Khruschev's January 1960 speech had been a landmark, should not be forgotten.

In October 1961, Marshal Malinovsky made a major speech on military strategy at the 22nd Soviet Party Congress. While he followed much of Khruschev's line on the paramount importance of strategic missile forces, Malinovsky reaffirmed the importance of traditional forces. He stressed that mass armies would be necessary for victory in a future war. In September 1962, the authoritative statement of Soviet military thinking, *Military Strategy – Soviet Doctrine and Concepts*, was published in Moscow under the editorship of Marshal Sokolovsky. This showed some signs of representing a compromise between those who concluded that the development of nuclear weapons greatly reduced the importance of large-scale armies and those who maintained that massive armies would still be necessary in future wars. For example in the chapter on 'Problems in the Construction of Armed Forces' it is stated that:

The advent of nuclear missiles ... revived ... the notorious theory that it is possible to conduct war with small armies that are technically well-equipped. The advocates of this theory do not take into account the fact that the new technology not only does not reduce but ... actually increases personnel requirements. Therefore massive multi-million-man armies will be necessary for waging the next war. ... For definitive victory it is absolutely necessary to defeat the enemy's armed forces, capture his military bases and occupy his strategically important areas. ... These and a number of other tasks can be performed by modern ground forces sufficiently strong in numbers ... therefore ground troops become the largest branch of the armed forces.[1]

Military Strategy also gives some clear signs of the impact on Soviet military thinking of the results of President Kennedy's measures on taking office to increase US military strength with their emphasis on developing conventional forces as a corollary to the adoption of the 'Flexible Response' strategy. Throughout the book stress is laid on the build-up of American forces. President Kennedy is quoted as outlining in 1961 a military

[1] Sokolovsky, op. cit., pp. 224–6.

programme for the build up and preparation of armed forces for either general nuclear or limited war.

The American plan, presented in the message of President Kennedy to Congress in 1961 and early 1962, provides for an increased rate of deployment of strategic rocket weapons in NATO countries and other alliances as well as for fully equipped and mobile conventional forces, especially ground troops. . . . Feverish preparations for all-out nuclear war against the Socialist countries are being made under cover of discussions of local war. We have reasonably convincing facts that show that the imperialists have not renounced their strategy of a surprise nuclear attack. True, the United States and its satellites have recently increased their defence budget for conventional weapons, but at the same time they are speeding up the development of strategic missiles. . . .[1]

'Flexible response' was in the Soviet view primarily a cover for a general increase in armaments to which the Soviet Union and its allies must respond.

These data show that modern armed forces are already mass armies . . . a future world war between the two coalitions of countries of the imperialist and Socialist armed forces will undoubtedly be waged by mass armed forces. . . . A new world war will be a coalition war. Entering it on one side will be the military coalition of capitalist states; on the other the coalition of socialist states.[2]

In this publication there is some, if carefully hedged, recognition of the possibility of 'small scale wars' for which Soviet military strategy must be prepared with the aim of preventing them from developing into a world war. The possibility of limiting any armed conflict if nuclear powers are involved is not however accepted.[3] A second edition published one year later (and of course after the Cuba crisis) retained the view that 'the concept of limited war contains many contradictions' but referred also to local wars in a way which suggested a move towards a less dogmatic view of the stage at which such wars would lead to a general nuclear war. The new edition also went as far as to suggest that in a local war tactical nuclear weapons

[1] *Military Strategy* (Praeger, 1963), pp. 71 and 264.
[2] Op. cit., pp. 201–203.
[3] Op. cit., p. 189.

might be used without resort to strategic nuclear weapons. An article in a Soviet military journal in May 1963, appearing between the two editions, referred to the possibility of the West launching a war without employing nuclear weapons, from which would flow the conclusion that Soviet forces must be prepared to react also by conventional means.[1] These indications of changes in Soviet military thinking combined with the emphasis in *Military Strategy* on the difficulty of mobilizing and assembling large forces in nuclear war conditions,[2] show that, quite apart from the international political climate and economic considerations, there were respectable military arguments from the Soviet point of view for greater emphasis on well-integrated, efficient mobile ground forces which would already be available in Eastern Europe if more life were given to the military side of the Warsaw Pact.

There are clear signs that from 1961 onwards the Russian aim was to enhance the military value of the Pact as well as its value for co-ordination of political policy. The period until the Czechoslovak crisis is marked by a series of joint manoeuvres and public statements by Soviet leaders implying efforts to step up the military integration within the Pact. Increased quantities of up-to-date equipment, including tactical nuclear missiles, were supplied by the Russians, though the nuclear war-heads no doubt remain under Soviet control. On the other hand this period also saw a steady trend towards greater autonomy and diversity among the East European countries, Rumania's moves in this direction receiving most publicity. The resistance to Soviet attempts to develop economic integration on a supranational basis through COMECON no doubt increased the importance from the Soviet point of view of military links in the framework of the Warsaw Pact. Russian moves to improve and strengthen military and political co-ordination interacted with the Pact members' own efforts to prevent the Pact from being used as an instrument for the reassertion of Soviet

---

[1] See Wolfe, *Soviet Strategy at the Crossroads*, chapter X, for discussion of the Soviet concept of limited war.
[2] *Military Strategy*, pp. 308 ff.

THE ROLE OF THE WARSAW PACT

leadership in face of the increasingly independent attitude of its members, some of whom, especially Rumania, were not slow to see the possibility of exploiting the Sino-Soviet dispute.

Between 1961 and the end of 1967 there were, according to published accounts, as many as 17 joint manoeuvres.[1] As early as 1962 the practice was introduced of these being at least nominally under the command of the Minister of Defence of the country in which they were held. (E.g. General Spychalski in Poland in 1962, General Lomsky in Czechoslovakia in July 1964, and Generals Hoffmann and Spychalski on East German and Polish territory in 1967.) The extent and tone of the publicity attending these manoeuvres has varied in accordance with the political climate. In 1962 *Red Star* in an editorial[2] stressed the joint forces' readiness 'to strike a retaliatory blow at an aggressor at any minute'. Czechoslovak radio described the 'Vltava' manoeuvres of September 1966, in which the Soviet Union, Hungary, East Germany and Czechoslovakia took part, as the biggest held in Europe either by the Warsaw Treaty or NATO countries since the end of the Second World War. Statements and speeches emphasized the close and friendly co-operation shown during these exercises. Warsaw radio, commenting on manoeuvres held in Poland in May and June 1967, referred to their contribution to the tightening of 'ideological bonds and brotherhood-in-arms' of the three armies taking part. The tone of statements by the Soviet Warsaw Pact commanders-in-chief also reflected increased reliance on the Warsaw Pact forces in the common defence plans.[3]

Reports on the earlier exercises implied a mainly conventional role for the East European forces, though Polish rocket units are mentioned as early as 1962.[4] By 1965 there was reference to an 'atomic thrust' to which the reply had been with 'the proper system of weapons'.[5] The 'Vltava' manoeuvres in Czechoslovakia in September 1966 were described as taking place 'in

[1] See Appendix 1, page 167.
[2] Quoted in *Soviet News*, 17 October 1962.
[3] E.g. Marshal Grechko, 'Fighting Alliance of Fraternal Peoples' in *Pravda*, 13 May 1965, and Marshal Yakubovsky, 'Fifty Years in Defence of Peace', *Izvestia*, 23 February 1968.
[4] E.g. Polish Radio (PAP) on manoeuvres in Poland in October 1962.
[5] East German Radio, 22 October 1965.

conditions of nuclear war'.[1] The pattern of these manoeuvres reflects a strong emphasis on the northern group of Poland, Czechoslovakia and East Germany. Of those announced there were not more than six on the territories of the southern members and only one (October 1962)[2] in Rumania. From the Soviet point of view the northern trio were both more reliable and strategically far more important in relation to the main threat of West Germany. The East German Minister of Defence referred in 1965 to the four northern members as 'the first strategic echelon'.[3] The Rumanian attitude towards the Pact is discussed below.

There was no doubt some truth in the repeated assertions by Soviet and East European leaders that the joint exercises had a unifying effect on the forces of the Pact members, but as these forces were brought up to date with modern equipment, including by 1964 tactical nuclear missile delivery systems, some of the stresses familiar to students of the western alliance could be detected. Soviet and Warsaw Pact warnings to the West against granting access to nuclear weapons to West Germany had been heard as early as the 1958 Political Consultative Committee meeting,[4] when Khruschev said that the Warsaw Treaty states were compelled to consider deploying missiles in East Germany, Poland and Czechoslovakia. The communiqué of the 1965 meeting held in January in Warsaw condemned any form of multilateral nuclear force which might be worked out in NATO as allowing West German access, direct or indirect, to nuclear weapons.[5] It may well be argued that part of the Soviet opposition to NATO nuclear sharing is due to fear of similar demands within the Warsaw Pact.[6] Marshal Grechko and other Soviet officers have stated that it is the missile strength of the Soviet Union which guarantees the security of the socialist countries.[7] There is no conclusive evidence that nuclear sharing was a major issue between the Rumanians and the Russians in

[1] Prague Radio, 20 September 1966.
[2] *The Times*, 19 October 1962.
[3] *Neues Deutschland*, 22 April 1965.
[4] *Pravda*, 24 May 1958.
[5] Polish Radio (PAP), 21 January 1965.
[6] Ermath Research Report Radio Free Europe, September 1965.
[7] E.g. Marshal Grechko in *Pravda*, 13 May 1965.

the widely publicized dispute between them in 1966, but it is very likely that control of the use of nuclear weapons was one of the points on which the Rumanians were standing when resisting Russian pressure to extend military and political integration within the Pact.

1965 saw, in addition to the meeting of the Political Consultative Committee, a little-publicized nine-day meeting in May of Pact defence ministers and commanders of armed forces in Carpathia at which 'views were exchanged on various questions of military development'.[1] On 14 September, speaking at a Soviet–Czech friendship rally in Moscow, Brezhnev said: 'The current situation places on the agenda the further perfection of the Warsaw Pact Organization.'[2] On 30 September he said that talks had been held with the East Europeans about the establishment within the framework of the Pact of a 'permanent and prompt mechanism for considering pressing problems'.[3] The Rumanians had in November 1964 reduced the length of compulsory service in their forces from 24 to 16 months.[4] In a speech at the celebration of the 45th Anniversary of the Rumanian Party in May 1966, the Party General Secretary, Nicolae Ceausescu, made quite clear the Rumanian opposition to military blocs, military bases and the stationing of foreign troops on other countries' territories.[5] There was no direct criticism of the Warsaw Pact, but the implication was picked up by the Western press[6] when the speech was followed by what appeared to be a hastily arranged visit by Brezhnev to Bucharest from 10–13 May. Immediately after that visit a story emanated from Moscow through the Agence France Presse that the Rumanians had circulated a document to members of the Pact raising objections to paying contributions to the cost of forces stationed on Pact members' territories, suggesting a rotation of the post of Commander-in-Chief of the Pact forces and also

[1] *The Times*, 19 May 1965. *Soviet News* (Soviet Embassy, London), 20 May 1965.
[2] Moscow Radio, 14 September 1965. *The Times*, 15 September 1965. *Manchester Guardian*, 15 September 1965.
[3] Speech at September Party Plenum, *Pravda*, 30 September 1965.
[4] Decree of Rumanian National Assembly, 14 November 1964.
[5] *Scinteia*, 8 May 1966.
[6] *Neue Zurcher Zeitung*, 16 May 1966. *New York Times*, 18 May 1966. *Humanité*, 18 May 1966.

that the use of nuclear weapons, whether strategic or tactical, should be subject to an agreement among the member states. The Rumanians, after some delay, subsequently denied the existence of the document and reaffirmed their loyalty to the Pact, but the impression was left that the story was not without foundation. Against the background of known Rumanian objections to any form of supranational control from Moscow, whether economic through COMECON[1] or political and military through Party channels or the framework of the Warsaw Pact, it is not unreasonable to conclude that Rumanian views were put forcibly to Moscow in advance of Brezhnev's visit. This may well have been planned for some time but possibly hastened by the tone of Ceausescu's May speech. The evidence of Brezhnev's own statements and the Pact meetings in 1965 strongly suggests that this was a time when the Russians were making determined moves to strengthen cohesion within the Pact. The Rumanians appear to have been concerned to preempt these. A further public indication of the independent Rumanian attitude was the visit (presumably planned some time before) of Chou-en-lai to Bucharest at the end of June. Apart from Tirana, Bucharest was the only East European capital where this visitor could be assured of a welcome.

The cohesion for which the Russians were working was not solely military. The Political Consultative Committee continued to be used for the purpose of issuing endorsements of Soviet policy, particularly at this time in connection with Soviet opposition to German nuclear participation. Brezhnev in his call for more effective Pact machinery would have had in mind the need to counter opposition to political co-ordination just as much as military. Again, as Ceausescu's speech on 7 May 1966 showed, the Rumanians were at the head of this opposition. Ceausescu's tactic was not to state his hostility to interference in Rumanian affairs, but rather to emphasize that socialist parties and governments naturally did not interfere in each other's development of a communist society, presumably on the assumption that such a statement would not be contradicted.

Divergent views within the Pact were again underlined by a

---

[1] Cf. the Rumanian Declaration of April 1964. M. Kaser, *Comecon*, pp. 108 ff.

Yugoslav report from Moscow in late May which referred to the forthcoming meeting of the Political Consultative Committee and reported a two-day meeting of Pact defence ministers in Moscow in preparation for the military discussions of the Committee. This was linked with a reference to a meeting of deputy ministers of defence in February described as discussing 'the improvement in the mechanism of military co-operation on the basis of proposals tabled by Rumanian and other representatives'.[1] Subsequently serious disagreements arising during a meeting of Pact foreign ministers, presumably also held in preparation for the meeting in Bucharest, were reported from Moscow.[2] It is very likely that the meeting, in July 1966 in Bucharest, was held at the instigation of the Rumanians who wished to use the occasion to put over their own views.[3]

In the event there was no public indication that there was any discussion of military matters at the meeting. The Declaration on Europe issued on 8 July[4] contained a proposal for a 'general conference' on European security in addition to the customary statements on European frontiers, a German settlement and the need for the Warsaw Pact powers to carry out 'the necessary defensive measures' if NATO were by any means to allow West German access to nuclear weapons. The relatively moderate tone of this declaration with its emphasis on intensifying contacts of all sorts between all European states, the fact that the well known Rumanian formula on respect between nations for sovereignty, equal rights and non-interference appears no less than four times and the call for the abolition of both alliances are probably signs of Rumanian hands in the drafting.[5] A declaration on Vietnam was also issued in tough language consisting mainly of a condemnation of the United States. Rumanian interest in maintaining relations with China may have contributed to the tone and content of this. Western press accounts have not been slow to draw a comparison between Rumania's position and that of France in NATO, on which an appropriate

[1] *Borba*, 27 May 1966.
[2] *The Times*, 12 June 1966.
[3] *Neue Zurcher Zeitung*, 15 May 1966. *The Times*, 18 May 1966.
[4] *Scinteia*, 9 July 1966.
[5] *The Times*, 9 July 1966. *Scinteia*, 9 July 1966.

gloss was provided by Rumania's establishment of diplomatic relations with West Germany in January 1967.

We thus have evidence of stresses within the Pact covering in some cases similar subjects to those known to have arisen within NATO. It is not possible to estimate reliably the degree of support Rumania may have received from fellow members in opposing Russian moves towards closer integration. The Hungarians would not be likely to have favoured anything resembling a return to the days of the Cominform and extensive supranational direction from Moscow. With Soviet troops on their territory they would have a direct interest in the question of support costs. The underlying Hungarian attitude towards the Czechoslovak crisis, shown by their sympathetic press reaction to the Czechoslovak Action Programme[1] and the publication[2] on 20 July 1968 by the Hungarian news agency of the Czechoslovak Praesidium's reply to the Warsaw Letter of 15 July is a sign of the way they would view the Rumanian stand. At the other extreme it must be recognized that there were those – notably the East Germans and Gomulka (even if many Poles thought very differently) – who favoured a tight rein from Moscow to prevent divergencies within the Communist bloc getting out of hand. These would also be able to exert influence through Pact meetings. The Czechoslovaks themselves under Novotny would not have been likely to oppose the Russians, and could no doubt have been expected to count in with those interested in keeping the Rumanians within bounds.[3] Discussions on the 'strengthening' of the Pact appear to have continued at least until the early summer of 1968 and there are signs that the process has been carried on with Marshal Yakubovsky's tour of capitals of all Warsaw Pact member states in September 1968.[4] At the same time it is now clear that the Czechoslovaks themselves, presumably with Rumanian support, have recently put forward proposals designed to increase the part played in decisions of the joint command by the representatives of member states other than the Soviet Union. General Prchlik revealed

[1] *Nepszabadsag*, 4 June 1968.
[2] The Hungarians were alone among the invading powers to do this.
[3] *Daily Telegraph*, 18 May 1966.
[4] Radio Sofia of 20 September referred to discussions on 'the further strengthening of the Warsaw Treaty'. Cf. *The Times*, 2 October 1968.

this at a press conference on 15 July 1968, when he described the function of these representatives up to that time as playing 'the role of liaison organs'.[1] The Czechoslovak Minister of Defence, General Dzur, on 5 October, explained that the Sofia meeting of the Pact Consultative Committee in March had been concerned with command problems and not the Czechoslovak crisis. He referred to documents, which he thought had Russian support, which would give 'even greater responsibilities and independence to the Defence Ministers and General Staffs'.[2]

It may be argued that the delay over the appointment of Marshal Yakubovsky to succeed Marshal Grechko on the latter's appointment as Soviet Minister of Defence provides further evidence of genuine consultation among the members of the Pact. Marshal Grechko was appointed Soviet Minister of Defence on 13 April 1967. His successor was not announced until 7 July.[3] It may well be that the Russians felt it necessary at least to appear to conduct genuine consultations about this appointment if only to deprive the Rumanians of grounds for securing support in other East European states for their attitude towards the Pact.[4] It is perhaps also significant that *Pravda* published a long article entitled 'Unity – the source of our strength' on 23 July. This was in effect a call for the maintenance of the unity of the Socialist camp and in particular support for the Warsaw Pact.

The Warsaw Pact emerges before the Czechoslovak crisis as an instrument of Soviet political and military policy, whose use and development has been closely related to the international climate and the development of Soviet strategic thinking. None of its known institutions is comparable in procedure or organization, so far as these are known, with those of NATO. The supreme organ, the Political Consultative Committee, has not met at regular intervals; in fact, there have only been nine such meetings since the Pact's conclusion in 1955. This cannot be

[1] Prague Radio Home Service, 15 July 1968.
[2] Prague Radio Home Service, 5 October 1968.
[3] Prague Radio, 7 July 1967 (SWB No. 2511).
[4] Radio Free Europe Report of 3 May 1967. 'New Warsaw Pact Commander likely to be Soviet.'

compared with the weekly meetings of the North Atlantic Council or the biannual meetings of NATO Ministers. The Secretariat located in Moscow with a Russian military Secretary General may well wield considerable power in the absence of regular meetings of the Consultative Committee. This is clearly the case with the Joint Command, also in Moscow, under the Soviet Commander-in-Chief. We have evidence from a Czechoslovak general of the insignificant part played in decision-making by the representatives of the other members on this command. In any case a special branch of the Soviet General Staff acts as the planning and co-ordinating centre for the Pact forces.[1]

The strict Soviet control over the military organization of the Pact is reinforced by the predominant role of the Soviet Union in the supply and manufacture of equipment and weapons which are standardized to a very high degree throughout the Pact forces. The regular Pact forces according to published information total in the region of 4 million, of which forces other than those of the Soviet Union make up about 850,000. This compares with a NATO total of about 6 million with the United States providing 3·5 million.[2]

Despite the greater emphasis since 1961 on the military side of the Pact, it is as an instrument of Soviet political policy that the Pact has acquired greatest importance. It is quite clear that it has been increasingly seen in Russian eyes as a means of securing a greater degree of unity among its members as the unity of the communist world has been steadily eroded. From the outset this aspect of the Pact was potentially significant in the post-Stalin era. In the absence of any other standing multilateral, political or military link the Warsaw Pact has more and more been used as a framework for working out and publicizing accepted Soviet (and East European) doctrine on international affairs. No doubt the permanent commission set up in Moscow

[1] Garthoff, *Eastern Europe*, September 1965, p. 13. Cf. Tirana Radio, 22 May 1965: 'The Treaty is in fact directed by the Soviet Minister of Defence. The C-in-C of the united armed forces ... is also Malinovsky's First Deputy Minister and General Batov the Chief of Staff ... is also Deputy Chief of the General Staff of the Soviet Army. The remaining Treaty personnel from first to last belong to the Ministry of Defence of the Soviet Union. Officially the deputy commanders are the Defence Ministers of the member countries but that is a mere formality'.

[2] Institute for Strategic Studies, *The Military Balance*, 1968–9.

THE ROLE OF THE WARSAW PACT

to advise the Consultative Committee on foreign policy plays an important part in this. This is not to say that the Russians see the Pact as a substitute for the wider communist unity for which they continue to strive. The European communist meeting at Karlovy Vary in April 1967 was intended as a step in the direction of a wider communist conference, and even in face of reactions to the invasion of Czechoslovakia, the international committee set up to prepare the conference planned for November 1968 decided to postpone and not to cancel it.[1]

But the evidence also shows that, despite Russian military predominance, the Pact has, in a similar manner to its economic equivalent COMECON, reflected the gradual assertion of varying degrees of national autonomy by its members. The Rumanians have been in the lead in resisting attempts to impose stronger central control; the Czechoslovaks have clearly held similar views, at least in the past few months, and we may assume that the Hungarians, whose press comment has continued to stress the right of the Czechoslovak Party to work out its own future, even while warning of the dangers of 'counter-revolution'[2], would also be opposed to any tightening of the Soviet reins. It is significant that, unlike the Russians and other invaders, the Hungarians have not criticized the Czechoslovak plans for economic reform based on decentralized planning. The Hungarians themselves embarked on a similar, and possibly more far-reaching, programme at the beginning of 1968.

So it appears that the Pact, while viewed by the Russians primarily as an instrument for retaining and tightening control in their 'Socialist Commonwealth', has shown some signs of acquiring, admittedly very gradually, a role as a forum in which the East Europeans themselves can exert some influence on their Soviet colleagues, whether in the direction favoured by the Rumanians or on the contrary to encourage a harder attitude toward such dissidents.

It remains to examine the use of the Pact in relation to the Czechoslovak crisis and to attempt to draw some tentative conclusions for the Pact's future development.

[1] *The Times*, 2 October 1968.
[2] E.g. *Nepszabadsag*, 24 July 1968.

THE CZECHOSLOVAK CRISIS 1968

The first thing that needs to be said is that there is no evidence that the machinery of the Warsaw Pact as such was used on any of the main occasions on which meetings were held between the Czechoslovak leaders and those of the Soviet Union and the four other invading powers. In any case the bilateral confrontations between the Russian and Czechoslovak leaders during Dubcek's January and May visits to Moscow, the visit of Kosygin and that of the Soviet Defence Minister, Marshal Grechko, to Czechoslovakia in May and the bilateral talks at Cierna-nad-Tisou at the end of July appear to have been those at which the real business was done. The Dresden meeting in March, from which Rumania was absent, was not described as a Warsaw Pact meeting, though the communiqué did refer to agreement on practical measures to strengthen the Warsaw Pact and its armed forces. Nor was there any sign that those at Warsaw and Bratislava were held under Pact arrangements. We know that the Political Consultative Committee meeting in March was not devoted to Czechoslovak affairs.[1]

The Russians certainly valued the co-operation of their allies from both the political and military points of view. The Rumanian attitude and the absence of a Czechoslovak 'invitation' precluded a unanimous Warsaw Pact reaction, whether political or military. If the Russians were to argue that events in Czechoslovakia threatened 'the interests of the entire Socialist system',[2] they must do this with other representatives of 'Socialism', and this is what they did, but without much emphasis on the Pact except where military measures were concerned. It is probable that other Pact members, especially the East German leader, Herr Ulbricht, influenced the Russians in favour of the use of force. We do not know, and perhaps never shall know, exactly how the Russian decision to invade was taken. But it must be remembered that this influence could be exerted through Party or Governmental channels quite independently of the Warsaw Pact and its institutions. Lastly it is noteworthy that the bilateral Treaty concluded on 16 October for the continued stationing of Soviet troops on Czechoslovak territory contains no mention of the Warsaw Treaty, and that, unlike the Hungarian

---

[1] See page 49 above.
[2] Warsaw Letter of 15 July.

intervention, the Russians have made no attempt to justify their invasion of Czechoslovakia by reference to the Treaty.[1]

Events in Czechoslovakia were bound to cause the Russians concern from a military point of view. The Czechoslovak forces occupied the Bohemian salient along the West German and Austrian borders without the support of any Russian troops stationed in Czechoslovakia. We have no reason to doubt that until 1967 the Czechoslovak forces under General Lomsky, who had served during the Second World War under Russian command, were trusted in this task by the Russians and their other allies.[2] Some of the changes introduced by the Czechoslovak leaders when their reform movement got under way were bound to undermine this confidence. First General Lomsky himself, the Chief of General Staff and the Head of the Political Directorate were replaced even before the publication of the Action Programme. The return of General Prchlik to army duty after his criticism of the July Warsaw meeting was accompanied by the abolition of the party central committee department for military and security affairs, of which he had been head. This, added to the apparent Czechoslovak reluctance to engage in large-scale Warsaw Pact exercises, was bound to arouse Russian suspicions. In the event the Russians described the manoeuvres which did take place as a field exercise, while the Czechoslovaks described them as a communications exercise, a significant difference.[3] The Warsaw Pact did of course provide the framework for these manoeuvres, though, in retrospect, they appear to have been primarily a Soviet reconnaissance from the military point of view. When it came to the invasion itself preparations were conducted by General Shtemenko who was appointed Chief of Staff of the Warsaw Pact a few days before the invasion and who had been Chief of Staff of the Soviet general forces (though this change may have been due in any case; Shtemenko's predecessor was 67).[4] Command of the invasion forces was given to General Pavlovski, Commander-in-Chief of the Soviet

[1] See pages 35-6 above.
[2] See *Red Star* of 22 and 23 September 1966 for a general account of the success of exercises held in Czechoslovakia under General Lomsky's command.
[3] Cf. *Rude Pravo* of 3 May 1968 referring to a 'communications exercise'. *Pravda* of 2 July described the exercise as an 'exercise with troops'.
[4] Keesing's Contemporary Archives, 1963, p. 22871.

ground forces, and not to the Warsaw Pact Commander-in-Chief, General Yakubovsky. This decision may have been partly due to the need to keep details of the preparations from Czechoslovak representatives on the Joint Command in Moscow, and is not necessarily a sign that the Pact machinery as such was not used to co-ordinate the invasion. In any case it could be argued that it was not appropriate for Yakubovsky himself to command a limited operation of this sort. The logistical military efficiency of the operation must certainly be partly attributed to the training provided by the series of Warsaw Pact exercises conducted since 1961. At the same time these arrangements and the predominant part played by Soviet forces are entirely consistent with the picture of the military organization of the Pact which had emerged by 1967.[1] It would be perfectly simple for the Russians with their tight control of all Pact military affairs to arrange the preparation and command of the invasion in whatever way suited them best. It is relevant that Sokolovsky's *Military Strategy* had contained the passage 'command of joint operations in major theatres remain in Soviet hands ... allied units in some areas might remain under national command'.[2]

What conclusions is it possible to draw from the role of the Warsaw Pact in the Czechoslovak crisis? First, the crisis effectively demonstrated that the working of the Pact, both military and political, reflects very accurately the military and political balance between its members. Examples of this are Rumania's complete absence from the operation and the Russian control of the planning and execution. The operation showed the East Europeans, if they needed to be shown, that the Pact is as much a limitation of their independence as a guarantee of their security. No doubt with this in mind Ceausescu in a speech on 17 July 1968 emphasized that the Pact was an instrument of collective defence rather than a justification for interference in the internal affairs of other states.

The efficiency of the Pact forces involved was also effectively demonstrated. The future reliability of the Czechoslovak forces

[1] See pages 49–51 above.
[2] Sokolovsky, op. cit. 368

THE ROLE OF THE WARSAW PACT

must remain in question from the Soviet point of view and this will provide an additional ground for the continued presence of Soviet forces in Czechoslovakia. Czechoslovak forces do appear to have remained in the vital frontier areas though this is a similar situation to that in East Germany, and can be seen as designed to avoid direct confrontation with NATO forces. The invasion of Czechoslovakia showed that the preservation of their position in Eastern Europe must be seen as a top foreign policy priority for the Russians. They have demonstrated their willingness to use force to secure this. The lesson will not be lost on the East Europeans and the political consequences will be reflected in future developments in the Warsaw Pact. This is likely to mean that the slight and gradual development of the Pact towards something more like what we understand as an alliance with a decision-taking and decision-influencing role will be slowed if not completely halted. The Russians are likely to want to take measures, at least in the short run, to halt if not reverse the process, and to strengthen their own ability directly to control the forces of their allies especially in view of the doubts about the reliability of those of Czechoslovakia. This interpretation of Marshal Yakubovsky's recent tour of East European capitals appears to have been circulating in Prague.[1] It may be long before we get reliable details of any changes in the command structure or procedure, but it is reasonable to conclude that, at least for the immediate future, the Pact will retain its primary importance as an instrument of Soviet political and military policy designed to maintain and strengthen Russian control of their 'Socialist Commonwealth'. Whether its primary importance is political or military from the Soviet point of view will depend on the particular circumstances in which it is put to use. It is perhaps revealing that in a recent *Pravda* article the 'Socialist Commonwealth' was apparently at least for present purposes equated with the Warsaw Pact.[2]

---

[1] *The Times*, 2 October 1968.
[2] *Pravda*, 27 October, contains an article entitled 'The implacable battle of ideas' which includes the passage: 'Today, when Czechoslovakia is a Socialist state, its sovereignty and independence is guaranteed by all the might of the countries of the Socialist Commonwealth – the members of the Warsaw Pact'.

4

NATO and the Crisis

Background

THE Czechoslovak crisis deeply involved the future of one international organization, if the Warsaw Pact can thus be described. It was also of profound concern to NATO, which was not technically directly concerned, but to whom the results and possible implications of the crisis had an immediate relevance. This relevance was emphasized by the statement of the foreign and defence ministers of the Alliance at the end of their meeting in November 1968 – the meeting itself having been brought forward by a month as a result of the crisis – to the effect that they 'could not remain indifferent to any development which endangers their security. Clearly any Soviet intervention directly or indirectly affecting the situation in Europe or in the Mediterranean would create an international crisis with grave consequences'.[1]

This statement was made at a time when the Alliance was being subjected to considerable criticism for having in some sense 'failed' before, during, and after the events of 20–21 August.[2] A careful examination of these charges requires consideration of the military and political purposes of the Alliance;

[1] Communiqué of the foreign and defence ministers of NATO, Brussels, November.

[2] See, for example, the allegation of the defence correspondent of the *Observer* (17 November) that NATO had suffered a communications breakdown in the critical period following 21 August, and the claim by the former Secretary of State for Foreign Affairs that resolute action by the NATO powers might have averted the invasion (*Evening Standard*, 15 November).

an examination of the way in which these purposes were being fulfilled prior to the crisis; and consideration of the alternatives open to NATO during the crisis. Inevitably, such an analysis will at this stage be incomplete, but it will not be without value if it assists to dispel certain widely held misconceptions about the nature of the Alliance.

The purposes of the North Atlantic Alliance are set out in the Preamble to the Treaty, of which the most significant section relates to the resolution of the signatories to unite their efforts for collective defence. The obligations assumed by the signatories are to uphold the principles of the United Nations; to strengthen their free institutions by the process of education, and to seek the elimination of economic conflicts; to maintain and develop their individual and collective capacity to resist armed attack; to consult freely together whenever any member believes that its territorial integrity, political independence, or national security is threatened; and to render such help as each considers necessary should any member be attacked. It is important to emphasize at this stage that there are several significant objectives which are deliberately excluded from the treaty. The military guarantee, couched in suitably cautious terms, applies only to the signatories. Furthermore, unless previously committed through military integration in the joint command structure, there is no hard and fast obligation to aid a fellow member if attacked; a member shall take only 'such action as it deems necessary, including the use of armed force, to restore and maintain the security of the North Atlantic Area'.

Those who condemn the Alliance because it has done no more than it set out to do should take some warning from the misfortunes of Lear, rejecting Cordelia because she loved her father – 'According to my bond; nor more nor less'. Nevertheless, the Alliance is clearly meant to have both a military and a political role to play in conditions short of an armed attack upon a member state. Because the invasion of Czechoslovakia was both a political and a military act, it is convenient to examine the political and military organization of the Alliance separately. It is, of course, open to dispute whether a clear distinction can in fact be made, or whether military problems and political relationships within alliances are so closely linked that the separate machinery for handling the two sets of problems in NATO should be more closely integrated.

Taking political relationships first, it is necessary to go no further back than 1956, the year of Hungary and Suez. Before the crises broke, a 'Committee on Non-Military Co-operation' had been set up by the North Atlantic Council 'to advise the Council on ways and means to improve and extend NATO co-operation in non-military fields and to develop greater unity within the Atlantic Community'. The report of the 'three wise men',[1] as it was later called, adopted by the Council in December 1956, remains the fundamental work on political consultation within the Alliance, and deserves extensive quotation. Noting that the first NATO objective was military security, the report observed:

Certainly NATO unity and strength in the pursuit of this objective remain as essential as they were in 1949. Soviet tactics may have changed, but Soviet armed might and ultimate objectives remain unchanged. Moreover, recent events in Eastern Europe show that the Soviet Union will not hesitate in certain circumstances to use force and the threat of force. Therefore the military strength of NATO must not be reduced, though its character and capabilities should be constantly adapted to changing circumstances. Strengthening the political and economic side of NATO is an essential complement to – not a substitute for – continuous co-operation in defence.[2]

Elsewhere, the report makes the more general observation:

The coming together of the Atlantic nations for good and constructive purposes – which is the basic principle and ideal underlying the NATO concept – must rest on and grow from deeper and more permanent factors than the divisions and dangers of the last ten years. It is a historical, rather than a contemporary development and if it is to achieve its real purpose, it must be considered in that light and the necessary conclusions drawn. A short-range view will not suffice.

The fundamental historical fact underlying development is that

[1] The three were: Dr Gaetano Martino (Italy); Mr Halvard Lange (Norway); Mr Lester B. Pearson (Canada). The Report was prepared after the circulation of a questionnaire to governments, a series of hearings in Paris in September, and a review in November following the Suez and Hungarian crises.

[2] 'Non-Military Co-operation in NATO', Report of the Committee of Three (NATO Information Service, Brussels), paragraph 25.

the nation state, by itself and relying exclusively on national policy and national power, is inadequate for progress, or even for survival in the nuclear age. As the founders of the North Atlantic Treaty foresaw, the growing interdependence of states, politically and economically as well as militarily, calls for an ever-increasing measure of international cohesion and co-operation. Some states may be able to enjoy a degree of political and economic independence when things are going well. No state, however powerful, can guarantee its security and its welfare by national action alone.[1]

Among the specific recommendations of the report, which served to transform NATO into something more than a purely 'functional' organization, concerned solely with defence, were the following 'principles and practices in the field of political consultation':

(a) members should inform the Council of any development which significantly affects the Alliance. They should do this, not merely as a formality but as a preliminary to effective political consultation;

(b) both individual member governments and the Secretary-General should have the right to raise for discussion in the Council any subject which is of a common NATO interest and not of a purely domestic character;

(c) a member government should not, without adequate advance consultation, adopt firm policies or make major political pronouncements on matters which significantly affect the Alliance or any of its members, unless circumstances make such prior consultation obviously and demonstrably impossible;

(d) in developing their national policies, members should take into consideration the interests and views of other governments, particularly those most directly concerned, as expressed in NATO consultation, even where no community of view or consensus has been reached in the Council;

(e) where a consensus has been reached, it should be reflected in the formation of national policies. When for national reasons the consensus is not followed, the government concerned should offer an explanation to the Council. It is even more important that where an agreed and formal recommendation has emerged from the Council's discussions, governments should give it full

[1] Ibid., paras. 35 and 36.

weight in any national actions or policies related to the subject of that recommendation.[1]

These extracts should make it clear that there is no such thing as 'NATO policy' existing independently of the consensus of the fifteen governments represented in the North Atlantic Council. A government may have cause for complaint if the processes of consultation have impeded it in the pursuit of a daring and original foreign policy. It has no ground for complaining that 'NATO' should have seen more clearly into the future than it had itself.

The normal processes of consultation, as outlined by the three wise men, have continued with varying degrees of intensity from 1956 to the present. In addition, an extensive review of the future tasks of the Alliance was carried out in 1967 as the result of an initiative by M. Pierre Harmel, the Belgian Foreign Minister. Although the French had, by that time, withdrawn from the integrated military organization of the Alliance they were (and are) represented on the North Atlantic Council, and the Report as approved, and issued to the public in December 1967 is a fifteen-power document. What is perhaps the most important passage in it now runs:

> The Atlantic Alliance has two main functions. Its first function is to maintain adequate military strength and political solidarity to deter aggression and other forms of pressure and to defend the territory of member countries if aggression should occur. Since its inception, the Alliance has successfully fulfilled this task. But the possibility of a crisis cannot be excluded as long as the central political issues in Europe, first and foremost the German Question, remain unsolved. Moreover, the situation of instability and uncertainty still precludes a balanced reduction of military forces. Under these conditions, the Allies will maintain as necessary, a suitable military capability to assure the balance of forces, thereby creating a climate of stability, security and confidence.
>
> In this climate the Alliance can carry out its second function, to pursue the search for progress towards a more stable relationship in which the underlying political issue can be solved. Military security and a policy of détente are not contradictory but complementary. Collective defence is a stabilizing factor in world politics. It is the

[1] Ibid., para. 51.

necessary condition for effective policies directed towards a greater relaxation of tensions. The way to peace and stability in Europe rests in particular on the use of the Alliance constructively in the interest of détente. The participation of the USSR and the USA will be necessary to achieve a settlement of the political problems in Europe.[1]

It was recognized that the political function of the Alliance should consist, not only of the improvement of relations among its members, but also of an improvement of relations with the Soviet bloc.

Before examining the ways in which the Alliance has been pursuing its political goal, it is necessary to examine how it fulfils the role of providing military security for its members. As with political questions, we first examine the goals as they have been stated by the alliance members themselves. In the military field it is convenient to go back as far as 1954, the year in which the French National Assembly blocked the proposal for a European Defence Community. The damage this caused to NATO plans for 'forward defence' was mitigated by the Paris Agreements of October 1954, which provided for the termination of the occupation régime in Western Germany and the recognition of the Federal Republic as a sovereign state; the accession of the Federal Republic and Italy to the Brussels Treaty[2] whose signatories were henceforth to constitute a 'Western European Union'; and an invitation to the Federal Republic to join NATO, thereby contributing to Western Defence by means of a national army integrated into the forces of the alliance.

Machinery was also set up to limit the number of forces and formations to be created within the WEU framework, and the UK gave a pledge to keep, on the mainland of Europe, the effective strength of the forces which, at that time, had been

---

[1] 'Report of the Future Tasks of the Alliance' (NATO Information Service, Brussels), para. 5, adopted by the NATO Ministers of Foreign Affairs at their meeting in December 1967.
[2] The Brussels Treaty of Economic, Social and Cultural Collaboration and Collective Self Defence had been signed on 17 March 1948 by representatives of Britain, France, Belgium, Luxembourg, and the Netherlands. It was a forerunner of the North Atlantic Treaty and may indeed outlast it – the Brussels Treaty was to last for 50 years; the North Atlantic Treaty provides for withdrawal after 20.

assigned[1] to NATO. Following a recommendation by Mr Dulles, President Eisenhower on 5 March 1955 gave a public undertaking to maintain American forces on the European continent for as long as would be necessary. It is worth noting, at this point, that the presence of British and American forces in Germany was underlined, not only on account of a Soviet threat, but also because of the re-creation of a German army. During this period, and for many years to come, it was possible to discover people who supported NATO both as a collective self-defence arrangement directed against the Soviet threat, and as that organization which kept German troops 'safely' integrated into a joint command structure.

With the accession of Germany to the North Atlantic Treaty, in 1955, the NATO 'family' was complete. Like any other military alliance it had to hammer out agreements on the nature of the threats which had brought its members together; on the correct doctrine which would determine the allied response; and on an appropriate system for the management of that response. Debates on these three distinct areas contributed much more to the tensions which grew up within the alliance, than did any purely 'political' issue. As an indication of the state of health within the Alliance before the Czechoslovak crisis, it is perhaps worth recalling some of the salient features of the major debates which have taken place in each category.

The nature of the threat
It is a 'straightforward', if difficult, intelligence problem to make a reasonable guess at the military capabilities of the Soviet bloc at any given time. What is much harder is to calculate the intentions of the Warsaw Pact High Command. In elaborating contingency plans for NATO, it is hard to determine whether a

[1] NATO forces are of three types: 'assigned to NATO' means that forces have already been placed under NATO operational command: so far, forces have only been assigned to the Supreme Allied Commander in Europe (SACEUR) who is responsible for their training in peacetime and military operation in wartime (although they remain under national control for administration and discipline); 'earmarked for NATO' means that forces will be placed at the disposal of the NATO Commanders in the event of mobilization or war; 'under national command' – those forces which ensure the defence of national territories as well as carry out security and garrison duties. Also any forces stationed outside the NATO area.

deteriorating political situation would be an essential precondition of an attack on NATO territory. If some sort of 'political warning time' can be counted upon; how long is it likely to be; and how many forces could, during that period, be rushed from England, for example, to the Central Front? Obviously, it is in the interest of the extra-continental powers if the alliance can agree that such a period can be counted upon – for this permits them, in peace time, to station more of their NATO-assigned forces at home, and thus to conserve foreign exchange. Debate on this point has taken place in the past, and between the most likely protagonists of the opposing schools. As Alastair Buchan has commented: '... the British view [is] that force levels in NATO should now be based on a reasonable view of Soviet intentions, and the German view [is] that they should be based on Soviet capabilities'.[1]

An unfortunate feature of these differences was the British tendency to back up their views with near-unilateral action, despite the formal obligation already referred to.[2] Writing before he became a Minister in the present government, Mr Mulley observed that 'The Council of Western European Union acquiesced in the withdrawal of 13,500 British troops from Germany in the financial year 1957–8 and in January 1958 authorized the withdrawal of a further 8,500. ... These reductions were extremely unpopular in Europe and undoubtedly contributed to the decline in British influence and prestige.'[3] Unlike the British, the Americans, as has been made clear in earlier sections, have no legal obligation to maintain forces on the continent of Europe, and her allies have been dependent on a series of unilateral guarantees, made without Congressional authorization. Were the Americans ever to believe that the situation in Europe was stable, only the anguished appeals of her allies would stand in the way of a complete military withdrawal. An appropriately low-key guarantee was, however, provided by Secretary of Defence McNamara in his last budget statement before the Senate Armed Services Committee.

[1] Alastair Buchan, 'The Future of NATO', *International Conciliation*, November, 1967, p. 15.
[2] See page 61.
[3] F. W. Mulley, *The Politics of Western Defence*, pp. 132, 133.

We recognize that our large military presence in Europe has acquired a particularly symbolic importance in the eyes of some of our allies. Accordingly, for nearly two decades, we have maintained substantial air and ground forces in Europe at a high state of readiness – as well as large forces in the Continental United States – in order to give concrete evidence to friend and foe alike of our commitment to NATO. In the course of 1968, we will, in agreement with our allies, re-deploy close to 34,000 United States military personnel from Europe to the United States . . .

I, for one, believe that the willingness of the United States to fulfil its obligations should no longer be in question, quite apart from the presence or absence of a particular number of US troops on the ground. . . . We will . . . continue to maintain forces in Europe for as long as they are desired.[1]

Doctrine

Quite apart from the debate about the nature of the Soviet threat there occurred a much more damaging difference of opinion about the way in which NATO should respond to the various forms of Soviet attack, should they ever take place. After an abortive attempt (launched at the ministerial meeting in Lisbon in 1952) to design a purely conventional defence of Europe, great – and indeed overwhelming – reliance was placed on the role of nuclear weapons.[2] The 'deterrent' aspect of these weapons was not the only role they were to play; NATO contingency plans were based on the assumption that, at some stage, the nuclear weapons would have to be employed if a major war occurred. During the Eisenhower administration large numbers of tactical nuclear weapons were introduced into Western Europe and held there under a 'double veto' system which required permission both from the host country and from the President of the US before they could be used. At the same time, intermediate range missile bases were constructed in Britain, Italy, and Turkey. The 1956 directives, under which the Supreme Allied Commander Europe had to operate, envisaged in effect a nuclear war in Europe. But in the later 1950s, European confidence in the US commitment to Europe was in-

[1] Robert S. McNamara, 'Fiscal Year 1969–73: Defence Program and the 1969 Defence Budget', p. 31.

[2] A fuller account of the debate on strategy is provided in Kissinger, *The Troubled Partnership*, pp. 91 *et seq.*

creasingly undermined by apprehensions that in the final analysis, once the US was threatened by Soviet rocket bombardment, no American government would be willing to risk such a possibility for any cause but the existence of the United States. European nervousness was reinforced when, early in the Kennedy administration, Secretary McNamara proclaimed the doctrine of 'flexible response'. Although this was no more than a straightforward adjustment to the technological facts of life, the Europeans flatly refused to accept the new doctrine until December 1967. It must be conceded that the new doctrine was not explained as clearly as it might have been, and the phrase 'flexible response' itself was ambiguous, containing as it did the possibility in certain circumstances of no response at all. Furthermore there is, unhappily, considerable justification in the comment of Dr Kissinger that 'American policy-makers often act as if disagreement to their views is due to ignorance which must be overcome by extensive briefings and insistent reiteration. They are less inclined to inquire whether there may be some merit in an opposing view than in overwhelming it with floods of emissaries, official or semi-official'.[1] The new doctrine, rather more accurately described as one of 'multiple opinions', has not remained static in the period 1960–67, but the central concept – well described by President Kennedy on 25 July 1961 as the provision of 'a wider choice than humiliation or all-out nuclear war' – has remained constant. McNamara subsequently summarized the debate in these terms:

> For six years the discussion has centred on the extent to which we should plan on the use of nuclear weapons as the main response to non-nuclear aggression. The United States has been firmly of the view that the threat of an incredible action is not an effective deterrent ... if the Soviets found the threat of an immediate nuclear response to limited aggression incredible, they could well be tempted to probe or experiment. ... Our NATO partners have now acknowledged the need to plan for a much larger range of contingencies than a massive NATO-wide attack.[2]

Whether or not the NATO ministers 'accepted' the doctrine, it was clear that the US could not be forced to use nuclear

[1] Kissinger, op. cit., p. 6.
[2] McNamara, op. cit., pp. 29–30.

weapons in circumstances that it considered inappropriate. Thus the debate was largely unreal, and the differences between the US and its allies served only to provide the French with ammunition in their campaign against US hegemony. Beaufre, for example, referring to the original US formulation of 'flexible response', says:

> This decision, it must be emphasized, was taken unilaterally by the Americans without consultation of any kind with their Allies. It led to very important consequences. The first was to give the Europeans the impression that they might once again become the arena for a trial of strength ... the Russians and the Americans meanwhile enjoying a kind of immunity in their home countries ... [The second] revealed the full extent of the contradiction within NATO between the principle of a common strategy discussed and approved by the alliance, and the secrecy in which the Americans shrouded their nuclear strategy.[1]

Emotion apart, the practical difficulties which the new doctrine posed for the Europeans were twofold. First, it presupposed a single, centralized control of Alliance nuclear weapons, which would make nonsense of any 'independent' nuclear weapon system of the type produced by Britain or France. Secondly, it required larger conventional forces to counter those Soviet attacks which would not provoke the Americans to use their strategic nuclear forces. But throughout the sixties the European allies, with the exception of Germany,[2] were allowing their conventional forces to run down.

Against the background of the protracted debate about nuclear strategy there took place a continuing argument about the number of troops required to implement NATO strategy

---

[1] A. Beaufre, *NATO and Europe*, p. 57. A clear statement of the basic French objection to the new doctrine may be found in the speech of M. Pompidou in the debate in the French National Assembly in April 1966: 'Nuclear weapons are all that count, and they are not integrated (in NATO). People believe that a war can be won, while in fact we can only hope to avert it by atomic deterrence.'

[2] The main increase in German strength during this period took place from 1960 to 1963. Relevant figures for the Defence Budget are:

1961 – 11·18 billion DM
1962 – 14·98 billion DM
1963 – 18·36 billion DM

For a detailed account of relevant German defence policy, see J. L. Richardson, *Germany and the Atlantic Alliance*, pp. 75–83.

in its existing form. The requirements for forces to be found by countries were set by the military commanders, and each year in an Annual Review process nations were asked to meet them. But for many years most nations had been unwilling to meet the goals set for them (lower than those contemplated under the new doctrine) and the whole planning process was gradually being stultified. In the spring of 1963, in Ottawa, ministers agreed on a new approach. They set up two new bodies: the Defence Planning Committee (which was really only the Council sitting under another name) and a lower level working committee. Their function was to bring into balance forces, resources and strategy, consulting nations when doing it. By the middle of 1966, when the French left the military organization, NATO defence ministers had finally agreed that, in a climate of progressive détente, the task of raising troops to match the doctrine was hopeless, and thenceforth the doctrine should be tailored to match the resources available.

Management
During the 1960s NATO was subject, not only to debates on the nature of the Soviet threat, and of the best way of meeting it, but also to arguments on the most efficient way of controlling nuclear weapons, and on the equitable division of foreign exchange burdens inherent in the way in which Alliance forces are distributed.

The nuclear sharing problem had, essentially, been solved before the Czech crisis; 'burden-sharing' had not. Taking the solved problem first, it is sufficient, for the purposes of this study, to recall that 1963 and 1964 saw intense argument within NATO about 'whose finger on the trigger?' of Alliance nuclear weapons. The general argument broke down into a dispute over the merits of an American-proposed 'Multilateral Force' or MLF, and of a British proposed 'Allied Nuclear Force' or ANF. Implicit in both plans was the assumption that West Germany, as the most exposed NATO member, and with a larger industrial base than either of the two minor nuclear powers, would want to possess nuclear weapons of her own. But, as both British and US spokesmen constantly affirmed in the context of negotiations over the non-proliferation treaty, none of the variants on the MLF/ANF theme would have involved the West Germans in any degree of control over nuclear weapons. It was never explained to anyone's satisfaction why the Germans should be prepared to contribute financially to a force that offered them a guarantee no more secure than the one they had already. Lippman described the MLF scheme, unkindly though not inaccurately, as a 'scheme conceived in distrust of the Germans, and designed to fool them' and it was duly pigeon-holed in 1965 in favour of a new consultative arrangement which permitted a freer exchange of views on the use of existing US nuclear weapons.[1]

Serious as the MLF debate had been, it was to some extent defused by the prevailing climate of détente. Of almost equal significance, in a period when both Britain and the US were suffering severe balance of payments difficulties and when the German economy was not maintaining its high rate of growth, was the question of offset costs, or 'burden-sharing'. At the NATO ministerial meeting in December 1967, McNamara stressed what he described as an anomaly in European attitudes.

> This is that on the one hand there should be no diminution in US forces, but on the other hand the responsibility for meeting the balance of payments deficit caused by such large scale continuing US deployments in Europe is none of Europe's affair. It is essential that deficits suffered by countries as a result of their stationing troops abroad in the common effort should be treated and solved by their allies on a co-operative basis. We would welcome suggestions from our allies on how to meet this pressing problem, since its solution cannot be further postponed.[2]

Before turning to the ways in which NATO, just before the Czech crisis, was attempting to achieve its political and military goals, it may be worth setting out the formal position following the 'withdrawal' of France in 1966. The French maintained a military liaison mission with the NATO Military Committee and with the Supreme Headquarters Allied Powers in Europe

---

[1] The formal structure, as finally agreed in 1966, includes two committees – the seven-member Nuclear Planning Group (NPG) where detailed discussion takes place, and the open ended Nuclear Defence Affairs Committee to which the NPG reports.
[2] Quoted in the 'Statement on Fiscal Year 1969 Program and Budget', p. 31.

(SHAPE), and continued to participate in some NATO agencies.[1] They withdrew from all integrated military commands and the NATO Defence College. They also did not participate in the SACLANT Anti-submarine Warfare Research Centre at La Spezia or the SHAPE Technical Centre at The Hague.

On the political side, the French remain members of the Alliance, have a Permanent Representative to the Council, and contribute to the International Staff. But, because France no longer takes part in NATO military discussions, the Defence Planning Committee, meeting at the level of permanent representatives under the chairmanship of the Secretary General, acts as the co-ordinating body of the 'Fourteen' for all matters concerning integrated defence. France retains the right to sit in the DPC but since 1966 has not in practice exercised it. Nevertheless, the French Delegation regularly receives the Agenda of the DPC and can, if it so wishes, raise in the Council any question which interests it concerning defence.

NATO activities in the pre-crisis period
Although it marked a formal turning point in the history of the Alliance, and inspired a great deal of effort in the period from January to June 1968, the Harmel report met with a significant amount of external criticism. It was contended that it made no contribution towards the search for a 'European Security System', proposed in the Bucharest and Karlovy Vary Declarations.[2] Perhaps a more practical criticism was that it did not deal with the relationships between Europe and North America. These omissions were the result of differences of view between the European members themselves, and not any reflection of tensions between the two sides of the Atlantic. Nevertheless, the Harmel Report contained some significant sections in paragraphs 12–14 relating to disarmament and arms control measures and the possibility of balanced force reductions in Europe,

[1] Notably NADGE, NATO Maintenance and Supply, the Central Europe Operating Agency (Pipelines), the Military Agency for Standardization, the Allied Long Lines Agency, the Allied Communications Security Agency, AGARD, the Von Karman Institute, Allied Naval Communications Agency, and the Conference of National Armaments Directors.
[2] For a text of the Karlovy Vary Declaration, see *Survival*, July 1967. See also page 15.

reflecting 'the will of the allies to work for an effective détente with the East'. The Report also stated that the allies would review policies to 'achieve a just and stable order in Europe, to overcome the division of Germany and to foster European security. This will be part of a process of active and constant preparation for the time when fruitful discussions of these complex questions may be possible bilaterally or multilaterally between Eastern and Western nations'. The Report also referred to 'the defence problems of the exposed areas, e.g. the southeastern flank. In this respect the current situation in the Mediterranean presents special problems, bearing in mind that the current crisis in the Middle East falls within the responsibility of the United Nations'.

It is convenient to deal separately with these three principal subjects; Germany, Disarmament and Arms Control, and the Mediterranean.

Germany

The most important new factor in any discussion of the German problem was, in NATO as elsewhere, the campaign mounted by the West German Government to improve relations with the Soviet Union and Eastern Europe. A typical description of that policy was given by the West German Chancellor in a statement of 18 January 1967 to the Bundestag, following his visit to Paris for talks with President de Gaulle:

> It is the aim of the Federal Government to loosen up German relations with the East European nations and the Soviet Union, and to reduce tension. This aim of ours conforms to the aims of the French President, chiefly because it is not directed against anyone, including Russia. ... So much has happened since 1939 that our scheme may seem to be unrealistic. But every people which wants to carry on policy according to a grand design, and not only with the aim of administratively dealing with single problems and questions of the day, needs what Toynbee called an historical challenge. We see such a challenge in the peaceful reformation of our relations with the East and, included in this, the solution of the German question.[1]

[1] Translation taken from *Keesing's Contemporary Archives*, p. 21856. A full statement of German views on the establishment of a European Peace Order may be found in the Federal Government's Declaration of 13 December 1966.

Two symbolic successes for this policy were the establishment of diplomatic relations with Rumania in January 1967, and the re-establishment of relations with Yugoslavia in January 1968. However, what the West Germans were gaining on the roundabouts of the East European mavericks, they were losing on the swings of East Germany and the Soviet Union. Although the fear of isolation may have been at the root of East German policies, the immediate irritant was the role of the Federal Republic in West Berlin.[1] Following Soviet protests in February 1968 to the French, British and US Governments, the East Germans imposed a series of restrictions on West German access to Berlin. On 10 March the East Germans banned members of the West German National Democratic Party (NPD) and other persons 'engaged in any kind of neo-Nazi activity' from staying on, or travelling through, East German territory. On 13 April the ban was extended to Ministers and senior officials of the Federal Republic. On 11 June, citing the recent passage of Emergency Laws by the Bundestag, the East Germans imposed additional restrictions on all West German and West Berlin citizens and goods.

Although the West German Foreign Minister declared that the restrictions did not amount to a new Berlin crisis, limited retaliation was set in hand. On 20 June the NATO Council announced that from that date stricter regulations would be applied by the Allied Travel Office in West Berlin on the issue of temporary travel documents to East German citizens who wished to visit NATO countries. The Council statement reaffirmed full NATO support for the maintenance of free access to Berlin, and Dr Kiesinger, speaking in the Bundestag on the same day, said that his government refused to be provoked into abandoning its declared policy of 'relaxation and co-operation' with Eastern Europe, including Eastern Germany.

Against this background, the Federal Republic continued to

[1] The relationship between West Berlin and the Federal Republic has been complicated by the German claim that the city is a 'Land' of the Federal Republic, although the jurisdiction of the Allied Military Government is recognized. As a result, the terms of Article VI of the North Atlantic Treaty make the legal obligations of the Parties unclear in the event of an attack on the *territory* of West Berlin. However, an attack on British, French or US forces in the city is an 'armed attack' within the terms of Article VI, and would therefore bring Article V into play.

pursue a dialogue with the Soviet Union. One incident in the series of exchanges was to appear in a new light after the invasion of Czechoslovakia. In a note of 5 July, the Soviet Government criticized the West German offer of a non-aggression pact on the grounds that this would serve only to release the Germans from constraints imposed by the 'enemy states' clauses in the UN Charter.[1]

Disarmament and arms control
With the resolution of the NATO debate on nuclear sharing, it had proved possible to achieve agreement on the key articles of a treaty on the non-proliferation of nuclear weapons. On 24 August 1967 the US and Soviet Union had presented a treaty text to the Eighteen Nation Disarmament Committee.[2] Although the draft dealt with the problem of the control of nuclear weapons, it left blank an article which was to provide for verification that fissile materials would not be diverted from peaceful to weapons purposes.

Argument on the nature of such 'safeguards' divided the nuclear states from the non-nuclear states and, more seriously, the member states of the EEC from all other potential signatories. Both difficulties were the subject of extensive discussion

[1] These run as follows:
Article 53
1. The Security Council shall, where appropriate, utilize such regional arrangements or agencies for enforcement action under its authority. But no enforcement action shall be taken without the authorization of the Security Council, with the exception of measures against any enemy state, as defined in paragraph 2 of this Article, provided for pursuant to Article 107 or in regional arrangements directed against renewal of aggressive policy on the part of any such state, until such time as the Organization may, on request of the governments concerned, be charged with the responsibility for preventing further aggression by such a state.
2. The term enemy state as used in paragraph 1 of this Article applies to any state which during the Second World War has been an enemy of any signatory to the present Charter.

Article 107
Nothing in the present Charter shall invalidate or preclude action, in relation to any state which during the Second World War has been an enemy of any signatory of the present Charter, taken or authorized as a result of that war by the Governments having responsibility for such action.

[2] The text was submitted to the ENDC by the US delegation as ENDC/192, and by the Soviet delegation as ENDC/193. The documents are identical.

in NATO. The first problem was the irritation of the non-nuclear states on discovering that the nuclear powers would escape any sort of inspection provision. This was inevitable, given that the Soviet Union remained adamantly opposed to accepting safeguards for itself. To ease acceptance of the arrangement by the non-nuclears, both Britain and the US declared unilaterally, in December 1967, that they would accept safeguards on their civil nuclear programmes, at the same time as they went into force for the non-nuclear signatories to the Treaty.

The more serious dispute was on the possibility that the EURATOM safeguards system should be as valid as the IAEA system for the members of the EEC. Any suggestion that the West Germans should be subject only to the controls of their EURATOM partners was, as might be expected, anathema to the Soviet Union. In an interview with *l'Unita* shortly after the tabling of the US–Soviet draft, Roshchin, the leader of the Soviet delegation at Geneva, said:

> ... the Euratom countries, namely Italy, Benelux and particularly West Germany, insist that the controls of the International Atomic Energy Agency (IAEA) of Vienna shall not apply to them. But we cannot allow a situation wherein a country, any country, is granted a privileged status. We favour one single system, recognized and accepted by all. We cannot and do not want to destroy EURATOM, but we do not want to create a situation of exceptions by making it possible for a country to evade the universal controls. In fact, all the Euratom countries would have the benefit of a different control. We shall continue our negotiations on the basis of the IAEA.[1]

Efforts to resolve this problem led to highly-coloured charges that the US was sacrificing the interests of its European NATO allies for the sake of a bilateral agreement with the Soviet Union. Such charges do not take adequate account of the fact that the Soviet position was basically reasonable, and widely supported by non-nuclear countries which were not members of the EEC whether or not they were members of NATO. Nevertheless, European fears of a Soviet–American 'deal' at their expense had not been stilled by 1 July 1968 when, after the

[1] *L'Unita*, 27 August 1967, pp. 1–2; US Department of State translation provided in *Documents on Disarmament*, 1967.

resolution of the safeguards and certain other disputes, the non-proliferation treaty was opened for signature in Moscow, London and Washington.

At the signing ceremony, President Johnson announced that agreement had been reached with the Soviet Union to begin 'in the nearest future' discussions on the limitations of offensive and defensive strategic nuclear weapons. Kosygin, at the same time, made public the contents of a Soviet memorandum on 'urgent measures on an end to the arms race and on disarmament in the near future'. Apart from the reference to a limitation and subsequent reduction of strategic nuclear delivery vehicles, perhaps the most striking feature was the statement that

> The Soviet Government also supports proposals concerning the implementation of measures for regional disarmament and for the reduction of armaments in various parts of the world, including the Middle East. The question of such measures for slackening the arms race in the Middle East, of course, could be considered only in conditions of elimination of the consequence of the Israeli aggression against the Arab countries and, above all, the full evacuation of the Israeli forces from the territory of the Arab states occupied by them.

At the resumed ENDC session in July both Britain and the US put forward their suggestions on the measures of arms control that might most appropriately follow the conclusion of the non-proliferation treaty. In July, the four Western negotiators at Geneva attended a special session of the North Atlantic Council for a discussion of these proposals, and of the Soviet nine-point memorandum.[1] Meanwhile, studies were proceeding in NATO about the possibility of mutual, balanced, force reductions. The defence ministers, meeting in May, had included in their communiqué the passage:

> In welcoming the fact that studies were now proceeding under the aegis of the Council on the subject of balanced force reductions, Ministers endorsed the proposition that the overall military capability of NATO should not be reduced, except as part of a pattern of mutual force reductions, balanced in scope and timing.

[1] This form of words made it clear that the French, who do not attend meetings of the defence ministers, were nevertheless taking part in the discussions of balanced force reductions.

In June, the foreign ministers, meeting at Reykjavik issued a clear 'signal' to the Warsaw Pact, in an annex to the communiqué in which they described, in general terms, the work that was going on in NATO, and their desire to co-operate with balanced force reductions in Europe with the Soviet Union and Warsaw Pact powers.

The Mediterranean

Since the Arab–Israeli War of June 1967 the Soviet presence in the Mediterranean has sharply increased. Reactions in the West had betrayed varying degrees of alarm but, prior to the Czech crisis, it had been generally accepted that Soviet motives were compounded of several elements.[1] These included: a desire to 'show the flag' in the Mediterranean, thereby ending the total American naval hegemony in the area; a general drive towards evolution as a 'global' as well as a 'super' power, with a consequent increase in the number of Soviet ships transitting the Mediterranean from Black Sea ports; an attempt to 'mark' the ships of the US Sixth Fleet, so achieving a counterforce capability in the event of general war; and the wish to complicate NATO contingency planning for maintenance of maritime supply lines in wartime to Italy, Greece and Turkey.

Although it was generally doubted that the Soviet Union was seeking to obtain permanent bases in the Mediterranean[2] the situation was nevertheless of great potential importance for NATO. The Reykjavik communiqué had said that 'Ministers examined and approved a report from the Permanent Council which dealt in detail with the situation in the Mediterranean and related defence problems. They directed their Permanent Representatives to consult fully on this situation and to extend their consultations in range and depth as circumstances required'. It was subsequently announced that a decision had been taken by representatives of the 'Fourteen' at Reykjavik in

[1] Compare, for example, F. J. Goodhart, 'Defence of the Mediterranean and the NATO southern flank', WEU Assembly Report, 1967; and C. Gasteyger, 'Moscow and the Mediterranean', *Foreign Affairs*, July 1968.

[2] See, for example, McNamara's statement in the Fiscal Year 1969 Budget Statement: 'We believe that those countries which have potentially useful facilities – primarily the UAR, Syria, Yemen, and Algeria – would probably resist granting full base rights on political grounds.'

June to establish a new NATO subordinate command called Maritime Air Forces Mediterranean (MARAIRMED). A primary objective of this new command is that Maritime Air Forces made available to NATO by member nations operating in the southern region of Europe should carry out co-operative surveillance of surface ships and submarines in the Mediterranean.[1]

The British at about this time decided to offer contributions to the NATO forces in the area, in addition to the permanent force which it was supposed to maintain in any case. These additions were: from 1969, a squadron of Shackleton long range maritime reconnaissance aircraft, later to be re-equipped with Nimrods, to be transferred to Malta from the United Kingdom; and, from 1970, the addition of a guided missile destroyer to the frigate force in the Mediterranean, and for part of that year one commando ship, with a UK-based Royal Marine commando group embarked.[2]

Reactions

It is a relatively simple task to present an analysis of the function and development of an organization over a period of years, as has been attempted in the first part of this chapter. 'Collective' decisions that did not accurately reflect the balance of forces within the organization may be expected to unravel. Themes that recur in policy pronouncements may be accepted as genuine with ever increasing confidence, while the considered pronouncements of the statesmen of member nations may be studied for the clues which they reveal to potential stresses within the organization. But in the short run, none of the investigatory techniques work. A hasty reaction by an Alliance member to an unexpected or a rapidly developing situation cannot give a reliable guide to the line which the corresponding national delegation may be taking within the organization. A collective statement by the organization as a whole may represent the best that can be hammered out at short notice under the pressure of events and in the absence of adequate information about the

[1] *NATO Letter*, October 1968.
[2] *Supplementary Statement on British Defence Policy* (July 1968).

situation on which the alliance is being forced to comment. Such statements may be relegated to a decent obscurity once the crisis is past. On the other hand, what may appear at the time as a 'post-hoc rationalization' may later be looked back on as the birth of a new doctrine, influencing alliance behaviour for years to come.

Any study of NATO's behaviour during the Czechoslovak crisis, based, as this one is, on a rapid and possibly incomplete survey of overt reactions by the organization, is necessarily of limited value. It will take years to determine whether the Czechoslovak crisis of 1968 should be ranked with the Cuban missile crisis of 1962 as a turning point in postwar history, or whether it should be seen (as at least one distinguished observer has described it) as an *'accident de parcours'*. Thus the analysis which follows should be regarded as highly speculative. The only reliable evidence which we have is of the 'dog which did not bark' variety, and although this may have been sufficient for Holmes to solve the mystery of 'Silver Blaze', it is not an adequate foundation upon which to base a firm pronouncement about the future of NATO.

One of the advantages which the North Atlantic Alliance offers to its members is a means of pooling, and jointly evaluating, information which may have a bearing on NATO security, and which has been collected by individual members. In the case of Czechoslovakia this process had been undertaken, from January 1968 onwards, by the North Atlantic Council, assisted as necessary by the Political Committee and Expert groups. Thus, as the situation developed following the fall of Novotny, NATO members had a common information base from which to develop their own estimates of what was likely to happen. From May the evidence of Soviet military preparation was clear for all to see, but it was also clear that these preparations formed part of the Soviet policy of pressure against Czechoslovakia and were not directed against NATO territory. It would however be surprising if NATO evaluations in May and June had included the suggestion that the Soviet Union would definitely invade Czechoslovakia. Whatever guesses NATO experts made before the invasion, they cannot reasonably be criticized after it on the grounds that they were no more accurate than those of the Russians and the Czechs.

An alternative criticism, that NATO was at fault for not manoeuvring to 'match' the Soviet deployment in some sense, deserves more careful examination. The obvious measure would have been for the NATO military authorities to arrange an 'exercise' in the area of the Czech–West German border which involved the forward deployment of substantial West German and US units. This build-up might have been interpreted within NATO as a contribution to the defence of Czechoslovakia. External observers would not, however, have been able to distinguish between a purely precautionary deployment and a systematic preparation for the invasion of Warsaw Pact territory. Indeed, the NATO manoeuvre to be effective would have had to be designed to lend itself to the latter interpretation. It may be argued that, under certain conditions of advanced détente, the Soviet and other 'authoritarian' parties may be prepared to tolerate democratic experiments elsewhere in the bloc. What is less credible is that the level of such toleration may be increased by a NATO military threat. Discipline is usually tightened rather than relaxed in any organization which believes itself to be 'under siege'. The principal concern of NATO in the summer of 1968 was to behave so as to avoid a Soviet occupation of Czechoslovakia; if this assumption is made – and on all the evidence it is an absolutely valid one to make – the Alliance hardly merits criticism for not adopting an aggressive stance before the invasion for this reason alone. On the contrary, it might reasonably expect congratulation for not doing anything stupid.

An alternative criticism might run as follows: recognizing that use of a NATO 'stick' would be self-defeating in the defence of Czechoslovakia, why was there not a more vigorous demonstration of carrots? On this argument, Western spokesmen should, before the invasion, have laid systematic stress on the benefits of détente and disarmament for the Soviet Union, and have pointed out that these benefits could not survive the invasion and occupation of Czechoslovakia. One form of this idea found expression, after the invasion, in the suggestion that the ratification of the non-proliferation treaty should be held up so as to 'punish' the Soviet Union.

Such suggestions are based on a complete misapprehension of the reasons for which NATO, in the pre-crisis period, had been seeking détente, including appropriate measures of arms control. These should not be seen as presents which the West offers the Soviet bloc from time to time as a reward for good behaviour. Arms control agreements can, if they are appropriately verified (or are self-verifying), be maintained under conditions of the deepest hostility and mistrust. For example, a tacit understanding on the non-use of chemical weapons was observed both by Britain and Germany throughout the Second World War, because it was in their mutual interest to do so. Détente and disarmament are *Western* interests, to be sought whenever possible. Whenever it is possible to demonstrate that Soviet and Western interests coincide in a particular area, progress can be made towards formal or informal agreements. The search for areas of common interest can be pursued, whatever the condition of inter-state relations in other fields. This basic principle is, in fact, well understood by the super-powers who could contemplate talks on the limitation of strategic missile systems at a time when Soviet-made anti-aircraft missiles were bringing down US aircraft over North Vietnam. Certain of the allies – both of the US and the Soviet Union – have what might be called a vested interest in ensuring that the search for super-power accommodation shall not be pursued at the expense of themselves, but their objections should not be confused with the assertion that post-Czechoslovak détente is impossible. On the whole, NATO members did not fall into the trap of threatening to sacrifice their own interests for Dubcek, however admirable his government may have appeared in comparison with the varieties of 'cold war communism' which have been observed in the past.

The only NATO activity undertaken before the crisis was to deny, collectively and individually, that there existed any Western plans for the subversion or occupation of Czechoslovakia, and to refrain from any actions or statements that might have given the opportunity for such an interpretation. In so far as this activity helped Dubcek to maintain that he was untainted by NATO support, it helped preserve the independence of Czechoslovakia. Although the Russians, and others, grew increasingly alarmed about the situation within Czechoslovakia, neither NATO nor the Czech Government gave them cause to fear that Czechoslovakia was on the point of 'changing sides'. Inactivity can be an effective policy, and of all the political virtues that of silence at the right moment is the least practised. Inactivity and silence are not, however, usually recognized as valid policies, and it is perhaps the besetting political disease of the present times that inactivity is assumed to be synonymous with indolence and ignorance. It requires emphasis that the attitude adopted by the NATO countries towards Czechoslovakia was a deliberate one, and there is no reason to doubt that the Czechoslovak leaders and their representatives urged such a policy as being the most helpful to their cause. After Cierna and Bratislava it appeared that NATO had played an important part in the retention of Czechoslovak autonomy in her internal affairs.

Nevertheless the invasion took place. On the night of 20–21 August various news agencies carried reports of the invasion, and a few of the Allied governments received Soviet diplomatic notification of the entry of Warsaw Pact troops into Czechoslovakia. During the night, NATO Headquarters alerted delegations and international staff, and the consultative machinery went promptly into operation (the North Atlantic Council was in session some 16 hours before the Security Council). The intensive analysis which was to occupy the weeks leading up to the Ministerial meeting of November must have concentrated, initially, on the military implications of the Soviet move for the East–West confrontation. The details of this analysis are, and must remain, a closely guarded secret, but it is possible to comment on the general problems which arise when one considers the 'military balance' in Europe and possible disturbances to it.

There are certain difficulties at the outset in deciding whether there is any real meaning in the concept of 'military balance' between NATO and the Warsaw Pact. The existence of strong NATO forces whatever their exact level will place certain constraints on the military options available to the planners of the Warsaw Pact. Similarly, the existence of Warsaw Pact forces will place a set of constraints upon the planners of NATO. The exact nature of the two sets of constraints depends as much upon what one side believes about the nature of the other's forces, including their size, readiness for combat, and likely employment, as upon the 'real' situation, difficult as this is to determine. However, if these constraints can be summed up by the statement that each side believes that an attack on the other would, on the whole, be militarily unprofitable, then it is possible to declare that there exists a 'military balance'. But the existence of a balance so defined can only be inferred from an absence of conflict, and it cannot be related in any simple way to the numerical strength of the forces on each side. Thus detailed arguments about the number of tanks on one side versus the number of anti-tank guns on the other have in reality very little to do with the evaluation of a military balance.[1] The history of warfare offers countless examples of numerically inferior forces launching an attack or embarking enthusiastically upon a war in the confident expectation of victory by reason of its superior morale or technology.[2] Despite this, enough people continue to believe in a close correlation between 'numerical strength' and 'military balance' for there to be pressures for 'matching increases' whenever any change is observed in the military strength of the other side. Classic examples of this type of pressure have been afforded by US debates over a 'missile' or even a 'megatonnage' gap.[3]

Efforts have therefore been made to establish some form of yardstick to measure the strengths of each side, bearing in mind the occasionally disastrous errors which this process has involved in the past. But the establishment of yardsticks is at best

[1] There is an interesting comparison between the contemporary debates on the military balance and those in the 1930s in Britain. The 'quantitative' argument between Winston Churchill and the Baldwin Government on German air rearmament between 1933 and 1936 missed the entire point of that rearmament programme and the nature of the real threat posed by Nazi Germany to Europe. It provides an admirable example to support the wise comment of Professor R. V. Hill in February 1942: 'The fundamental axiom in modern war is that an exact knowledge of weapons and equipment is necessary at the highest level of all as the essential basis, not only of strategy and tactics, but even . . . of policy itself.' (House of Commons, 24 February 1942).

[2] See, for example, the opening chapters of M. E. Howard, *The Franco-Prussian War* (Hart-Davis, 1961).

[3] This was a central theme in President Kennedy's campaign in 1960, and strong echoes were to be found in President Nixon's 1968 campaign.

a subjective process. Indeed, given a result which one would like to 'prove', the design of the corresponding 'yardstick' to provide 'supporting evidence' often demands only a modicum of ingenuity. It may be observed, for example, that those who wish to demonstrate Warsaw Pact superiority frequently measure in 'divisions present in Central Europe after a short period of reinforcement'. Those who wish to demonstrate a rough equality measure in 'men', while a NATO superiority can be demonstrated by measuring in 'deliverable nuclear weapons'. This is not to impute intellectual dishonesty to the protagonists in these somewhat sterile arguments. All the 'yardsticks' mentioned would have a degree of relevance, given certain assumptions on the way in which conflict between NATO and the Warsaw Pact might come about. A recent report by Senator Cooper delivered to the Military Committee of the North Atlantic Assembly drew upon a series of yardsticks provided by the US Department of Defense to 'prove' that, before the Czechoslovak crisis, there existed a rough equality of strength in Central Europe between NATO and the Warsaw Pact. He argued from this that the changes in Soviet forces must there have 'upset' the balance and that some NATO response was therefore required.

On the morning of the invasion, however, the more immediate question was the nature of any possible threat to NATO, rather than the longer term implications. No one believed that the Czechoslovak crisis had been engineered simply to provide a cover for the necessary forward deployment of troops directed against NATO. It is therefore not surprising that no announcements emerged on 21 August of any NATO alert. What form of 'quiet' precautions were taken on that and succeeding days is not, and should not be expected to be, known – given that the main purpose would be to avoid exacerbating an already tense situation. That some form of precautionary measures were in fact taken may however be reasonably inferred from various facts, including the press announcement on 23 August that West German army leaves were being cancelled.

In the uncertain period which followed the invasion it was obviously unlikely that NATO would implement any force reductions which might previously have been envisaged. On 4

September the Defence Planning Committee issued a statement which announced that an assessment was in the course of preparation, and said that:

Meanwhile, the Defence Planning Committee has recalled the position taken by Defence Ministers on 10 May 1968 in Brussels, subsequently reaffirmed by Foreign Ministers at Reykjavik on 24 and 25 June 1968, to the effect that the Alliance must maintain an effective military capability and must assure a balance of forces between NATO and the Warsaw Pact. At that time Ministers also endorsed the proposition that the overall military capability of NATO should not be reduced except as part of a pattern of mutual force reductions balanced in scope and timing. The Defence Planning Committee has confirmed the validity of this position and deplores the fact that the prospects for progress in the field of balanced mutual force reductions have suffered a severe setback.

The members of the Defence Planning Committee have accordingly affirmed the necessity of maintaining NATO's military capability and of taking into account the implications of recent developments in Eastern Europe in the planning of their national forces. . . .

Press reports suggested that the main NATO response in the military field would consist of remedying those structural weaknesses which had been observed before the Czechoslovak crisis. These problems related mainly to the lack of a well-organized system of reserves, adequate mobilization plans, and to the rate at which the West German Air Force had been converting its F-104s from a nuclear to a conventional role. That improvements in these areas would be part of the NATO response was confirmed by the communiqué issued after the meeting of foreign and defence ministers in November. This included the passage:

The Allies participating in NATO's integrated defence programme have . . . been obliged to re-assess the state of their defences. They consider that the situation arising from recent events calls for a collective response. The quality, effectiveness, and deployment of NATO's forces will be improved in terms of both manpower and equipment in order to provide a better capability for defence as far forward as possible. The quality of reserve forces will also be improved and their ability to mobilize rapidly will be increased. Renewed attention will be directed to the provision of reinforcements for the flanks, and the strengthening of local forces there. The conventional capability of NATO's tactical airforces will be increased. Certain additional national units will be committed to the major NATO commanders. ...

The detailed version of these measures is intended, at the time of writing, to be reflected in the NATO force plans for 1969–73 which should be submitted in January 1969. Some advance indication of their nature was, however, provided by a NATO spokesman immediately after the ministerial meeting. He described them, on a country by country basis, as follows:

Belgium: the recruitment of 'career volunteers', which had been interrupted for a considerable time, would be re-opened. It was proposed to recruit 4,000 volunteers a year in this way. A decision had been taken to maintain in Germany for the time being four battalions of armoured infantry whose withdrawal had previously been foreseen. Belgian forces in Germany would be reinforced by the movement from Belgium to Germany of some HAWK and NIKE anti-aircraft missile units. A light anti-aircraft artillery battalion destined in due course for the forces in Germany would be established this month in Belgium.

Canada: the Canadian Government is in the process of conducting a comprehensive review of its defence policy and the Canadian minister emphasized that this would naturally take the Czechoslovak situation into account. Meanwhile the Canadian Government is planning to maintain its present commitments to NATO both in Europe and in Canada. Current plans include the construction and commitment to NATO of four modern anti-submarine destroyers equipped with helicopters and two big support ships which would enable Canada to expand her anti-submarine activity in the North Atlantic. In the light of the present situation, a decision has been deferred concerning a possible reduction in the number of aircraft stationed in Germany.[1]

Germany: some units that were to have been turned into training formations are now going to be retained as combat units. The capability in reconnaissance aircraft is to be improved and it is planned to purchase 88 Phantom aircraft for this end. The German

---

[1] A certain degree of controversy subsequently developed as to the definiteness of the Canadian statement. In the light of subsequent events it became apparent that the first sentence of the paragraph was the most significant.

Government's 1969 Defence Budget includes an increase of 740 million DM. The artillery's conventional firepower is to be improved and this could lead to as many as 30 additional batteries for NATO. It is planned to order four anti-submarine frigates and 135 transport helicopters.

Greece: the Greek Minister had stressed the measures his government was taking to strengthen its defences and to increase its Defence Budget. But, as the Greek economy could not bear its defence burden alone, he welcomed the reference which had been made in the discussion to the continuing validity of previous Council decisions regarding defence aid to both Greece and Turkey.

Italy: the defence budget for 1969 is to be increased by as much as seven per cent over last year. Numerous measures are being taken to improve the effectiveness of Italian forces, including an order for modern anti-submarine aircraft. All three services, army, navy, and airforce, would be subjected to a continuing programme to increase their efficiency.

Netherlands: the Netherlands Defence Minister had said that a number of measures were being considered but these would only be implemented as part of a collective and co-ordinated effort. . . . The measures under consideration include a strengthened anti-tank capability in some army units, an improvement in electronic warfare and anti-submarine equipment for the navy, and, in the airforce, an increased number of planes.

Norway: Norway aims to improve its defence posture in the north. For example, the manning level of forces in northern Norway is to be increased by sending soldiers from training units to northern Norway at an earlier stage and after more intensive initial training. Over the next five years, the procurement of certain equipment will be speeded up. In financial terms, this will amount to something like 100 million Kroner over the next five-year period.

Turkey: the Turkish Minister had, in general, welcomed the main theme that had run through the meeting and he, too, pointed out that his country's defence effort requires, and receives, augmentation in the form of aid from some of her partners.

United Kingdom: the British Defence Minister . . . had said that the United Kingdom would be ordering an additional squadron of 20 Harrier vertical take-off aircraft.[1]

[1] Mr Healey subsequently announced that the UK would also make an aircraft carrier or commando or assault ship available in the Mediterranean from January 1969 'on an almost continuous basis', and would assign a further infantry battalion to NATO 'for the next two years or so' (*The Times*, 15 November).

United States: The United States announced a considerable number of measures. For example, they are going both to increase and accelerate the programme of exercises for ground and airforces committed to NATO, including, particularly, exercises involving the units that have been re-deployed to the United States, and also units of their Strategic Reserve. They are making certain improvements in the manning levels, and in the state of readiness of Strategic Reserve units in the United States committed to NATO. They will be enhancing the US tactical air power in Europe both in quantity and in quality.[1]

Whatever the military significance of these measures, the list, taken as a whole, served the important psychological function of demonstrating that NATO was determined to maintain that level of forces which it considered adequate for collective self defence. It is hardly appropriate for anyone writing without access to classified information to attempt an 'independent' assessment of the post-invasion strengths of NATO and Warsaw Pact forces in Central Europe. It would be even less appropriate to pronounce on possible disturbances to the 'military balance'. All that can usefully be said at this stage is that the scale, timing and military efficiency of the occupation had evidently served to impress the Western cognoscenti. Senator Cooper noted that:

Within a period of 24 hours the Soviet Union and its allies moved into Czechoslovakia a force of approximately 25 divisions or about 250,000 men. Of these, 22 were Soviet divisions. Eight Soviet divisions were moved from East Germany, 11 from the Western part of the Soviet Union, two from Hungary, and one airborne division was flown from the Soviet Union and quickly took over airfields and facilities at Prague. In addition, three Polish divisions and smaller units from Hungary, Bulgaria and East Germany took part in this invasion.[2]

Turning to the political consequences of the Czech crisis for NATO, one is struck by a certain enthusiasm, manifested in the post-crisis atmosphere, for some extension of the NATO commitment to what are often called the 'grey areas' of Europe.

[1] Report of the NATO spokesman's statement is taken from 'NATO Latest No. 4'.
[2] North Atlantic Assembly, November.

One of the more dramatic examples of this 'forward policy' was afforded by a speech by President Johnson in San Antonio, Texas, on 30 August, in which he appeared to be warning the Soviet Union against an invasion of Rumania. A realistic US or NATO guarantee to Rumania appears so militarily improbable that it can only be concluded that this statement – which appears so strangely in the speech that it reads unmistakably like a last-minute addition – was designed as 'cover' for a considerably more plausible warning concerning a possible invasion of Yugoslavia. There are strong indications that this was deliberate, and that no doubts existed in the Soviet Government concerning the real significance of the San Antonio speech. This would not mean that NATO really believed that the Soviet Union, after enduring Yugoslav heresies for over 20 years, should have found its patience suddenly exhausted. The Yugoslavs might however have been intended for inclusion in the 'Socialist Commonwealth' whose affairs were, according to what has been described as the 'Brezhnev Doctrine' to be collectively organized henceforth.[1] A NATO reply to this doctrine may be discerned in the following passage of the November Communiqué.

> The members of the Alliance urge the Soviet Union, in the interests of world peace, to refrain from using force and interfering in the affairs of other states.
> Determined to safeguard the freedom and independence of their countries, they could not remain indifferent to any development which endangers their security.
> Clearly any Soviet intervention directly or indirectly affecting the situation in Europe or in the Mediterranean would create an international crisis with grave consequences.

It is difficult to see what this response might mean in practice. Certain scenarios have been published in the US press involving a Soviet attack on Yugoslavia, a dramatic intervention by aircraft of the US Sixth Fleet, and NATO support for Yugoslav guerrillas. Some versions of this scenario even include a role for the militarily insignificant Soviet Mediterranean fleet. Such developments should not automatically be relegated to the category of political science-fiction, but their study would take us

[1] See pages 114–116 below.

rather far from an examination of the likely implications of the Czechoslovak crisis for NATO.

In the first place, it can immediately be said that the twin goals of détente and defence set out in the Harmel Report remain completely valid. The November Communiqué notes that:

... the political goal remains that of secure, peaceful, and mutually beneficial relations between East and West. The Allies are determined to pursue this goal, bearing in mind that the pursuit of détente must not be allowed to split the Alliance. The search for peace requires progress, consistent with Western security, in the vital fields of disarmament and arms control and continuing efforts to resolve the fundamental issues which divide East and West.

Thus, although the Czechoslovak crisis does not require any radical change in the purposes of the North Atlantic Alliance, the impact of the crisis on NATO has been very considerable. Since it has long been a principal object of Soviet policy to divide and disrupt the Western alliance, the signs of renewed vigour and purpose in NATO must be regarded as a substantial debit entry in Soviet costing of the invasion. This conclusion would be further strengthened if it is the case, as several indications suggest, that French interest in NATO has been revived by the Czechoslovak invasion and its implications for the policy towards Eastern Europe and the Soviet Union pursued by the French Government since 1966; in addition, fears that Algeria may permit the Soviet fleet in the Mediterranean to use the former French naval base at Mers-el-Kebir may be another significant factor.

It is argued in this chapter that the collective behaviour of the NATO allies before the invasion was right. Those who do criticize them for the calculated silence and inactivity in the summer of 1968 should seriously address themselves to a discussion of what else could have been done to assist the Czechoslovak leaders. The argument of these critics is largely based upon an assumption which the authors of this study do not accept – that the invasion had been long planned, and could have only been averted by the possibility of active intervention by the West. But even if the argument set out in chapter 2 of this study is disproved, it is still very difficult to accept the proposition that the invasion could have been averted by any declaration by the West, even if it had been possible to have obtained such a declaration from the NATO alliance. It may also be doubted that a warning by the United States similar to that given in the San Antonio speech of President Johnson on 30 August could have had any effect upon the Soviet decision.

The subsequent action of the Alliance with regard to possible Soviet ambitions in Europe outside the NATO area carries implications which could be serious. An imprecise declaration of interest in areas outside the Alliance[1] was perhaps the least that the Alliance members could do in the context of the autumn of 1968. It is possible that such a declaration may have some effect on Soviet strategy, but it would appear improbable; and it also seems that the fears expressed of possible invasions of Yugoslavia and Austria were not based on the reality of the situation at that time. If the essential features of the policy of peaceful coexistence are maintained by the present and immediate future Soviet leaders, the possibility of military invasion outside the bloc area must be regarded as so remote as to be virtually discounted. This thesis does not deny the possibility of the Soviet leadership taking advantage of situations to further their national interests in what have become known as the 'grey areas' in Europe; it does contend, however, that in present circumstances any general declaration of interest by NATO in such areas cannot be of real value unless it is militarily and politically plausible. Any extension of the Alliance's role requires very careful consideration. Not the least of its possible consequences would be a further polarization of the two-bloc system, and the tacit abandonment of the movement towards joint forces reductions and the lessening of European tensions.

If the Czechoslovak crisis has made the prospects for the North Atlantic Alliance look much brighter than they did early in 1968, it must also be recognized that the crisis has also demonstrated certain weaknesses in the Organization and in its alliance concept. The whole issue of 'political warning', discussed earlier in this chapter, must require detailed re-examination. NATO's own detailed analysis of the crisis should furnish certain lessons

[1] It has been argued that the studied imprecision of the communiqué – 'could not remain indifferent to any development which endangers their security' – cannot be described as amounting to a commitment. But its very imprecision can well lead to the assumption that some form of commitment is intended.

in the techniques of crisis management and contingency planning. But the central problem for NATO will be to decide whether in fact its members now consider it as something more than a defensive alliance. If it is to move in the direction of a guarantor of European protection from possible Soviet expansionist plans, this extension of its original purpose must be recognized and understood. Above all, it must be recognized that such an extension would be a virtual total abandonment of the policy adopted in 1968 prior to the invasion, and such an abandonment must carry with it the acceptance of a failure in tactics. It is contended in this study that, given the nature of the Alliance, no such failure occurred. It is also the contention of this study that the Soviet action in Czechoslovakia was essentially defensive and reluctant, and that no threat to NATO interests existed. It may well be that a NATO guarantee of the independence of nations outside the two Alliances is desirable; but it must be emphasized that such a guarantee contains implications which are very serious.

It should also be emphasized that moves to 'strengthen' NATO must be political and organizational as well as military. The *raison d'être* of the organization has been increasingly doubted over the past ten years, and the movement towards converting the Alliance from a purely military-defensive organization into one that actively promotes the reduction of tension in Central Europe has been questioned by those who are unimpressed by the argument that the Soviet capability to invade the Alliance area does not imply any intention of doing so. The proponents of this criticism have used the Czechoslovak invasion as a powerful argument to point to the perils of relaxing the political and military vigilance of the West. No observer of NATO can fail to detect the note of satisfaction in certain quarters at the invasion to underline the warnings they have been delivering in public as well as in private for many years. There is, however, a very important middle ground between extreme attitudes towards possible Soviet ambitions in Europe. NATO's value to its members goes far beyond the provision of armed forces and an integrated command structure, and it can be argued that what might be loosely called the non-military aspects of NATO collaboration could and should be expanded further, to provide additional political and economic strength. A reading of the Czechoslovak invasion that concludes that the intention of Soviet policy towards the West is still based primarily upon the use of conventional military forces in an aggressive role must be regarded as a dangerously superficial one.

It can be argued that the determination to strengthen the Warsaw Pact imposes upon NATO the necessity to do the same. Again, the definition of strength is crucial. Whether the existence of NATO is in the long-term interests of full European pacification is a matter for considerable debate. But even if it is accepted that, in present circumstances, it still plays a vital role, it must be recognized that that role is political as well as military. The most dangerous result of the Czechoslovak crisis for NATO and for Europe would be for the Alliance to expand its military commitments while abandoning the concept of political initiative. The dangers of doing the exact opposite have been argued on countless occasions, and are manifestly valid. It would be tragically ironic if NATO's new lease of life were utilized to return to concepts which were appropriate to the circumstances of the early 1950s, and thereby forfeit the very real long-term advantages for the Alliance members and Europe as a whole of a genuine relaxation of tension in Central Europe. A careful reading of the entire Czechoslovak crisis, therefore, should lead NATO to the conclusion that it would be perilous and foolish to abandon the ideal of relaxing tensions in Central Europe and to engage upon an extension of NATO military commitments outside the Alliance. If the revivication of NATO may be one result of the Czechoslovak invasion, it is of crucial importance to ensure that this revival is used properly for the good of Europe as a whole.

5

The United Nations and the Crisis

Introduction
On 21 August a UN spokesman issued a statement which deplored resort to force 'in contravention of the Charter of the United Nations'. It continued:

> In the present case the Secretary-General regards the developments in Czechoslovakia as yet another serious blow to the concepts of international order and morality which form the basis of the Charter of the United Nations and for which the United Nations has been striving all these years.

As the first of the purposes of the Organization, the Charter of the UN lists the maintenance of international peace and security.[1] Three important chapters of the Charter are concerned with the fulfilment of this purpose, and many of the functions and powers of the principal organs are related to it. In consequence the United Nations has frequently been judged solely on its ability to settle or avoid international disputes. By this criterion many would say that the UN failed totally in its handling of the Czechoslovak dispute. The object of this chapter is to examine the role played by the UN (principally the Security Council and the General Assembly) in relation to the Soviet invasion of Czechoslovakia, to assess the Organization's capabilities of action in a case of this sort and the effectiveness or otherwise of the action taken in New York.

At the outset two essential points should be made. First,

[1] Article 1 (1), UN Charter.

while in certain situations an international organization may be greater than the sum of its members, it can only achieve as much as its members allow. So, although member states undertake to settle disputes peacefully,[1] the role of the UN is necessarily very different in a dispute involving a permanent member of the Security Council and one which does not. Mr Shahi (Pakistan) put the position as he saw it after four days of debate in the Security Council on the Czechoslovak intervention as follows: 'When the permanent members of the Security Council stand diametrically opposed, the capacity of the organization to act effectively is paralysed.'[2]

Secondly, account must be taken of the present character of the United Nations with a membership of 126 states as compared with the original 51 which attended the first Session of the General Assembly in London in 1946. This means that neither of the present two super-powers, the United States and the Soviet Union, can now count on a built-in majority. A large number of the additional members (especially after 1960 when, of 17 new members, 16 were newly-independent African states) adopt a policy of non-alignment between what they see as rival East and West European, and therefore relatively distant, blocs in whose disputes they wish to avoid becoming involved. At the same time there is a greater number of member states such as Algeria, with her interest in continuing Soviet support in the Middle East, or India and Pakistan in connection with the Kashmir dispute, who feel either an obligation towards or a need to avoid antagonizing the Soviet Union, just as some Latin American states, who were among the original UN members, can be said to have a special relationship to the United States. It is in the light of this background that the action, or failure to act, of the United Nations should be seen.

The Security Council
It was clear that New York was the place where an effective world protest against the Soviet action could be recorded. From the point of view of those nations which saw it as vital that the Organization should publicly condemn a clear contravention of

[1] Article 2 (3) of Charter.
[2] S/PV 1445, p. 112.

the Charter, it was important to bring the question before the Security Council as quickly as possible and in a way calculated to secure the maximum support by members from all parts of the world, including those who would aim to avoid involvement in what they would see as a 'cold war' issue.[1] The best solution from this point of view would have been for the Czechoslovaks themselves to appeal to the Council. But, unlike the case of Hungary in 1956, the Czechoslovak Government never sought to leave the communist camp or the Warsaw Pact and believed that it would not be to their advantage to take the initiative. During consultations which began early on the morning of 21 August it became clear that the Czechoslovaks would not themselves appeal. In the event the Security Council was convened within twenty-four hours of the Soviet invasion by a representative group of six members, Canada, Denmark, France, Paraguay, the United Kingdom and the United States, to consider 'the present serious situation in the Czechoslovak Socialist Republic'.

The debate began at 5.30 p.m. on 21 August and was to occupy almost twenty-four of the next seventy-two hours. It was marked by a series of delaying tactics by the Soviet representative supported by his allies and friends, the steadily sharpening tone of the debate as it proceeded, and the impact of the balanced statements by the representatives of Czechoslovakia. The veto by the Soviet Union of the first draft resolution tabled on behalf of seven Council members was no doubt inevitable, but Soviet attempts to delay the inscription of the agenda item and to postpone a vote on the resolution are not consistent with the view that the United Nations proceedings were seen by the Soviet representative as of no account.

The initial debate, theoretically concerned only with the question of inscription,[2] produced a Soviet statement more than three times the length of that of the United States representative, even allowing for interruptions of the latter by the Soviet and Hungarian representatives on points of order. Mr Malik (USSR) argued that the situation was outside the competence of the

---

[1] The General Assembly reaction to the crisis over UN expenses and to the opinion of the International Court of Justice are good examples of this.
[2] S/P V 1441.

THE UNITED NATIONS AND THE CRISIS

Security Council, being a matter purely within the domestic jurisdiction of Czechoslovakia,[1] and one which that state had not sought to bring to the United Nations. Somewhat inconsistently he alleged that the Western bloc had been guilty of interference in Czechoslovak domestic affairs and yet had initiated the debate.

'What,' asked Malik, 'could be more ridiculous and more tragic than to be a communist being defended by an Imperialist and a lord?'

For the invasion, Malik provided two justifications. First, that the forces concerned had been invited in.

The Soviet Government and the Governments of other allied States have decided to meet the request of the Czechoslovak Government for military assistance in accordance with the existing treaty obligations and on the basis of the relevant provisions of the United Nations Charter.[2]

Secondly he considered the intervention as one to preserve the 'Socialist Commonwealth' and hence European peace and security.

The threat to the Socialist system in Czechoslovakia is, at the same time, a threat to the foundations of European peace. This is why the actions of the Soviet Union and other socialist countries are motivated by a desire to strengthen peace and not to tolerate the undermining of the mainstays of European security.

Malik ended his main statement at this stage by quoting a Tass statement (previously cited by the US delegate Mr Ball)

[1] The Soviet argument was based on Article 2 (7) of the Charter. In fact in Security Council practice a decision to adopt an item on the agenda is without prejudice to the ultimate question of competence. For an examination of the practice see Jimenez de Arechaga, *Voting and the Handling of Disputes in the Security Council* (1950).

[2] Malik later referred to Article 51 of the Charter in justifying the intervention, but while that Article permits individual and collective self-defence in certain circumstances it also provides that 'measures taken by members in the exercise of this right of self-defence shall be *immediately* reported to the Security Council and shall not in any way affect the authority and responsibility of the Security Council under the present Charter to take at any time such action as it deems necessary in order to maintain or restore international peace and security'. This article would appear to undermine rather than support Soviet objection to consideration by the Security Council of the intervention.

referring to an invitation for the intervention from 'party and government leaders of the Czechoslovak Socialist Republic'. In his final words he appeared to underline the basic Soviet approach to what they saw as an area to be recognized as a sphere of vital Soviet interest. 'Nobody will ever be allowed to wrest a single link from the community of Socialist states.'[1]

In a further attempt to delay inscription Malik disputed the President of the Council's procedural move to take a vote by arguing that while he objected to inscription, he did not insist on a vote. 'When the one who objects does not insist on a vote things may not be pushed as far as a vote. The one who objected set out his position in his statement and this suffices.' Ball's rejoinder was to the point: 'It seems to me that if the Council is going to consume all the time we have consumed this evening on this matter ... I think it would be quite frivolous procedure if we did not now express the views of the Council on this matter.' A vote was taken and the agenda was adopted by thirteen votes to two.[2]

The resumption of the debate after this vote was begun with the acceptance, in accordance with Article 31 of the Charter, of a request from a representative of the Czechoslovak mission to the UN, Mr Muzik, to participate in the debate (without the right to vote). Muzik's first statement consisted of quotations from statements by Czechoslovak Government and party organs and members of the Czechoslovak Government, including the Party Central Committee, the Praesidium, the National Assembly, President Svoboda and the Czechoslovak Minister of Foreign Affairs. These stated in effect that the intervention had not been by invitation and was unanimously regarded by the authors of all the statements as contrary to international law. Muzik was careful to stress that he was speaking on the

---

[1] The Soviet doctrine on the inviolability of the socialist commonwealth was later elaborated in *Pravda* and by Gromyko at the General Assembly. See also page 114.

[2] Voting was: *In Favour* Algeria, Brazil, Canada, China, Denmark, France, India, Pakistan, Paraguay, Senegal, UK, US, Ethiopia.
Against Hungary, USSR.

NB. The adopting of an item on the Council agenda is a procedural question not subject to veto. (Statement of Four Sponsoring Powers at San Francisco, 7 June 1945; UNCIO Docs Vol. II, pp. 711–14, para. 3.)

explicit instructions of Mr Hajek, the Czechoslovak Foreign Minister.[1] Czechoslovak hopes of preserving at least something of what had been achieved since January 1968 by persuading the Russians that their aims were not 'anti-socialist' were illustrated by Muzik's concluding words: 'the changes in Czechoslovakia since January were aimed only at improving the socialist system to bring the Republic closer to the lofty goals of freer socialism.'[2]

The speech of the United States delegate following Muzik was a violent attack on Russian policy towards Czechoslovakia going back to the death of Jan Masaryk in 1948.

Thus Czechoslovakia, wedged between more powerful States, has been the victim of two foreign tyrannies in succession: first that of Hitler and then that of the Soviet Union. Hitler's oppression, savage though it was, lasted for the comparatively brief span of seven years and ended with the downfall of the tyrant himself. But the Soviet tyranny that followed has lasted from 1948 to the present, for twenty years.[3]

This evoked a response in similar tone from Malik, who read out what he described as 'an appeal to allied states, including the Soviet Union, with an insistent demand for direct immediate assistance to the Czechoslovak people, including assistance through armed force'. This was said to have been sent by 'a group of members of the Czechoslovak Central Committee, of the Government and the National Assembly'. Apart from this attempted justification of the intervention, the emphasis of Malik's speech was on what he described as 'imperialist machinations' in Czechoslovakia. 'The Soviet Union has irrefutable data showing that events in Czechoslovakia can be traced outside that country.'[4]

Ball pointed out the inconsistency of Soviet insistence that events in Czechoslovakia were an internal matter, in which the Soviet Union was nevertheless not only free but under some obligation to interfere. Muzik replied to some of the points

---

[1] Mr Hajek was on holiday in Yugoslavia at the time of the invasion.
[2] S/PV 1441, p. 77.
[3] S/PV 1441, pp. 79–80.
[4] S/PV 1441, pp. 103–5.

made by Ball about events in 1948 and the comparison he had drawn between events in Hungary in 1956 and the Czechoslovak situation. He also stressed (speaking in Russian) the loyalty of the Czechoslovak Government and Party to socialist principles and the 'socialist camp'. The debate was adjourned at 11.5 p.m. after it had been agreed through informal consultations that the Council would meet at 10.30 on the following morning.

At the next meeting, at which the Czechoslovak representative was not present, the Danish representative introduced the first draft resolution on behalf of Brazil, Canada, Denmark, France, Paraguay, the United Kingdom and the United States. Senegal later also became a co-sponsor.[1] This included both condemnation of the armed intervention and a demand for the withdrawal of the troops. The Canadian representative described the resolution as 'the least we can do if the fundamental principles of the Charter have any meaning'.[2]

The debate continued in the same key, with the emphasis of the statements by Western representatives on concern for the safety of the Czechoslovak leaders. The morning debate ended with a procedural dispute on the timing of the next meeting. Whether or not in agreement with the Soviet representative, the Algerian, Mr Bouattoura, in effect assisted the former in trying to avoid setting a definite time for a resumption. He argued the need for time to consider 'certain important developments' and suggested that, in the absence of any listed speakers for the afternoon's meeting, the customary practice of arranging the next meeting through informal consultations should be conducted through the President. The Algerian suggestion was supported by the Hungarian representative and Malik. Ball objected to indeterminate delay because 'the world is watching this body to see how it responds to the very dangerous and grievous situation with which it is presented'. The Canadian representative made explicit the new developments to which the Algerian had referred. 'We are aware that there are new elements. They have been only too frequently referred to, that is, that the

---

[1] See Appendix 3 for text. Compare the broad base of the sponsorship with the initial resolution on Hungary in 1956 which was sponsored only by France, UK and USA.

[2] S/PV 1442, pp. 18–20.

THE UNITED NATIONS AND THE CRISIS

Government of Czechoslovakia is in the process of being changed today. I do hope that we are not going to wait until we receive representations from a new government which says, and confirms the statement which the representative of Hungary has made, that the new government would of course not wish to continue this discussion.'[1] In the event the point was put to the vote on a formal proposal made by the United Kingdom representative that the Council meet at 5 p.m. 'on the understanding that if consultations make it desirable we can postpone the meeting beyond the time arranged'. This was agreed by 11 votes with five abstentions (Algeria, Hungary, India, Pakistan, Soviet Union).

The third meeting did not in fact take place until 9 p.m. The first speaker was the representative of Czechoslovakia who announced the impending visit of the Czechoslovak Foreign Minister and read out two cables, which he underlined came from the Czechoslovak Ministry of Foreign Affairs. These described the activities of those members of the Czechoslovak Party and Government who were free. The first referred to allegations that a 'factional collaborationist Central Committee' was being formed. Muzik commented that, despite the situation, the occupation forces had not 'succeeded in imposing on the Czechoslovak people representatives whom it did not elect'. Muzik's statement made a considerable impact. Immediately after it the representative of Senegal declared his co-sponsorship of the draft resolution. The remainder of the debate, until the adjournment at 3.55 a.m. on 23 August after the vote on the first draft resolution and the subsequent introduction by the Canadian representative of the second draft resolution requesting the Secretary-General to seek the release and ensure the safety of the Czechoslovak leaders, was almost exclusively occupied with what, if read in the context of the whole debate, can only be seen as determined attempts by the Soviet Union and its allies to delay the proceedings. A procedural debate on whether the Bulgarian representative was to be allowed the right to speak at the following meeting *and* before the vote was a transparent example of this. If Ball may be criticized for the sometimes excessively polemical tone of his statements, he was

[1] S/PV 1442, p. 56.

surely justified in saying that it was a matter of grave concern 'to find this solemn body turned into a circus by the most absurd ridiculous proposals obviously intended to obstruct the exercise by this body of the expression of its opinion, which is long overdue on a crisis which is confronting the world . . .' The Hungarian representative made a lengthy, if in the circumstances somewhat inappropriate, statement devoted mainly to quotations from Western publications regarding the events in Hungary in 1956. Malik himself made one of his longest and apparently least directly relevant statements when the Bulgarian move seemed unlikely to delay a vote.[1] The Bulgarian spoke at length after the prolonged wrangles over the timing of his intervention.[2]

When the vote was finally taken the Indian, Algerian and Pakistani representatives abstained.[3] The Indian explained this on the ground that the urgent need was for the withdrawal of the Soviet troops. The condemnation would not be helpful and Indian efforts to have this part of the resolution amended had been refused. The Pakistani stated that he had not had time to secure instructions from his government. The Algerian considered the Council proceedings to have been misconceived in the absence of opportunity for real discussion and consultation, the importation of the 'cold war', and what he saw as the double standard demanded of the Council as between Europe and the Middle East or South-East Asia. He nevertheless stressed the importance of the withdrawal of the Soviet troops. The Soviet representative left the Council in no doubt as to his views: 'This paltry piece of paper is only a summary of these slanderous inventions which we have heard at such length by the representatives of the United States and Great Britain.'[4] He defended his veto as enabling the Soviet Union to 'defend a just cause and the interests of very many peoples of other countries . . . against

---

[1] S/PV 1443, pp. 78–125.
[2] S/PV 1443, pp. 128–147.
[3] The vote was: *In Favour* Brazil, Canada, China, Denmark, Ethiopia, France, Paraguay, Senegal, UK, USA.
Against Hungary, Soviet Union.
Abstaining Algeria, India, Pakistan.
[4] S/PV 1443, p. 161.

imperialist aggression'.¹ He was also quick to brand the resolution introduced by the Canadian (on behalf of the same members as the first draft resolution) as a 'new trick of the NATO countries' and an attempt 'to drag the Secretary-General of the UN into the dirty business of intervention in the affairs of a Socialist state....'

The resumed debate,² which began at 5 p.m. on 23 August, revealed little new. Representatives of Bulgaria and Poland were again present and, for the first time, a representative of Yugoslavia who read into the record the Yugoslav Government's statement of 22 August calling for the withdrawal of the 'occupation forces', and attacked the 'policy of spheres of interest' and 'blocs' which created conditions for the 'subjugation of the interests and independent policy of a member of an alliance'.³ The emphasis was again on the safety of the missing Czechoslovak leaders, a point on which the Soviet delegate returned no reply. He again condemned the draft resolution introduced by the Canadian and exchanged polemics with Ball. The Council adjourned at 8.35 p.m. after the Canadian representative had explained that the co-sponsors of the draft resolution would be prepared to consult on the precise wording of the resolution, provided that its basic objectives were pursued. This he said in response to the representative of Ethiopia who, while supporting the idea of using the Secretary-General's good offices, had emphasized the need for the Secretary-General to enjoy the widest possible support if his mission were to be successful, and also the risk of limiting the scope of his action by too restrictive a resolution.

The last Council session concerned with the Czechoslovak situation lasted from 11.30 a.m. until 4.15 p.m. on Saturday 24 August. Three quarters of this time was spent in argument over whether an East German representative should be seated. This began with objections by the Soviet representative to the procedure whereby, in accordance with precedent, a telegram received from the East German Foreign Minister had been

¹ S/PV 1443, p. 171.
² Although again invited to be present under Article 31 of the Charter, the Czechoslovak representative did not appear.
³ S/PV 1444, pp. 58-60.

circulated to members of the Security Council but in a manner indicating that it was not an official document. This part of the debate was theoretically concerned with the procedural question of whether an East German representative should be seated. In practice it developed into a lengthy justification by the Soviet and Hungarian representatives of the East German Government as worthy of normal treatment and an attack on the Western and other powers who refused recognition. The Bulgarian representative was allowed to speak during this 'procedural' debate. The President made clear that, in permitting this, he was making no ruling on whether non-members of the Council should be allowed to intervene in procedural debates, but he put the point to the Council and allowed the Bulgarian to participate when there was no objection. After the Bulgarian had spoken, Lord Caradon (UK) emphasized the importance for the Council of avoiding setting a precedent of this sort.[1] Again in the context of the whole debate, and taking account of the fact that all representatives, including Mr Malik, were aware that the move to seat an East German representative could only lead to dispute and could also provide an opportunity for speeches on another subject, it is clear that this whole episode was another example of delaying tactics by the Soviet Union and its allies. In the event the Soviet proposal to seat an East German representative was defeated by 9 votes to 2 with 4 abstentions.[2] The Brazilian representative explained that he abstained only because he was President of the Council for the debate. 'My sole personal judgement indicated for the President the exercise of restraint, discretion and silence. It does not in any way reflect . . . any change in the attitude of the Government of Brazil.'[3] The high point of this meeting was the statement by the Czechoslovak Foreign Minister, Hajek, who gave a measured account of the Czechoslovak attitude towards the invasion, emphasizing Czechoslovakia's continued loyalty to the cause of socialism and communism, membership of the Warsaw Pact

---

[1] S/PV 1445, p. 47.
[2] The voting was: *In Favour* — Soviet Union, Hungary.
Against — Canada, China, Denmark, Ethiopia, France, Paraguay, Senegal, UK, USA.
Abstaining — Brazil, Algeria, India, Pakistan.
[3] S/PV 1445, p. 111.

and her other obligations to the 'socialist community', and also the Czechoslovak leaders' belief that the developments in Czechoslovakia had strengthened the 'socialist and patriotic feelings . . . as well as the leading role of the Communist Party'.[1]

After the Soviet representative had read out a *Tass* report that the talks in Moscow between the Soviet leaders and the Czechoslovak delegation led by President Svoboda would continue on 25 August, the Council adjourned at 4.15 p.m. on the understanding that it would meet again on Monday 26 August at 10 a.m. In the event Mr Hajek asked that the Security Council cease its consideration of the Czechoslovak situation to avoid prejudicing the Moscow talks which finished on 26 August. The item remains on the Security Council agenda.

General Assembly

After the Security Council meetings there was no move to call an Emergency Special Session of the General Assembly on the Czechoslovak situation, nor did it appear as an item on the agenda of the 23rd Session.[2] It was, however, inevitable that there would be fairly extensive reference to Czechoslovakia during the session, both because of the general debate which is used for an overall review of world affairs, and because the agenda for the Assembly contained a number of items relevant to what occurred in Czechoslovakia.[3]

In the general debate Western and Latin American representatives referred to Czechoslovakia in terms clearly disapproving of the invasion. Few Afro-Asians mentioned it and most of those representing 'non-aligned' countries either made no reference or referred to the situation with great caution.[4] Mr Gromyko's clear statement on 3 October of the Soviet Union's determination to preserve the 'Socialist Commonwealth' at the cost, if necessary, of the sovereignty of individual socialist

---

[1] S/PV 1445, p. 97.
[2] The Czechoslovak situation might have been submitted either as a Supplementary Item (Rule 14 General Assembly), or as an Additional Item (Rule 15).
[3] E.g. the Third Committee's consideration of the violation of human rights and freedoms and the current 'International Year for Human Rights'.
[4] Ethiopia and Japan referred to the intervention. Such an influential member of the non-aligned group as the United Arab Republic made no reference.

countries[1] evoked a response from the American Secretary of State, Mr Rusk, and the British Foreign Secretary, Mr Stewart, who both stressed the conflict of this attitude with the basic principles of the UN Charter. Stewart on 14 October, after quoting Gromyko's assertion that the Soviet Union could not tolerate a situation where 'the vital interests of socialism are infringed upon and encroachments are made on the inviolability of the boundaries of the Socialist Commonwealth', pointed out that this meant that the Soviet Union would judge the interests of certain other states. Placing this Soviet assertion beside what was done in Czechoslovakia it was clear that the Soviet Union could and would, if it saw fit, 'take military action outside its own territory in accordance with its judgement of what the interests of other states may be'. This Stewart described as 'wholly repugnant to the Charter'.[2]

Among the seven main committees and other subsidiary committees and bodies comprising the apparatus of the Assembly, Czechoslovakia has come up on a number of occasions. The special Committee on Friendly Relations is concerned with those principles to which the intervention was directly opposed. Despite Soviet moves to postpone a further meeting of the Special Committee on the Question of Defining Agression (a question proposed by the Soviet Union herself in 1967), Czechoslovakia has come up in the Legal Committee's consideration of this question. On 19 November the US representative (Senator Cooper) made a long and highly political statement in this Committee to which the Soviet representative replied at length. His lack of usable legal arguments may have been partly responsible for the Soviet representative's concentration of much of his attack on the fact that the proceedings were being televised. Czechoslovakia was a major element in debate in the Third Committee under 'The International Year for Human Rights'. It should also be noted that there was a heated debate resulting from the Soviet intervention in Czechoslovakia at the 1968 General Conference of UNESCO in the course of discussion of that organization's contribution to peace.

---

[1] A/PV 1679, pp. 28–31; see also page 114 below.
[2] COI Publication No. 39267, text of Mr Stewart's speech.

THE UNITED NATIONS AND THE CRISIS

Questions and conclusions
What then should be the verdict on the handling of the Czechoslovak crisis by the United Nations? There is no doubt that the Charter provisions regarding the use of force have been flouted.[1]

The essential fact in considering the Security Council's role is the involvement of one of the permanent members with the right of veto in the case of all votes on all substantive as opposed to procedural proposals. The whole concept of the Charter was based on Great Power co-operation in the functions allotted to the Security Council for the pacific settlement of disputes and also as having the 'primary responsibility for the maintenance of international peace and security'.[2] The Council's role as an instrument of peaceful settlement is envisaged by the Charter as following the use of such traditional means as negotiation, enquiry, mediation, conciliation or arbitration,[3] but it is empowered to investigate any international dispute or potential dispute; and UN members have an obligation to refer to the Security Council any dispute they have failed to settle by the traditional means described above.[4] The Council's role in enforcement action for the maintenance of peace and security is limited. It does not have at its disposal a force as envisaged under Article 43 of the Charter. In practice the establishment by the Security Council of a UN peacekeeping force is dependent on the agreement or at least acquiescence of the permanent members. Even where this exists, the practice has always been that the deployment of such forces only takes place with the agreement of the states on whose territory the forces are to operate. In these circumstances action of this nature was not possible even had the Czechoslovaks asked for it. Similar considerations would have applied to action under Article 40 calling upon the parties to a dispute to observe provisional measures pending settlement, or Article 41 imposing sanctions. In this context it is of little value to attempt to assess the action of the Security Council in these terms.

In the event the Security Council meetings served the purpose

---

[1] In particular Article 2 (4) of the Charter.
[2] Article 24 of the Charter.
[3] Article 33 of the Charter.
[4] Article 37 of the Charter.

of providing a focal point for protest from most quarters of the world at the action taken by the Soviet Union and its allies. The weakness of the Soviet case in terms of respect for the Charter or international law was shown quite clearly. It was obvious that the Soviet attitude in the Council was dictated by the need to hold up the proceedings by any feasible means in the expectation at first of a change of government in Czechoslovakia and later of the agreement imposed in Moscow. The failure of the Soviet delegate to provide answers to the basic questions of the identity of those Czechoslovaks alleged to have invited the intervention, and the whereabouts and safety of the Czechoslovak leaders, was effectively publicized and convincingly demonstrated to the representations of the non-aligned countries who might be expected to suspend judgement as long as possible. The failure of Malik to refer at all to the Czechoslovak representative's statement at the third meeting on 22 August and the failure of attempts to create a collaborationist government no doubt allowed other members to draw their own conclusions about the real situation.

The abstention of Algeria, India and Pakistan on the first draft resolution requires comment. It is not the case that the resolution had no non-aligned support. Even if Brazil and Paraguay are to be regarded as partially aligned as a result of their geographical position and relationship with the United States, Ethiopia and Senegal cannot be described as clear supporters of any Western or Eastern grouping. It is therefore reasonable to see self-interest as the prime cause of the abstentions. All three had good reasons to avoid antagonizing the Soviet Union.

This being so, it is not very convincing to argue that the sharp and polemical tone of the debate and the insistence of the sponsors of the resolution on retaining condemnation of the intervention were decisively instrumental in preventing non-aligned support, although these factors may have helped to provide pretexts for abstention. The tactics of the US delegate may be seen as having helped the Soviet delegate in his task of delaying the whole proceedings by providing targets at which the latter could effectively tilt. A reading of the debate strongly suggests that the quieter, more balanced and more succinct approach of Lord Caradon was more effective.

THE UNITED NATIONS AND THE CRISIS

It is not possible to state definitely whether or not the debate tangibly affected Soviet actions, though the strenuous efforts of the Soviet representative to hamstring the proceedings and introduce new subjects show Soviet sensitivity to the prospect of condemnation by representatives of four continents. The debate may have given some encouragement to the Czechoslovaks themselves and it is possible, although this cannot be assumed, that the evidence of world-wide concern about the safety of the Czechoslovak leaders had some effect on the Soviet attitude.

The debate also served to highlight another aspect of East-West relations which, though neither necessarily encouraging nor hopeful for the future, should be fully realized if not accepted. As the Yugoslav representative and a number of other delegates pointed out, the invasion was based on the principle of spheres of vital interest of the Great Powers. In face of the involvement of such interests the Security Council was shown to be powerless to take practical action. On the positive side the removal of any illusions about these realities is much less likely to harm the United Nations than criticism based upon them.

What of the role of the General Assembly? It has been suggested that an item should have been inscribed on the agenda, or that an initiative should have been taken to call an Emergency Special Session under the 'Uniting for Peace' procedure[1] as in the case of Suez and Hungary in 1956. We have seen how, despite the absence of either of these moves, the Czechoslovak crisis was far from forgotten at the 23rd Session of the General Assembly. A primary consideration was bound to be the wishes of the Czechoslovak representatives themselves and their estimate of what would be helpful. It could certainly not be argued that they had had to surrender the power of expressing an individual view on this. They were opposed to either course. In the General Assembly general debate the Czechoslovak representative, Mr Pleskot, said: 'We expect that the Governments of all States and their representatives at this session of

---

[1] The 'Uniting for Peace' procedure was designed to avoid frustration of the UN from action to maintain peace and security because of the negative vote of a permanent member. It is based on a General Assembly Resolution (No. 377(V)) of 3 November 1950.

the UN General Assembly will understand this situation and do nothing that would be at variance with the will of the Czechoslovak Government to find a solution for the existing situation on the basis of the results of the Moscow discussions.'[1] The trend of the Security Council debate had emphasized that a detailed discussion on a draft resolution would have been likely to result in Czechoslovakia becoming, in the context of the UN as such, little more than a stereotyped cold war issue. This would not have been likely to further her interests. There is also the attitude of the large non-aligned membership of the UN to be taken into account. The Afro-Asians who comprise the majority of this group are not concerned about what they see as purely European problems. This, combined with their reluctance to become involved in East-West disputes, must have rendered it hazardous to assume that any resolution as clear as that which secured 10 votes in the Security Council would get enough affirmative votes in the General Assembly to be an effective register of protest. A Special Representative, as in the case of Hungary, might have been appointed, but it is hard to see such a representative playing even a humanitarian role. As regards positive action, similar political difficulties apply to the General Assembly as to the Security Council where a permanent member is involved in a dispute. Furthermore, an item on the agenda of the 23rd Regular Session would necessarily have suffered in effectiveness from the fact that events outside the UN would, by October 1968, have rendered a condemnatory resolution and concern for the safety of leaders of the Czechoslovak Party and Government much less apparently relevant. This would not have applied to an immediate move after the end of the Security Council meetings, but on this point the other considerations and particularly the Czechoslovak attitude seem overriding.

Some comment should be offered on the role of the Secretary-General. The statement issued on his behalf on 21 August was strong and clear. The resolution requesting the Secretary-General's good offices was never put to the vote. But it would not be unreasonable to expect that the Soviet representative's violent attack on it would have found an echo in reluctance of non-aligned members to risk the public integrity of the Secretary-

[1] A/PV 1682, pp. 58-60.

General and his office, bearing in mind the results of his predecessors' involvement in actions which did not throughout have the approval or acquiescence of the Soviet Government.[1] The Ethiopian representative's attitude towards the draft was indicative of this. It would certainly have been extremely unlikely that U Thant would, in the present climate of the UN, have considered any independent action in the absence of a clear mandate.

The general conclusion is that, operating within the limits which have been described, the United Nations acquitted itself reasonably effectively. For the future, the overall interest of the majority of member states in a renewal of progress towards détente is likely to prevent any strong or effective protest against a growing encroachment in Czechoslovakia, unless this were achieved by open violence.

[1] Mr Hammarskjold's actions in the Congo, as those of Trygve Lie over the Korean question, were principally responsible for their losing the confidence of the Soviet Government.

6
Interpretations and Conclusions

THE narrative of the development of the crisis in Czechoslovak–Soviet relations in Chapters 1 and 2 ended with the events of 20–21 August, when the invasion took place and many of the Czechoslovak leaders were arrested by the invading forces. It is appropriate to attempt an analysis of motives and purposes of the invasion before briefly describing events between the end of August and December.

It is argued in Chapter 2 that the Soviet leaders were by mid-August prisoners of a time limit that was to expire on 9 September, when the 14th Party Congress was to meet, and that the publication of the Draft Statutes on 10 August probably played an important part in convincing the Soviet leaders and their allies that the policy of pressure had definitely failed. The Party Congress, it was now clear, would complete the removal of the remaining elements in the Party sympathetic to Moscow, and would confirm those features of the Action Programme which were most unacceptable to the Soviet leaders. In these circumstances, the first Soviet priority was to prevent the assembly of the Congress and the virtually irreversible decisions which it would take. Even if there had been time available for a renewal of a policy of pressure it must have become quite apparent to a majority of the Soviet leaders that there was no reasonable expectation of a retreat by the Czechoslovak Party from the position its leaders had reached, and that the most drastic measures were required to save the situation. The delicate balancing of factors is unknown, but it is reasonable to conclude

INTERPRETATIONS AND CONCLUSIONS

that the decision was reached that the possible unpleasant consequences of the use of force were secondary to the very real immediate dangers and the strong possibility of even more serious future ones.

The historian of any crisis who ignores the importance of human factors omits a central point. It is subsequently easy to rationalize actions, and to remove from their analysis factors which seemed unimportant when viewed later, but which at the time played a significant role. We do not know, and are never likely to know, the arguments that took place within the Soviet leadership and with their Pact allies throughout the summer of 1968. If it seems reasonable to conclude that although there was general agreement on the necessity to bring the Czechoslovaks to heel there were strong differences over the methods that should be adopted, such a conclusion can only be hypothetical. It may be said that factors quite unconnected or only remotely connected with the immediate problem, including the unrest within Russia itself, the developing relationship with the United States, the Middle East and Vietnam, and the fears of West German economic and political expansion, must have played some part. The student of Soviet policy towards Czechoslovakia between April and August can see the outlines of the objections to the Czechoslovak reforms clearly enough; what he cannot see is the weight attached in Moscow to each factor in the equation.

Several strong indications lead to the supposition that it was anticipated in Moscow that control would have passed to a new government within a few hours of the invasion, and that the *coup d'état* would have been followed by an immediate *post facto* justification of the invasion by the new authorities. No effort was made to disarm Czechoslovak army units; the apparatus of an army of occupation and its attendant police units was absent. The operation depended for success upon speed, the deployment of overwhelming force to deter organized resistance, and the swift proclamation of a new government.

The outstanding features of the invasion and the immediate aftermath were the complete success of the military side of the operations – even though it may be remarked that a well-prepared move of this nature against an ally of whose military capability the invader has complete knowledge and over whose prior

111

dispositions he has a considerable degree of control cannot be numbered among the most difficult of military operations – and the almost complete failure in the immediate political objects of the exercise. It is this failure that gives further strength to the belief that the decision to invade was taken at a relatively late stage and was based upon a very considerable misapprehension of the political realities within the Czechoslovak Party. The total failure to provide anything resembling a convincing legal[1] or political justification was the first clear sign that, despite the total military success, the immediate objective of the operation had not been achieved. The explanation moved rapidly away from the claim of an 'invitation' by the Czechoslovak Government to one by 'Party and Government leaders';[2] when no names materialized, the justification became one of the need to deal with the designs of 'imperialists and counter-revolutionaries', to which were added allegations of plots by 'Fascist saboteurs' from West Germany. As has already been emphasized in Chapter 5, it was one of the most notable contributions of the Security Council debates that the Soviet representative was exposed to the need to furnish these successive improvised justifications at the moment when the Soviet leaders were grappling with the unexpected situation that confronted them on the morrow of the invasion.

It is possible to see where part of this miscalculation lay. A *Pravda* article of 22 August, evidently prepared before the invasion, significantly referred to Dubcek as the leader of a 'minority revisionist group' in the Praesidium, which had prevented the implementation of the Cierna and Bratislava agreements. There is further evidence that points to the fact that the Soviet leaders had expected Dubcek to have been outvoted at the meeting of the Praesidium on the evening of 20 August, or at least that his opponents would be in a position to appeal as a group for Soviet assistance.[3] In the event, the invasion took

[1] See Appendix 5.
[2] The Polish Press referred to 'Party and State activists'.
[3] A broadsheet issued by *Rude Pravo*, and reproduced in the Austrian newspaper *Die Presse* on 28 August, contained an account of the meeting by a participant. From this it appears that a conservative group hoped to be in a position to ask for Soviet help either as leaders of a majority or as a group determined to end Dubcek's revisionism.

INTERPRETATIONS AND CONCLUSIONS

place before the meeting ended and before the invitation, an essential part of the propaganda aspect of the invasion, could be sent. The prepared political justification for the invasion accordingly disintegrated at the very outset. This major setback was compounded by the solidarity of the Czechoslovak leaders and the virtually total popular support for them in the country. Perhaps the most remarkable indications of this support were the declaration of the National Assembly on 22 August reaffirming loyalty to Svoboda and the legal government and Party leadership, and the clandestine meeting of the 14th Party Congress in a Prague factory.

In the week following the invasion, culminating in the Moscow Agreement of 26 August[1] and the return of Dubcek and Cernik to Prague, the failure of the initial Soviet plan was manifest. It had proved impossible to discover an alternative government which would have had any real chance of retaining power when the Soviet forces were withdrawn.[2] The Czechoslovak leaders retained their unity – a unity, indeed, greatly strengthened by the invasion – and the role of President Svoboda in Moscow appears to have been crucial. The Moscow Agreement formalized the Soviet acceptance of the Czechoslovak régime and represented the abandonment, for the time being, of the attempt to replace the Czechoslovak leadership. The price paid for this can only be inferred, since the text of the Agreement has not been published. But it can be assumed that it contained provisions restricting the implementation of the liberalization movement.

The subsequent events were in effect a return to the policy of pressure, undertaken this time with the advantage of the physical presence of substantial Soviet forces on Czechoslovak territory, but in the context of a strengthening of popular support for the policies for which the Czechoslovak leaders had stood. As in the previous period of pressure, the actions of the Soviet leadership do not lend justification to theories of a clearly thought out

[1] See Appendix 4.
[2] It was significant that the lengthy appeal for assistance published in *Pravda* on 22 August, allegedly signed by 'a group of members of the Central Committee of the Communist Party of Czechoslovakia, of the Government and the National Assembly who turn for help to the Governments and Communist parties of fraternal countries', gave no names.

programme, and tend to confirm an impression of an essentially cautious, pragmatic and unimaginative leadership seeking, by a series of *ad hoc* measures, to achieve the elimination of Czechoslovak heresy for which it had been groping since March.

The most significant Soviet justification for the invasion was given in a major *Pravda* article on 25 September, and whose theme was reiterated by Gromyko on 3 October at the UN General Assembly. The article expressed matters that had been stated before, but its salient feature was the bluntness and clarity with which the rules for the Soviet bloc were set out. It stated that 'The peoples of the socialist countries and Communist parties ... have freedom for determining the ways of advance of their respective countries. However none of their decisions should damage either socialism in their country or the fundamental interests of other socialist countries and the whole working class movement'. 'The sovereignty of each socialist country cannot be opposed to the interests of the world of socialism', and 'naturally the Communists of the fraternal countries could not allow the socialist states to be inactive in the name of abstractedly understood sovereignty when they saw that the country stood in peril of anti-socialist degeneration'. Gromyko put the argument in even blunter terms, in which there was an interestingly dominant note of defiance:

> The countries of the socialist commonwealth have their own vital interests, their own obligations including those of safeguarding their mutual security. ... This commonwealth constitutes an inseparable entity cemented by unbreakable ties such as history has never known. ... To damage the position of socialism in the world is tantamount to increasing the dangers of a new world war. ...
>
> The Soviet Union and other socialist countries have on many occasions warned those who are tempted to try to roll back the socialist commonwealth, to snatch at least one link from it, that we will neither tolerate nor allow that to happen. ... The socialist states cannot and will not allow a situation where the vital interests of socialism are infringed upon and encroachments are made on the inviolability of the boundaries of the socialist commonwealth and therefore on the foundations of international peace.[1]

[1] See *Pravda*, 25 September, and General Assembly Record A/PV 1679, pp. 28–31.

INTERPRETATIONS AND CONCLUSIONS

These statements were of course *ex post facto* justifications for what had been done, and a period of well over a month elapsed between the invasion of Czechoslovakia and the publication of the *Pravda* article. But, more important, they were clearly designed to warn both the West and the entire Soviet bloc of the Soviet determination to preserve the cohesion of an inviolable Socialist Commonwealth. The declaration that it was the function of the Soviet Union to define the acceptable limits of deviation, and the equation of the Socialist Commonwealth with membership of the Warsaw Pact,[1] may also be noted as significant. The declarations are, in tone as well as in content, essentially defensive *vis-à-vis* the West, while being minatory towards Eastern Europe.

The presentation of the terms of membership of the Socialist Commonwealth is of substantial importance in the context of the Soviet attitudes towards Eastern Europe since the death of Stalin. The degree of autonomy to be tolerated by the Soviet Union had not been made clear either in the Khruschev era or thereafter. The Soviet leaders had acquiesced in the movement by Rumania towards a limited degree of autonomy, principally because it had not been accompanied by the loss of Party authority comparable to that which they believed to be taking place in Czechoslovakia in 1968. The Czechoslovak leaders may have believed that the avoidance of Nagy's disastrous error of 1956 would be sufficient, and that constant pledges of loyalty to the Soviet Union, the Warsaw Pact, and COMECON would be adequate indications of Czechoslovak reliability. If so, they wholly failed to appreciate that their definition of 'Czechoslovak internal affairs' about which their allies were not concerned was not the same as that of the Soviet leaders and other Pact members. Was there, accordingly, a serious misunderstanding between the two sides? The Soviet leaders had given warning after warning of the features of the Czechoslovak situation that caused them the greatest concern, and it can be argued that it was the fundamental misunderstanding over the definition of 'internal affairs' that bedevilled the tortuous dialogue between the two sides. The fresh definition of the rules of the Socialist

[1] See Chapter 3, page 55, and the reference to the *Pravda* article on 27 October.

Commonwealth may therefore be regarded as one of the most important results of the Czechoslovak crisis.

Soviet policy towards Czechoslovakia between the end of August and December was directed towards the whittling away of the Action Programme and the restoration of at least the pre-April situation. Press censorship was reimposed, the implementation of the Action Programme checked, and agreement secured to the stationing of Soviet forces in Czechoslovakia by the Treaty signed on 16 October and ratified by the National Assembly two days later. The fate of the economic reforms is not clear; Sik resigned, and was described by *Tass* as 'one of the most odious figures among the right-wing revisionist forces'; the Czechoslovak–Soviet meeting at Kiev on 6–8 December was primarily concerned with economic matters and 'the deepening of co-operation within the framework of COMECON'.[1] The arrival in Prague on 17 December of Nikolai Baibakov, the Soviet chief economic planner, together with reports of Soviet refusal at that time to grant economic aid, point strongly to the use being made by the Soviets of the economic predicament of Czechoslovakia in order to increase pressure upon the leadership.

But it is not really possible, at this stage, to draw up a complete assessment of the post-invasion situation. In the short term, the invasion – despite the failure of the immediate plan – achieved its main objective of reasserting Soviet control over the country. The student of the subsequent events is, however, more impressed by the relativeness rather than the completeness of this success. The fact that the Soviet leaders were compelled to recognize the régime they had deposed was surprising enough; the fact that, up to December, the Czechoslovak leaders had managed to avert the worse consequences of occupation was another unexpected development. The invasion itself had caused an immediate revival of interest in NATO among its members, which might have long-term effects, and had at least strengthened the hand of those in the United States who

[1] *Rude Pravo*, 10 December.

INTERPRETATIONS AND CONCLUSIONS

had been arguing against any major American withdrawals from Europe. Although the ultimate consequences may not be great, the image of the Soviet Union as a peace-loving nation had been severely harmed by the invasion.[1] More serious for a leadership that had placed such emphasis upon the World Communist Conference had been the reaction within the world communist movement. The postponement of the Conference, decided by the Preparatory Committee on 30 September–1 October in Budapest, was confirmed at a subsequent meeting in November. It was announced that the Conference would be held in Moscow in May 1969, but it is possible that further postponements will be necessary unless the Czechoslovak problem is satisfactorily resolved.

It was in the achievement of the latter objective that the relativeness of Soviet success between the end of August and December was so marked.

The Soviet leaders, having failed to find the expected political support within the Czechoslovak Party, apparently realized that their most realistic chance of securing their main objectives lay in the use of the existing Czechoslovak Government. This was at best an uncomfortable solution, and the signs of Soviet dissatisfaction with the pace of 'normalization' have been clear from the tone of the Russian press,[2] the lengthy periods spent by First Deputy Foreign Minister Kuznetsov in Prague, and the several visits paid by the Czechoslovak leaders to Moscow followed by declarations of Czechoslovak determination to 'intensify the struggle against anti-Socialist forces'.[3] Although the Soviet leaders have continued to exert pressure, the fundamental dilemma of Soviet relations with members of the bloc has not been removed. The Czechoslovak leaders, while accepting changes, have continually emphasized their determination to adhere to the 'post-January policy' while avoiding anything

---

[1] The reluctance of several non-aligned countries to denounce the invasion is commented upon in *The Times*, 20 November, and the *Morning Star*, 22 November.

[2] E.g. *Pravda*, 10 September, accusing Czechoslovak newspapers of speaking from 'anti-socialist' positions; ibid., 3 October, accusing the Czechoslovak media of not exposing the 'hostile activities of anti-socialist and rightist revisionist forces'.

[3] E.g. the communiqué of 4 October issued after the visit to Moscow of a delegation from the Praesidium.

which previously obstructed 'its consistently Socialist character'.[1] The violence of Soviet attacks on Czechoslovak national unity behind the government,[2] and their efforts to support the activities of the conservatives in the Party emphasize the understandable Soviet desire to have a more congenial régime with which to deal; but the care that was taken to avoid clashes between the Soviet forces and demonstrators, and the absence of the imposition of anything resembling a full occupation régime, also illustrated the appreciation by the Soviet leaders of the need to move with circumspection. The question arises as to whether they achieved any real progress between the end of August and December.

The Resolution of the November meeting of the Czechoslovak Party Central Committee[3] was generally interpreted as a substantial climb-down from the principles of the Action Programme. A close reading of the Resolution shows that this is a misleading verdict. Leaving aside the frequent assertions of loyalty to the 'post-January policy' there are as many as five specific references to the Action Programme which should have been the 'basis for the process of unification in the Party and in society'. There is the admission that 'Right-Wing and anti-Socialist tendencies' frustrated the post-January policy and seriously 'complicated the political situation in the country and our relations with the allies', but there is no reference to 'counter-revolution', and the Resolution strongly criticizes the 'serious resistance of the dogmatic and conservative forces'. As a whole, the Resolution reveals a careful balance between the acceptance of points insisted upon by the Soviet leaders and determination to adhere as far as possible to the Action Programme. It is, for example, made quite clear that while the unity of the Party must not be jeopardized there must be no attempt to suppress the rights of a Party member to express freely and openly 'his views on Party policy and the activities of all Party bodies from top

[1] President Svoboda, 11 October.
[2] E.g. *Pravda*, 22 September, denouncing the newspaper *Lidova Demokracie* for interpreting the unity of the people from a 'non-class attitude'; Moscow Radio, 18 September, attacking Sik for making statements 'typical of tactics of right-wing forces ... who disguise their anti-socialist pro-Western views by false statements on ... national unity'.
[3] Summarized by Prague Radio Home Service, 18 November.

INTERPRETATIONS AND CONCLUSIONS

to bottom'. The passage relating to the role of the press, radio and television has been emphasized in most reports as epitomizing the retreat from previous policy. The very considerable curtailment of the freedom of the mass media should nevertheless be seen in perspective. There had been several indications of the unease of the Czechoslovak leaders before the invasion at the results of the total abandonment of censorship,[1] and it was wholly unrealistic to expect that the removal of restrictions could survive the events of 20–21 August. The interpretation of the provisions governing press freedom must depend on the way government and party policy develops. It is of importance to note several indications. The journalists do in practice appear to have exerted some influence upon the government's handling of press relations. After well-publicized protests[2] against censorship and the banning of the publications *Reporter* and *Politika*, the former was permitted to reappear. The Director of the Government Committee for Press and Information, Deputy Prime Minister Colotka, left this post on 5 December, to be replaced by a relatively unknown ex-deputy Minister of Education and Ambassador to Sweden, Havelka, who is certainly not known as a 'conservative', and who took care to emphasize in an interview broadcast by Prague Radio on 10 December that his appointment did not herald a tougher line but rather a more intensive effort to 'maintain a constant dialogue with journalists' and win their support for government policy. This appointment could mean that the function of the Government Committee was intended to be less rather than more important, and future policy was to be to rely more on self-censorship, with the powers to ban publications held in reserve, rather than on direction. The appointment – also on 5 December – of Josef Smidmajer as Director-General of Tele-

[1] See, for example, Dubcek's rebuke at the May Plenum of the press for getting ahead of the Party organs in advocating changes.
[2] E.g. the statement issued after a meeting of Prague journalists on 18 November, reported on Prague Radio in German on the same day. See also the statement issued after the Plenum of Czech journalists' union on 5 December, reported on Prague Radio on 6 December, expressing satisfaction at the 'positive results' of talks between journalists and political leaders.

It must be noted that the quite understandable outrage of the Western Press at the re-imposition of censorship in Czechoslovakia has in most cases concealed the fact that some gains had been retained.

vision provided another indication that the trend was not then in the direction of complete control. Neither of these appointments could remotely be regarded as a victory for freedom of speech in the mass media, but neither did they represent the imposition of authoritarian control. This is not, however, to underestmate the possible consequences of future Soviet pressure.

Up to December there were no signs that major non-governmental institutions were giving up their newly acquired rights to criticize government policy and make suggestions. The Chairman of the Central Committee of the Czechoslovak Trade Unions, Polacek, in his speech to the tenth plenary session of the Committee on 5 December, said that the working people wanted the trade unions to revert to their prime purpose 'to protect the justified interests of the workers'. In a television programme Polacek said that he had written to the Prime Minister stating that the unions could not accept the government's approach to price policy because it involved greater price increases than those previously agreed. These and other indications showed that the role in the Novotny régime of the unions as little more than agencies for promoting Party and Government policies had definitely ended.

So far as the economic reforms are concerned, it may be noted that the Central Committee Resolution states that the Party intended to continue on the road of the reforms,[1] and subsequent speeches reiterated this point. Although the economic field is one in which the Czechoslovak leaders have limited room for manoeuvre, it would be unwise to assume at this stage that the economic reforms are doomed to complete abandonment. Nevertheless, a combination of price rises, economic failure, apathy and discontent with the leadership could well undermine the unity of the Party and its popular support. Such a situation would give further opportunities for the installation of Soviet nominees in key positions.

---

[1] The Resolution stated that 'The Central Committee considers it necessary to declare . . . that it regards it as the basic line in the economic policy of the Party to continue the road of the reforms it has entered'.

INTERPRETATIONS AND CONCLUSIONS

The Czechoslovak crisis must be seen in a wider context if its full implications are to be properly assessed. This study has examined it from the points of view of NATO, the United Nations, and the Warsaw Pact, and some further attention must be given to the possible consequences upon the freshly-defined Socialist Commonwealth.

A consideration that goes far beyond Czechoslovakia alone is the evidence provided by the events of 1967-8 of the consequences of the breakdown of a Stalinist type of government and the failure to provide an effective substitute. If it is the case that the invasion taught the members of the Soviet bloc a lesson, one has also been offered to the Soviet leaders. It is probable that most if not all the East European régimes will be inclined to tighten their control,[1] but the dilemma of finding the right balance is bound to remain after Czechoslovakia. Several of the elements that caused the Czechoslovak hostility towards the Novotny régime are present in every country in the Soviet bloc. All suffer from over-centralized, inefficient economies. Attempts to reform these have not made very substantial progress, although it may be noted that the Hungarians introduced considerable decentralization measures at the beginning of 1968, and – unlike the Russians and the Poles – have been significantly quiet about the Czechoslovak reforms. All the other countries had by then also introduced, or had resolved upon, some measure of economic decentralization, beginning with East Germany in April 1964 and ending with Rumania in December 1967, but to nothing like the degree introduced in Czechoslovakia or even Hungary.

Reference has already been made to the essential differences between the situations in Rumania and Czechoslovakia. It should also be noted that comparisons between Poland and Czechoslovakia cannot be pushed too far. There has been some speculation about the possibility of economic and political changes in Poland, where there have been disturbances and protests by students and intellectuals, including the student

[1] See *The Times*, 10 November, on the forthcoming Polish Party Congress, and *The Observer*, 17 November, on the outcome. The theme of the Central Committee Theses described revisionism as 'contrary to the basic principles of Marxism-Leninism' and 'an illness gnawing the organism of Communist and workers' parties'.

riots in March 1968. Before similarities between Czechoslovakia and Poland are drawn, however, it may be emphasized that there is no minority problem in Poland comparable in importance to that of the Slovaks, and that the Polish intellectuals have tended to operate outside rather than within the Party. The more prominent members of the Polish Writers' Union are not members of the Party, and it is difficult to envisage a similar coalescing of forces against the régime developing within the Party structure as happened in Czechoslovakia. This latter difference is of importance in any assessment of the possibility of lasting and effective change. The March riots, although symptomatic of the unrest which has erupted at Warsaw University sporadically over the past few years, emphasized the essential differences between the Polish and the Czechoslovak situations. Mishandling by the authorities, including forcible removal of students and sympathizers, materially contributed to the spread of the trouble.[1] The Church, a vital factor in any Polish movement, remained silent until the disturbances had been brought under control, and there was no evidence of working-class support for the students.[2] The support of the Writers' Union was, in immediate political terms, an irrelevancy.

It may also be emphasized that the economic situation in Poland is also very different to that in Czechoslovakia during the period leading up to Novotny's overthrow. It is possible that similar troubles can be expected in Poland if greater emphasis is not laid upon market forces and greater freedom of choice for factory and enterprise management. But at present the Party's insistence on the dangers of economic 'revisionism' of this kind is reinforced by the relatively satisfactory growth of the Polish economy in recent years,[3] even though 1968 may prove to have been a less satisfactory year. Moreover Poland, unlike Czechoslovakia, is not suffering from having known a higher standard

[1] Polish Radio, 12 March 1968; *Le Monde*, 13 March; *Observer*, 17 March.

[2] See, for example, the *Morning Star*, 18 March, reporting workers' 'demands for a speedy purge' of all responsible for the demonstrations.

[3] Deputy Prime Minister Waniolka said in October 1968 that industrial production had increased by about 38% between 1964 and 1967; output in the chemical and electrical engineering industries rose by 70% and 54% respectively in the same period (Polish Radio, 19 October 1968).

of living and a more efficiently managed industrial economy in the past.[1]

The Polish Government and Party do not appear to be vulnerable to a comparable threat to that facing Novotny by the autumn of 1967, and it is difficult to envisage a Czechoslovak-type situation developing in Poland. There is no reason to suppose that the known likely successors to Gomulka within the Party – notably General Moczar and Edward Gierek – would follow a more liberal policy, or abandon the Party's strict line of orthodoxy in the wake of the Czechoslovak crisis and its total condemnation of revisionism contained in the recent Central Committee Theses.

Sufficient emphasis has already been placed upon the uniqueness of the situation in Czechoslovakia and the means whereby the Novotny régime was replaced. It would be dangerous to look at other members of the Soviet bloc in similar terms. Nevertheless, the main problems of adapting an autocratic system to changing circumstances in Eastern Europe in the post-Stalin world are, in their essentials, common to each. To these problems must be added that of the reminder of Soviet determination to specify the limits of tolerance in order to maintain the bloc in its present form, which will limit the freedom of manoeuvre of individual régimes for at least a period. Some commentators have applied Imperial analogies to the Soviet concept of Eastern Europe.[2] The analogy is in some respects a convenient one, and particularly in the context of the pejorative contemporary usage. It is also tempting for former imperial powers to throw back at the Soviet Union the charge previously brought against themselves. It is an analogy which is at once both relevant and superficial. It is relevant in the sense of the

---

[1] Estimates presented to the Joint Economic Committee of the US Congress (*New Directions in the Soviet Economy* (Washington, 1966), p. 887) showed as a percentage of the West German consumption per head Poland as 45 in 1937 and Czechoslovakia as 95; by 1964 the corresponding figures were 40 and 57. Overall consumption per head has of course increased in both countries since the war (by 97% in Poland and 35% in Czechoslovakia; both figures from the same source, to 1964, p. 886)), but comparative standards had dropped.

[2] See, for example, the reference by Mr Healey in the House of Commons in November to the dangers of 'an Empire in decay'.

concept of the Socialist Commonwealth as an entity reliant upon and subservient to the Soviet Union, and upon which no attack from outside or from within will be tolerated. It is superficial because the degree of authority and control varies so greatly, and because the ideological aspect of the bloc adds a dimension of great importance which was absent in most previous Empires. If the Czechoslovak movement is viewed purely in terms of a member of an Empire seeking greater freedom and autonomy, a crucially important aspect of why the crisis with the Soviet Union developed so rapidly is missed entirely.

How will the Czechoslovak crisis affect the future evolution of the international organizations involved and the situation in Eastern Europe? Although it is too early to attempt an assessment of the long-term results and implications, the significance of what has already occurred must be recalled and emphasized.

An attempt was made, and with some success, to transform a communist régime in Eastern Europe. This attempt was launched from within a communist party, and although it was checked by the use of armed force by the Soviet Union and its Pact allies, it was not completely ended. It was checked because a majority of the Soviet leaders and their advisers considered that the experiment had got out of control and threatened the preservation of the authority of all communist parties in Eastern Europe, including that of the Soviet Union itself. The intervention was accordingly a defensive measure to preserve the *status quo*, and was not an indication of Soviet aggressiveness or expansionism. The employment of other Warsaw Pact forces was designed to emphasize the collective interest in such a preservation. The complex long-term problem of how to preserve the bloc as a whole has not been solved at all.

So far as the United Nations was concerned, the crisis had been a vigorous reminder of the fact that the UN can only reflect the reality of the world power structure. But it has also demonstrated the fact that it can play a role in such circumstances by exposing the super-powers to uncomfortable challenge before the representatives of the world. This is a factor that cannot be wholly dismissed by the super-powers, since

INTERPRETATIONS AND CONCLUSIONS

many members of the UN are in the position of assisting or obstructing their interests. The United Nations, in short, reflects the reality of the world power structure in more senses than one. Many commentators in crises of this kind emphasize the helplessness of the United Nations to intervene. The limitations of UN action in such circumstances have already been described in Chapter 5, but it may also be remarked that national interpretations of the value of UN intervention tend to vary drastically according to the balance of national interests involved. To read the UN debates on Czechoslovakia without a full comprehension of the wider implications and undercurrents is to see only one aspect of the situation during the Security Council meetings in the week that followed the invasion.

It seems probable that the development of the Warsaw Pact will be increasingly in the direction of political as well as military consolidation. In the past it was seen by the Soviet leadership as a useful part of the process of binding the East European bloc together, and it would appear that its importance in this role is now greater than before. It would also appear that any tendency towards making it into something resembling a genuine international organization will be suspended.

It is more difficult to assess the effects upon NATO, beyond the resurgence of immediate interest in the Alliance that was occasioned by the invasion of Czechoslovakia. Whether it will have a real effect upon relationships within NATO remains to be seen. The central point emphasized by the crisis was the importance of the dialogue between the super-powers and the extent to which NATO provides a mechanism whereby the other members of the Alliance are enabled to participate. The crisis itself, and the immediate aftermath, left this particular problem unchanged.

Finally, what are the implications for the future of East–West relations, so far as they can be tentatively assessed in December 1968? First, the development of a tacit understanding between the Soviet Union and the United States of spheres of influence must be recognized. The Czechoslovak crisis reminded us of this fact. Second, although the crisis itself and the handling of the pre-invasion situation by the NATO powers recognized this fact, subsequent NATO statements run the very real risk of introducing a note of ambiguity into an otherwise clear understanding. Third, that it is important that the twin Harmel objectives – vigilance and the pursuit of détente – be maintained. One further consequence of the events of 1968 could be a reassessment of the real objectives of détente, and a more precise definition of a word that contains many shades of different meanings. The crisis may at least emphasize that détente is not more than an intermediate stage in the development of East–West relations, but it would be of value if a greater measure of agreement could be secured in the West as to the limits of détente.

The most important lesson of all from the whole Czechoslovak crisis for the West is that in pursuing initiatives with East European countries it is not to be expected that any one of them can move substantially ahead of what is sanctioned by the Soviet Union. The West has tended to draw encouragement from the fact that certain East European countries have been more forthcoming in response to their initiatives than the Soviet Union; but the events of 1968 have emphasized once again the limitations of the influence that can be exerted upon Moscow by individual East European leaders. It can indeed be said that the Czechoslovak crisis of 1968 has been a reminder of the fact that it is only through the patient working towards a realistic *modus vivendi* between competing systems and groupings that the best hope lies for the attainment of the ultimate objective that events such as the invasion of Czechoslovakia will not be repeated. It has been a salutary reminder that *realpolitik* remains the dominant factor in European, and world, politics. And it is here argued that such a conclusion is not necessarily a depressing one.

Selected Chronology
January–December 1968

5 January.	Czechoslovak Communist Party Central Committee plenum decides to separate the functions of party First Secretary and President of the Republic, 'in accordance with the process of democratization which has begun'. Antonin Novotny, while retaining the Presidency, resigns as First Secretary and is succeeded by Alexander Dubcek, previously First Secretary of the Slovak Communist Party.
29–30 January.	Dubcek pays unaccompanied visit to Soviet Union. The communiqué at the end of the visit announces 'full identity of views on all questions discussed'.
5 March.	Czechoslovak Party Praesidium transfers responsibility for ideology from the conservative, Jiri Hendrych, to Josef Spacek.
6–7 March.	The Political Consultative Committee of the Warsaw Pact meets in Sofia.
16 March.	Dubcek, in a speech at Brno, reaffirms that the alliance with the Soviet Union remains the basis of Czechoslovak foreign policy.
23 March.	Meeting in Dresden of Bulgarian, Czechoslovak, East German, Hungarian, Polish and Soviet party leaders. Communiqué refers to a forthcoming economic summit meeting and to agreement on practical measures to strengthen the Warsaw Pact and its armed forces.

THE CZECHOSLOVAK CRISIS 1968

26 March.	Speech by Hager, Secretary of the SED Central Committee, criticizing Czech policies and Smrkovsky's speeches. (Later the subject of formal exchanges between the Czech and East German Governments.)
1 April.	At resumed meeting of the Czechoslovak Party Central Committee Dubcek says: 'We must continue to build up our army and improve it according to Socialist principles; as a defensive barrier against the enemy outside, the imperialist aggressors. We must build it up as a firm link in the alliance of the armies of the Warsaw Treaty.'
3 April.	Resignation of Czechoslovak Minister of Defence, General Bohumir Lomsky.
4 April.	New Praesidium of Czechoslovak Communist Party elected.
6 April.	Oldrich Cernik succeeds Jozef Lenart as Prime Minister.
8 April.	New Cabinet announced.
9 April.	Czechoslovak Party's Action Programme published.
23–26 April.	Session of Rumanian Central Committee adopts resolution noting that the Rumanian Party had not been invited to Dresden Meeting at which questions of importance to Warsaw Pact and CMEA were discussed.
24 April.	Announcing in the National Assembly the programme of Czechoslovak Government, Prime Minister Cernik says: 'As long as NATO exists, we shall contribute to the strengthening of the Warsaw Treaty, we shall strive to make the Czechoslovak People's Army a firm link of this alliance, and we shall develop greater initiative towards the intensification of the work of its joint command. The government will ensure the needs of defence in harmony with the possibilities of our State.'

SELECTED CHRONOLOGY

26 April.	Czechoslovak–Bulgarian Treaty of Friendship, Co-operation and Mutual Assistance renewed.
30 April.	*Pravda* carries account of Czechoslovak provincial party meetings, quoting fears expressed by conservatives of consequences of lifting of Press and TV censorship and expressing anxiety over subversive attacks against the Action Programme.
4–5 May.	Dubcek accompanied by Cernik, Smrkovsky and Bilak had what *Tass* describes as a 'brief friendly meeting' with Soviet leaders in Moscow.
6 May.	*Le Monde* reports a CPSU meeting of 23 April. Brezhnev described as worried over Czech developments and believing Dubcek a prisoner of 'reactionary and anti-Communist elements'. General Epishev (head of the political control department of the Soviet armed forces) quoted as speculating on appeals for intervention from 'faithful communists' in Czechoslovakia. Should this happen the Red Army would be 'ready to do its duty'. The same article claims that a similar line is prevalent in Bulgarian Party circles. Polish Government protests to Czechoslovakia about 'anti-Polish campaign'. New Czechoslovak Ambassador to Moscow, Vladimir Kouchy, presents credentials; President Podgorny refers to 'anti-Socialist' elements in Czechoslovakia.
6–7 May.	Czechoslovak Foreign Minister, Jiri Hajek, visits Soviet Union.
7 May.	Czech trade union newspaper, *Prace*, takes up Epishev's remarks, saying it is 'unbelievable' that Soviet Central Committee would consider military intervention.
8 May.	Meeting in Moscow of leaders of Soviet, Polish, East German, Hungarian and Bulgarian parties. There is little publicity and no communiqué.
15 May.	Statement by Chairman of the Czechoslovak National Assembly, Josef Smrkovsky, on

	Dubcek's visit to Moscow, says: 'We must understand the fears of the Soviet Union which has in mind not only Czechoslovakia but the security of the whole Socialist camp. Even so, the Soviet comrades declared that they do not want to, and will not, interfere in Czechoslovakia's internal affairs.'
17–22 May.	Soviet Defence Minister, Marshal Grechko, and General Epishev visit Czechoslovakia. Communiqué states, *inter alia*, '... concrete steps have been outlined for the further development of the friendships between the Soviet Army and the Czechoslovak People's Army and the strengthening of their co-operation within the framework of the Warsaw Treaty'.
17–25 May.	Soviet Prime Minister, Mr Kosygin, visits Czechoslovakia for cure and consultations.
18 May.	Czechoslovak protest to East Germany about article in *Berliner Zeitung* of 9 May alleging US and Western German military units in Czechoslovakia.
19 May.	Czechoslovakia news agency, *CTK*, reports denial by General Epishev of *Le Monde* report on possible Soviet Army assistance to loyal communists.
24 May.	Announcement in Prague that Warsaw Pact command staff exercises will take place in Czechoslovakia in June.
30 May.	Novotny dismissed from the Party Central Committee and suspended from Party membership.
1 June.	Czechoslovak Central Committee decides to convene an extraordinary party congress on 9 September.
3–15 June.	Czechoslovak National Assembly delegation, led by Smrkovsky, visits Soviet Union.
4 June.	Dubcek, addressing meeting of party activists at Brno, says: 'Anti-party and anti-Communist tendencies exist ... what do we mean by the

	anti-Communist danger? The danger arises from tendencies to weaken our relations with the Soviet Union. Our whole policy is based on our relations with the Soviet Union – our foreign policy, our economic policy.'
12 June.	Soviet–Czechoslovak economic agreement signed.
16 June.	Treaty of Friendship, Co-operation and Mutual Aid between Hungary and Czechoslovakia signed in Budapest.
17 June.	Czechoslovak Foreign Minister, Jiri Hajek, goes to East Germany for a two-day visit. He says his talks with his East German counterpart, Otto Winzer, had taken place in a 'friendly and cordial atmosphere'. Smrkovsky and the Vice-Chairman of the National Assembly, Josef Zednik, give interviews on the visit by the National Assembly delegation to the Soviet Union, and say that the Soviet Union had no intention of interfering with Czechoslovak internal affairs. The highest Soviet officials had confirmed this, he says.
20 June.	Warsaw Pact command staff exercises in Czechoslovakia and Poland begin.
26 June.	National Assembly passes law abolishing advance censorship.
27 June.	Prague newspapers, *Prace, Mlada Fronta, Zemedelske Noviny* and *Literarni Listy* publish the manifesto '2,000 Words' by Ludvik Vaculik, demanding an acceleration of the democratization process and calling on workers to demand the departure of those who had abused their power. The manifesto is criticized the same day by Dubcek and the party Praesidium.
2 July.	Announcement in Prague that Warsaw Pact exercises have ended.
4 July.	Prague newspaper, *Vecerni Praha*, reports that leaflets attacking 'progressive representatives' of the Communist Party have been found in the street.

5 July.	In a note to the West German Government, the Soviet Union refers to the 'enemy states' articles in the UN Charter. Smrkovsky criticizes the '2,000 Words' for 'political romanticism', while admitting the 'honourable intentions' of its author.
8 July.	Czechoslovak Communist Party Praesidium issues a statement expressing willingness to confer bilaterally with any of their allies.
8–10 July.	Czechoslovak Foreign Minister, Jiri Hajek, visits Bulgaria.
9 July.	Bill granting every Czechoslovak citizen right to obtain a passport without restrictions passed by National Assembly. General Dzur, Minister of National Defence, announces that 35 per cent of the troops in the Warsaw Pact exercises have returned to their permanent garrisons.
10 July.	Czechoslovak General Vaclav Prchlik announces that a 'new situation' had developed since the original official statement that the troops in the Warsaw Pact exercise would be withdrawn immediately on July 2. The Soviet *Literaturnaya Gazeta* attacks '2,000 Words'.
11 July.	Article in *Pravda* attacks '2,000 Words' and compares situation with that in Hungary in 1956. *Prague Radio* broadcasts rejoinder deploring attempts to 'spread among the inadequately informed public the false belief about the dangers threatening Czechoslovak Socialism'.
12 July.	Soviet Defence Ministry organ, *Krasnaya Zvezda* (Red Star), denies that Warsaw Pact exercises were intended to force Soviet strategic concepts on the allies.
13 July.	Yugoslav news agency, *Tanyug*, quotes President Tito as expressing disbelief that there could exist in the USSR elements so short-sighted as to resort to a policy of force over Czechoslovakia.

SELECTED CHRONOLOGY

The East German party newspaper, *Neues Deutschland*, attacks '2,000 Words' and Czechoslovak developments in article entitled 'The Strategy of Imperialism and the Czechoslovak Socialist Republic'.

Kosygin, at Press conference in Stockholm, expresses confidence that Czechoslovak party will not surrender its leading role and recommends correspondents to read the assessment of events in Czechoslovakia in *Pravda* of 11 July.

Letter of the Czechoslovak Army, declaring support for the party, handed to military attachés of other Warsaw Pact countries and Yugoslavia.

14–15 July. Bulgarian, East German, Hungarian, Polish and Soviet leaders meet in Warsaw. Meeting sends letter to the Czechoslovak party saying that the signatories are 'deeply disturbed' by events in Czechoslovakia.

14 July. Polish party newspaper, *Trybuna Ludu*, criticizes 'reactionary forces, supported by centres of imperialist subversion' for their 'offensive' against Communism in Czechoslovakia.

15 July. Rumanian Head of State and party leader, Nicolae Ceausescu, in a speech at Galati, and the party organ, *Scinteia*, express confidence in the Czechoslovak party and its leadership.

General Prchlik, head of the Party Central Committee department for Military and Security Affairs, criticizes the Warsaw meeting and claims that the Warsaw Pact does not allow the troops of any party to the Treaty to stay in the territory of another without the latter's consent.

16 July. Czechoslovak Minister of Defence, General Dzur, writing in *Rude Pravo*, recommends reform of Warsaw Pact command.

17 July. *Neues Deutschland* adduces 'illuminating details' of 'massive' West German intervention in Czechoslovakia.

	Speech by Ceausescu describing Warsaw Pact as instrument of collective defence rather than a justification for interference in the internal affairs of other states.
18 July.	Czechoslovak Praesidium issues reply to Warsaw letter refuting its allegations.

Dubcek broadcasts to the nation, thanking citizens for their support and observing that 'we have no alternative but to complete the profound democratic and Socialist changes in our life, together with the people'. Reaffirms Czech loyalty to the Warsaw Pact.

The Bulgarian party newspaper, *Rabotnichesko Delo*, in a leading article headed 'The counter-revolution should be routed', alleges 'disorganization of the State and entire party life' in Czechoslovakia.

US Secretary of State Rusk denies rumours that US had warned Soviet Union against intervening by force in Czechoslovakia. |
| 19 July. | Dubcek, addressing Central Committee plenum, reaffirms adhesion to the Action Programme. All speakers express agreement with the Praesidium.

Tass announces Soviet proposal for meeting between Soviet Politburo and Czechoslovak Praesidium on 22 or 23 July in Moscow, Kiev or Lvov.

Pravda claims that on 12 July Czechoslovak security forces found a secret cache of American arms near the West German border. It also claims that documents are in Soviet hands describing a NATO and CIA plot to subvert the East European countries, particularly Czechoslovakia and East Germany. (This allegation was subsequently denied both by a State Department spokesman in Washington and a NATO spokesman in Brussels.)

Hungarian party newspaper, *Nepszabadsag*, says that Hungarian sympathy for Czechoslovakia remains unchanged but has been overtaken by concern that her 'Socialist achievements are imperilled'. |

SELECTED CHRONOLOGY

	The Rumanian party organ, *Scinteia*, carries full texts of the joint Warsaw letter and the Czechoslovaks' reply.

The Rumanian party organ, *Scinteia*, carries full texts of the joint Warsaw letter and the Czechoslovaks' reply.

Marshal Grechko cuts short visit to Algeria and returns to Moscow.

19–20 July.   Waldeck Rochet, General Secretary of French Communist Party, visits Prague. Dubcek speaking to Central Committee reacts cautiously to Waldeck Rochet's proposal for a meeting of European Communist Parties.

20 July.   Hungarian news agency, MTI, publishes summary of the Czechoslovak Praesidium's reply to the Warsaw letter. But this step is not followed by any of the other countries which met in Warsaw.

Scinteia carries article entitled 'Full Confidence in the Czechoslovak People, in its Communist Party', expressing 'serious alarm' at 'tendencies towards interference from outside' which could only damage the international communist movement.

Krasnaya Zvezda joins other major Soviet newspapers in commenting on Czech internal developments.

21 July.   President Svoboda, in a speech at Javoruna, reaffirms loyalty to the Warsaw Pact.

22 July.   The *Pravda* revelations about an arms cache (see entry for 19 July): *CTK* reports the official Prague view that the hiding of the arms was a provocation to dramatize the situation. *Prace* notes that the weapons were hidden inexpertly and conspicuously.

Agreement reached on meeting between Soviet Politburo and Czechoslovak Praesidium, on Czechoslovak soil.

CTK reports acceleration in withdrawal of Russian troops.

Announcement in Bonn that, in view of the political situation, the Defence Ministry would try to reschedule or relocate Exercise Black Lion (previously planned for Autumn 1968; and which would have taken 3 West German divisions, with US and French support, to the Czech frontier area).

23 July. General Karel Peprny, Commander of the Czechoslovak Border Guards, refuting allegations of laxity, states that Czechoslovakia is perfectly able 'to protect its state borders with its capitalist neighbours'.

UN spokesman announces the Czech permanent representative's denial that the situation in his country constituted a menace to international peace and security.

Krasnaya Zvezda attacks General Prchlik for his Press conference of 15 July. Western observers note that *Krasnaya Zvezda* takes care to distinguish between the General and the rest of the Czech Army, and even leaves the impression that reforms of the Warsaw Pact organization would not be rejected out of hand by the Soviet Defence Ministry.

Izvestia accuses Czechoslovak Minister of the Interior Josef Pavel of having been responsible for the conviction of innocent persons in the early days of the communist régime.

Izvestia announces Soviet exercises on the western frontiers of the Soviet Union.

Further Moscow statements that reservists were being called up and that civilian transport would be requisitioned for these exercises, which would continue until 10 August.

25 July. Announcement in Prague of the abolition of the party department for military and security affairs, and return of its head, Gen. Prchlik, to the army.

Pravda article accuses certain Czechoslovak party leaders of conniving at the activity of 'Right-wing anti-Socialist revisionist forces'.

Soviet and Polish government halt the movement of Soviet and Polish tourists into Czechoslovakia without explanation.

Nepszabadsag calls on the Czech leaders to take action against a 'bourgeois counter-revolution', accusing them of an 'erroneous interpretation of democracy and freedom' by abolishing press censorship, and exhorts them not to permit developments which had led in Hungary to a 'counter-revolution'.

26 July. *Pravda* article expresses fears that Czechoslovakia is moving towards the restoration of a 'bourgeois régime' and attacks Deputy Prime Minister Sik.

Berliner Zeitung article denounces West German aid for 'creeping counter-revolution' in Czechoslovakia.

Polish Army newspaper, *Zolnierz Wolnosci*, denounces danger to socialism in Czechoslovakia created by 'external imperialist forces, internal forces of reaction and revisionist forces actively co-operating with them'.

Literarni Listy appeals to Czech Praesidium: 'You are writing a fateful page in our history. . . . Write with deliberation but, above all, with courage.'

27 July. Professor Sik, writing in *Rude Pravo*, recalls Brezhnev's refusal to support the 'old guard of discredited politicians' in December and reaffirms the view that the Communist Party's leading role should rest not on repressive force but on the conviction of ideas.

CTK publishes official statement criticizing General Prchlik's statement of 15 July.

28 July. Bulgarian frontier authorities refuse admission to 50 young Czechoslovaks planning to take part in World Youth Festival.

Professor Sik, writing in *Rude Pravo*, demands a public correction of statements in *Pravda* article of 26 July.

Marshal Grechko's Order of the Day on Soviet Navy Day refers to 'imperialist attempts to force a breach in the Socialist system and change the balance of power in their favour'.

29 July Talks between Czechoslovak Praesidium, accompanied by Svoboda, and the Soviet Politburo open at Cierna-nad-Tisou, near Czechoslovak border.

Pravda publishes article stressing Czechoslovak indebtedness to and dependence on the Soviet Union.

Czech Ministry of the Interior issues, for the guidance of chief editors and publishers, a list of items which may not be published in the mass media.

Hungarian daily newspaper, *Magyar Hirlap*, states that 'the tragic experience of Hungary has not been taken into consideration in Czechoslovakia'.

30 July. *Pravda* leader says: 'We cannot remain indifferent to attacks by revisionists on Marxism-Leninism as a unitary international doctrine, attacks which have recently become stronger.'

Article in *Zycie Warszawy* quoted by PAP discusses 'the satisfaction of the anti-Communist experts in the West German Press' about the situation in Czechoslovakia.

Neues Deutschland publishes full-page article headed 'Overcome Mistakes so as to strengthen the Socialist worker-peasant power', stating that the 'profound disquiet' expressed in the Warsaw letter is becoming 'daily more justified as the result of growing activity by hostile forces'.

Rabotnichesko Delo, quoted by *BTA*, says that 'the threat to Socialism in Czechoslovakia, that fraternal country, is getting greater every day'.

Rude Pravo, quoted by *CTK*, describes 'the idea that relations between Communist parties can be successfully solved by methods of propagandistic, political or military pressure' as a 'dangerous illusion'.

Belgrade *Politika Express* publishes the results of a public opinion poll on Czechoslovakia under the heading 'Support for Prague with heart and mind'.

31 July. *Scinteia*, in an article entitled 'The road to strengthening the unity of the Socialist countries', says: 'The Communists, all working people in our country, follow with a feeling of sympathy

SELECTED CHRONOLOGY

1 August.	the renewal and transformations in the friendly country (Czechoslovakia).' *Pravda* suspends attacks on Czechoslovakia. A short joint communiqué issued on the conclusion of the Cierna talks speaks of the 'atmosphere of frankness, sincerity and mutual understanding in which the talks had been conducted and announced that the Czechoslovak leaders would meet the signatories of the Warsaw letter in Bratislava on 3 August. Smrkovsky tells a large crowd in the Old Town Square, Prague, that the Czechoslovak delegation had 'succeeded in securing the sympathy of the Soviet comrades for our internal affairs. Our internal affairs will not be the subject of discussion at the Bratislava meeting'.
2 August.	Dubcek, in a broadcast, thanks the people for their 'wise and circumspect attitude' and assures them: 'You can be completely satisfied with the results and the spirit of the negotiations. . . . We kept our promise to you.' At the same time he stresses the need to maintain a 'prudent and statesmanlike attitude', adding: 'There must be no misuse of spontaneous . . . meetings for the expression of anti-Socialist and anti-Soviet sentiments. . . . All of us, and also our friends abroad, must see to it that we seek ways, patiently and calmly, of strengthening our co-operation. . . . By so doing we shall create favourable conditions for the 14th Congress of our party.'
3 August.	Participants in Bratislava meeting issue a Declaration which makes no reference to the internal situation in Czechoslovakia. Kadar, on his return home from Bratislava, says: 'It is a very great thing that it has been possible partly to clear up the misunderstandings and differences.' *Prague Radio* and *CTK* announce that the last Soviet troops have left Czechoslovak territory.
4 August.	Dubcek, in a television broadcast, gives an assurance that no secret agreement was reached

	at either Cierna or Bratislava, and says that the meetings had opened up new scope for the revival process in Czechoslovakia.
5 August.	*Pravda* editorial describes the Bratislava talks as an important step along the road of consolidating the unity of the socialist countries, and as a crushing blow to imperialist plans to sow discord. *Trybuna Ludu* expresses satisfaction with the Bratislava talks, calling the declaration a 'momentous document of the international Communist movement'. *Rabotnichesko Delo* acclaims the Bratislava document as of 'enormous importance for the triumph of Socialism in the world and for strengthening the unity of the Socialist community and the international Communist movement'.
8 August.	Josef Valka publishes article in *Literarni Listy* entitled 'From Warsaw to Bratislava' attacking the Russians for interference in Czechoslovak affairs. Another article in the same number warning the Russians that they had forfeited Czechoslovak friendship.
9–11 August.	President Tito visits Czechoslovakia and is given an enthusiastic welcome.
9 August.	Hungarian party secretary, Zoltan Komocsin, quoted by *Budapest Radio* as saying that the Bratislava meeting had 'restored the unity which had suffered a certain rupture'. Moscow *Pravda* article by Rodionov on democratic centralism and danger of permitting factions in communist parties.
10 August.	Draft party statutes published as a supplement to *Rude Pravo*. They assert the right of an outvoted minority to adhere to its views, secret voting and the limitation on period of term of office by one person.
12–13 August.	Ulbricht visits Czechoslovakia and meets Dubcek at Karlovy Vary.

SELECTED CHRONOLOGY

14 August.	Moscow *Literaturnaya Gazeta* accuses *Literarni Listy* of 'attacks on the principles of Marxism-Leninism and seditious attacks on the Soviet Union'. Marshal Grechko meets East German Defence Minister, General Hoffman, to 'exchange views on general political questions and co-operation between the fraternal armies'. Moscow *Red Star* article by Brigadier-General Baranski, Deputy Chief of Polish Armed Forces, 'Our common concern and common responsibility' expressing concern at the 'growth of hostile and dangerous trends in fraternal Czechoslovakia', declaring 'readiness to aid' the Czechoslovak Party and people and asserting the indivisibility of the defence of Eastern Europe.
15–17 August.	President Ceausescu of Rumania visits Czechoslovakia and is warmly received by the people.
16 August.	Twenty-year Czechoslovak–Rumanian Treaty of Friendship, Co-operation and Mutual Aid signed in Prague. *Pravda* article by Yurg. Zhukov attacking items in Czechoslovak Press underestimating the importance and finality of the Cierna and Bratislava declarations.
17 August.	Prime Minister Cernik reported to have stated that Czechoslovakia was contemplating a World Bank loan.
18 August.	*Pravda* article by Kolesnichenko ('Loyalty to international duty'), and by Aleksandrov ('Blatant outbursts of reaction') denouncing the 'noticeable intensification in Prague of late of subversive activities by anti-Socialist forces against the foundations of the Socialist system in Czechoslovakia'.
19 August.	*CTK* denies that Cernik had said that Czechoslovakia was considering a World Bank Loan, but only loans from individual countries. *Pravda* article alleging victimization of 99 Auto-Prague workers for writing to *Pravda*.

20 August. The East German Party newspaper, *Neues Deutschland*, says that socialist internationalism includes a readiness to enlist help from the fraternal countries.
Emergency session of CPSU Central Committee.

21 August. Soviet ambassadors in London, Paris and Washington inform the Governments to which they are accredited that troops from the five Warsaw Pact countries, Soviet Union, Poland, Hungary, Bulgaria and East Germany have crossed the Czechoslovak frontier.

Tass announces that the troop movement is in response to a request from the Czech party and Government leaders.

Ceausescu in Bucharest denounces the invasion as a 'Flagrant violation of the national sovereignty of a fraternal, socialist, free and independent state'. He announces the formation of 'new armed patriotic detachments' to defend the independence of the country.

NATO Council sets aside regular business for an all-day discussion of Czechoslovak events. Spokesman refers to impact on détente and on plans for mutual force reductions.

Individual NATO Governments reacted as follows:
UK: 'A flagrant violation of the UN Charter and of all accepted standards of international behaviour.'
France: 'The armed intervention by the Soviet Union in Czechoslovakia shows that the government of Moscow has not freed itself of the policy of blocs which was imposed on Europe by the effect of the Yalta agreements.' (President de Gaulle)
Canada: Mr Sharp said that the invasion will set back the East/West détente but 'there's little we can do or little that we need fear concerning any outbreak of hostilities.'
US: 'The tragic news from Czechoslovakia

SELECTED CHRONOLOGY

shocks the conscience of the world. The Soviet Union and its allies have invaded a defenceless country to stamp out a resurgence of ordinary human freedom. It is a sad commentary on the communist mind that a sign of liberty in Czechoslovakia is deemed a fundamental threat to the security of the Soviet System.'

Netherlands: After a special meeting of the Dutch cabinet, Prime Minister Piet de Jong announced that a visit of Soviet warships to Amsterdam planned for September will be cancelled.

West Germany: Condemns the Soviet military intervention as a clear violation of Czechoslovak sovereignty and as interference in that country's internal affairs.

U Thant issues an appeal to the Soviet Union to exercise the greatest possible 'moderation' in regard to Czechoslovakia, and to withdraw her troops.

The Security Council meets at the request of Canada, Denmark, France, Paraguay, the UK and the US.

22 August.　The Security Council votes to inscribe on its agenda 'the present serious situation in Czechoslovakia'.

Voting:

For:	Algeria, Brazil, Canada, China, Denmark, Ethiopia, France, India, Pakistan, Paraguay, Senegal, UK, US.
Against:	Hungary, USSR.
Abstentions:	None.

A draft resolution (S/8761) is introduced by the Danish representative on behalf of Canada, Brazil, France, Paraguay, UK and the US. (Senegal later became a co-sponsor.) Then follows a procedural vote on the conditions under which the Council would temporarily adjourn, in which the Soviet Union and Hungary were joined in their abstention by India, Pakistan and Algeria.

143

Further NATO reactions include:

Italy: communiqué following an emergency cabinet meeting says that in the face of the crisis Italy believed that the Atlantic Alliance provides the only real guarantee 'against all external attempts at its free institutions'.

West Germany: weekend Army leaves are cancelled.

Denmark: cancelled visits planned for September by Zhukov and Peter.

Norway: cancelled planned September visit by Zhuvov.

Czechoslovak National Assembly issues declaration reaffirming loyalty to President Svoboda and the legal Government and Party leadership, and calls on the people to maintain dignity. The declaration is sent to the embassies of the invading powers; all accept the documents except the East Germans.

Pravda publishes a 2-page report on developments in Czechoslovakia, in justification of armed invasion. Dubcek leader of a minority, revisionist group in Czechoslovak Praesidium which 'adopted right-wing opportunist attitudes' and prevented implementation of Cierna and Bratislava agreements.

23 August. Security Council continues discussion of the first resolution on Czechoslovakia. Acting Czechoslovak permanent representative announces that Hajek (who had been on holiday in Yugoslavia) is on his way to address the Assembly.

Voting on the resolution:

For: Canada, China, Denmark, Ethiopia, France, Paraguay, Senegal, UK and US.
Against: Hungary and USSR.
Abstentions: Algeria, India, Pakistan.

SELECTED CHRONOLOGY

A second resolution (S/8767) is introduced by Canada on behalf of Brazil, Denmark, France, Paraguay, Senegal, UK and US.

NATO spokesman says that the Council 'closely and thoroughly analysed the political and military situation in Europe, by the Soviet invasion of Czechoslovakia' and will continue to watch developments and will consult on their political effects.

Further individual NATO reactions were:
Italy: announces indefinite postponement of an industrial show, scheduled to be held in Moscow in December.
UK: Foreign Office announces that Secretary of State Stewart has cancelled official visits to Hungary and Bulgaria.
Belgium: announces that it will not participate in economic, cultural and technical contact with the five Warsaw Pact countries which have invaded Czechoslovakia until further notice.
Turkey: expresses the hope that the Security Council will find a just solution to the Czechoslovak question, and that foreign forces will leave the country as soon as possible.

President Svoboda leaves for Moscow with Husak, Dzur, Bilak, Piller, Indra and Kucera. On arrival there are greeted by Brezhnev, Kosygin, Podgorny.

Husak, from Moscow, tells members of the Slovak Party Central Committee that Dubcek and Cernik are in Moscow.

Tass publishes address to Czechoslovak 'brothers' from governments of USSR, Bulgaria, Hungary, East Germany and Poland. Soviet and other troops did not come to interfere in Czechoslovak internal affairs.

Rumania broadcasts reaffirm solidarity with Czechoslovakia.

New patriotic detachments in Budapest take part in military parade.

The Central Committee of the Albanian Communist Party denounces the 'barbarous aggression' undertaken by the 'five' and declares that the Warsaw Pact has been transformed into a treaty of aggression.

24 August. Procedural debate in the Security Council on seating an East German representative. The East German request is defeated.

Voting:
For: Hungary, USSR.
Against: Canada, China, Denmark, Ethiopia, France, Paraguay, Senegal, UK and US.
Abstentions: Algeria, India, Pakistan, Brazil.

Hajek addresses the Security Council which is adjourned on the assumption that it will reconvene on Monday, 26 August.

AFP reports from Moscow that Svoboda is requesting Hajek to ask the Security Council to end its discussions on the Czech Crisis.

Sources in the West German Ministry of Defence are reported by the Press as saying that the occupation force has made a definite attempt to jam West German radars.

Moscow Television denies rumours of a concentration of troops on the Soviet and Bulgarian borders of Rumania.

Tass attacks Rumania for aiding anti-socialist forces in Czechoslovakia. *Tass* accuses Rumania and Yugoslavia of giving 'active assistance to anti-Socialist forces' in Czechoslovakia, and of taking the same line as the 'imperialist NATO' powers and the 'Maoist group' in China. *Tass* also speaks of 'Czechoslovak political adventurers' being active in Belgrade and Bucharest. *Izvestia* attacks Ceausescu by name and accuses him of assisting Czechoslovak 'counter-revolutionaries'.

Presidents Tito and Ceausescu meet at Urchatz, on the Yugoslav–Rumanian frontier, in secrecy. Brief official communiqué states that there had been an exchange of views 'concerning problems pertaining to bilateral relations and

SELECTED CHRONOLOGY

	present-day international problems of interest to the two countries'.
25 August.	Press reports from Bonn speak of a request from Kiesinger for 'a NATO Summit'. US Embassy in Prague publishes an appeal asking all US Nationals to leave the country as soon as possible. *Radio Free Slovakia* issues a warning that spurious tracts are being distributed by collaborators, proposing that Slovakia should withdraw from the Czechoslovak State, and become a Soviet Republic. *Pravda* leader refers to Soviet troops having to act under extremely difficult conditions in Czechoslovakia.
26 August.	Additional request from Foreign Minister Hajek that the Security Council ceases discussion on the Czechoslovak Situation, lest it should prejudice the Moscow talks.
27 August.	President Svoboda and other Czech leaders return from Moscow. A second communiqué confirms the presence in Moscow of Bulgarian, Hungarian, Polish, East German leaders.[1] Czechoslovak delegation at UN announces it will not take part in any further Security Council discussions on Czechoslovakia.
28 August.	West German cabinet issues a demand for complete restoration of Czech sovereignty and the pull-back of all Soviet invasion forces. Svoboda reaffirms adhesion to the Action Programme; calls for continued unity, wisdom and prudence. Dubcek, on radio, states that Government seeks 'the complete removal' of Pact forces at the earliest possible date, and that 'normalization' requires suppression of 'passion and psychoses'. Extraordinary Congress of Slovak Communist Party replaces Bilak as First Secretary by Husak, and elects new Central Committee.

[1] For communiqué, see Appendix 4.

29 August.	Rumanian Communist Party Central Committee issues a statement that it 'considers of the utmost importance the carrying into effect of the complete withdrawal, in the shortest time, of the Armed Forces of the five Socialist states from Czechoslovakia'. Smrkovsky, in radio broadcast says that only national unity had prevented imposition of even harsher terms in Moscow.
30 August.	President Johnson in a speech at San Antonio, Texas issues a stern warning against a Soviet attack on Rumania. Deputy Minister of the Interior commits suicide after refusing to hand over documents to Russian secret police. Ceausescu, at Cluj, says that use of forces by one Socialist country against another is incompatible with Communism.
31 August.	Consultations between NATO ambassadors and the State Department take place in Washington in the morning. In the afternoon the following statement issued by the State Department:

There are larger Soviet forces now present in Central Europe than at any other time since the early post-war period. The changed East–West military situation in Europe is of significance to the security of the US and its allies.

In the light of these events we are reviewing with our allies what the implications may be for existing arrangements to provide for our common security.

In the evening Dobrynin, Soviet Ambassador in Washington, informs Mr Rusk that he is authorized by his government to deny rumours cited by Johnson that Russian troops were preparing for action against Rumania.

Central Committee Plenum of Czechoslovak Communist Party announces new Praesidium of 21 members. Plenum told by Dubcek that the leadership 'had failed to appreciate the collective strategic interests of the Soviet Union and its four other Warsaw Pact allies as a concrete and

SELECTED CHRONOLOGY

	objective factor in determining the pace of Czechoslovakia's internal development' and that temporary censorship of the mass media would have to be introduced.
1 September.	Dubcek announces indefinite postponement of the 14th Party Congress.
3 September.	Opening the general debate of the UN-sponsored conference of non-nuclear states, Brandt appeals for a global convention to prevent any use of nuclear, biological, chemical weapons. Svoboda accepts Professor Sik's resignation as Deputy Prime Minister. *Izvestia* announces indefinite postponement of the 14th Party Congress.
4 September.	Following a meeting of the Defence Planning Committee (on which France is not represented) an agreed NATO statement is issued referring to the review which is now being undertaken of defence arrangements. Press reports from Bonn claim that seven new Soviet divisions have moved into East Germany. Chancellor Kiesinger is reported as 'unsatisfied with the Western allied response'. *Pravda* describes as 'wild lies' reports that Washington had been told in advance of its plan to invade, and had received a White House assurance that the US would not react. *Tass*, reporting Sik's resignation, describes him as 'one of the most odious figures among the right-wing revisionist forces'.
5 September.	US cancellation of the first planned event under the US–Soviet cultural exchange agreement; a second 'inaugural' flight by Aeroflot officials from Moscow to New York was also cancelled.
6 September.	Secretary of Defence Clifford, speaking to the National Press Club, says that Moscow's action 'clearly demonstrated that a significant American presence in Western Europe is still needed'. He went on to say that work must proceed on the anti-missile system, so that the Americans can

negotiate with the Russians from a position of strength.

V. Kuznetsov, Soviet First Deputy Foreign Minister, arrives in Prague. Czechoslovak Party Praesidium expresses opposition to 'extremes in politics, irresponsible tendencies of any kind, efforts to endanger the post-January policy and the conclusions of the Moscow negotiations from whatever side'.

8 September. Senator Mansfield, speaking on 'Face the Nation', referring to actions that should be taken in the aftermath of the Czech crisis, said: 'Primary responsibility should not fall on us, but should fall on our allies, who are there in the immediate area of concern, who are fully capable of meeting the requirements which they have agreed to under the NATO agreement.'

Gomulka justifies invasion by the existence of a 'concrete threat of detaching Czechoslovakia from the ranks of the Warsaw Pact countries'.

9 September. *New York Times* news service reports that the US is pressing its European allies to:
(*a*) restore to full strength the divisions that they had assigned to NATO;
(*b*) speed up the re-equipment of the German Air Force for a conventional, and not just a nuclear role;
(*c*) improve long-neglected contingency plans for a quick call-up of forces and an effective mobilization of reserve units in the European countries.

In the course of his Press Conference, General de Gaulle says that France will not participate in any special NATO ministerial meeting.

Rude Pravo estimates production loss as a result of the invasion at 1,626 million crowns (£94,308,000).

10 September. Clifford, briefing a House armed services subcommittee, says that Czechoslovakia will not cause an increase in US defence spending.

SELECTED CHRONOLOGY

Cernik, Hamouz (Deputy Prime Minister) and Vales (Foreign Trade Minister) go to Moscow for economic talks and sign economic agreement.

Svoboda, Dubcek, Smrkovsky, Cernik and Husak issue statement reaffirming policy of 'strengthening the Socialist order of society and developing its democratic and human character', and appealing to Czechoslovaks abroad to return.

Tass and *Pravda* accuse some Czechoslovak newspapers of continuing to 'speak from anti-Socialist positions' and of alleging that there had been no counter-revolution.

11 September. President Johnson says:

The leaders of the Soviet Union seem to have decided that a movement toward a humane version of Communism in a small friendly country is a threat to their security – despite the fact that the Czechs remained their ally in the Warsaw Pact.

New military and political risks have arisen from this aggressive act, which demand ever closer co-operation among the Western Allies. For our part, we have made it unmistakeably clear that the use of force and the threat of force will not be tolerated in areas of common responsibility like Berlin.

Czechoslovak Government approves Czech–Soviet economic agreement.

12 September. Dubcek, in public speech, says that Czechoslovakia wishes to fulfil Moscow Agreement, but would allow no retreat to pre-January conditions.

13 September. Albanian National Assembly votes unanimously in favour of withdrawal from Warsaw Pact.

Czechoslovak National Assembly approves Bill setting up Office for the Press and Information, and another 'on some measures to secure public order,' which limits the right of assembly.

Dubcek, on radio, reaffirms there will be no return to pre-January conditions, and warns against clashes with occupying forces.

16 September. Exercise 'Black Lion', involving West German,

US and French forces, begins in Southern Germany well to the west of its originally planned area, near to the Czech border.

Thirteen leading economists publish defence of Sik in *Rude Pravo*.

Smrkovky, referring to 15 articles of agreement signed in Moscow, declares that some of them say that the Czech Communist Party will continue to implement policy which had been planned in January.

Soviet statement declares 'the firm intention of proceeding against those forces which want to use the positive process which has been under way in Czechoslovakia since January for an overt or covert attack on Socialism'. *Tass* accuses Czechoslovak information media of 'wrecking' the Moscow Agreement, and charges Yugoslav press of spreading 'bourgeois propaganda' about Czechoslovakia.

17 September. Clifford announces that 20–40,000 US troops may be sent to Europe shortly as a 'temporary measure' to take part in NATO exercises.

19 September. Prague announces resignation of Dr Hajek.

Pravda article (by Lomakin) says that theory and practice of Yugoslav leaders 'served as an example for revisionist elements in Czechoslovakia'.

20 September. *Izvestia*, replying to 16 September statement by Czechoslovak economists, attacks Sik reforms, and alleges that the statement could only impede the implementation of the Moscow Agreement.

23 September. Smrkovsky, at Zalvzi chemical works, speaks of national unity, and the unity of the Czechoslovak leaders as 'an arch from which not a single stone must be allowed to fall'.

24 September. Fifty leading Czechoslovak economists reaffirm support for economic reform in *Rude Pravo*.

25 September. The Czechoslovak Ambassador to the United Nations says in New York that his government

SELECTED CHRONOLOGY

opposes any discussion of the Soviet invasion and occupation of his country by the General Assembly. 'We hope that world opinion will understand that we wish to settle our problems within the Socialist community', he told reporters.

Kiesinger addressing the Bundestag in its first meeting since the invasion says that pending a withdrawal of the Warsaw Pact occupying troops, 'a reappraisal of the NATO forces in Europe is unavoidable'. He adds that West Germany reserves the right to increase its defence budget beyond scheduled plans.

Heads of Czechoslovak radio and television (Hejzlar and Pelikan) are dismissed.

Federation proposals are published.

Pravda article (by Kovalev) emphasizes that independence of socialist countries is subordinate to interests of world communist movement.

27 September. Yakubovsky reported by Prague Radio to have been received by Svoboda in the presence of Dubcek, Cernik and Dzur. Bucharest Radio announces Yakubovsky's arrival there on the same day.

29 September. Husak claims on television that the Party had, prior to the invasion, planned to take action against the excesses of the mass media. He announces plans for a new party action programme, 'valid for several months or a year, and concerning both internal and external policy'.

1 October. Announcement that the World Communist Summit, previously planned for November in Moscow, will be postponed.

Tass alleges establishment of terrorist groups in Czechoslovakia with connivance of 'imperialist intelligence services'.

3 October. Gromyko, speaking in the UN General Assembly, defends Soviet intervention in Czechoslovakia as essential for world peace and emphasizes the need for disarmament.

THE CZECHOSLOVAK CRISIS 1968

3–4 October.   Dubcek visits Moscow for two days of talks on the Czechoslovak normalization programme. Czechoslovak Government represented by Dubcek, Cernik, and Husak; Soviet Union by Brezhnev, Kosygin and Podgorny.

Communiqué speaks of a treaty on the temporary stationing of Warsaw troops in Czechoslovakia, and Cernik, on return from Moscow, says that this will be signed within the next few days.

Communiqué also states that Czechoslovak Government and party 'will intensify the struggle against anti-Socialist forces, will take the necessary measures to place all mass media at the service of Socialism and will strengthen the party and state authorities with men firmly adhering to positions of Marxism-Leninism and proletarian internationalism'.

4 October.   Czechoslovak permanent representative at the UN confirms that his country does not wish its affairs to be discussed in the General Assembly.

Announcement from Brussels that the NATO Council will advance the date of its December ministerial meeting to the second half of November. (It was also reported that the various members were expected to have an early opportunity for an informal discussion in New York on 7 October.)

5 October.   General Dzur expresses his confidence that the 'overwhelming majority' of the occupation troops will have left by 28 October, but that 'a certain part of the troops, however, will definitely stay in our country through the winter'.

7–9 October.   Kosygin visits Finland for talks with President Kekkonen. Communiqué states that they had reaffirmed their intention 'to continue to adhere in international affairs to the aims of presenting peace, strengthening security in Europe and throughout the world, and developing peaceful co-operation among all peoples'. (Finnish Prime Minister, Dr Koivisto, began a two-week visit to Soviet Union on 22 October.)

SELECTED CHRONOLOGY

11 October. Dubcek, addressing meeting of party officials, reaffirms intention of adhering to Soviet alliance, also to 'the permanent and positive features of our post-January policy', and to continue trading with the West.

Svoboda states adherence to post-January policy, avoiding those things 'which previously obstructed its consistently Socialist character'.

Three Soviet citizens convicted of violating public order by staging protest against Soviet invasion of Czechoslovakia. Pavel Litvinov, 29, sentenced to five years imprisonment at Chita; Mrs Larissa Daniel sentenced to four years to the Irkutsk region; Konstantier Babistsky sentenced to three years in the Omsk region of Siberia.

14–15 October. Cernik leads Czechoslovak Government delegation to Moscow to discuss treaty provisions relating to stationing of troops in Czechoslovakia.

16 October. Treaty signed in Prague by Cernik and Kosygin, the latter being accompanied by Gromyko and Marshal Grechko. Ratified in Moscow by Praesidium on 18 October, and approved by Czechoslovak National Assembly by 228 votes to four, with ten abstentions, and ratified by President Svoboda on same day. Cernik speaks of the 'new reality' the country had to face, and states that the Soviet forces would not interfere in Czechoslovak internal affairs and would respect Czechoslovak law. Kosygin, however, states that 'to defend the achievements of Socialism in Czechoslovakia' is 'a sacred internationalist duty'. The treaty gave the Soviet Union the right for the first time since 1945 to station troops in Czechoslovakia. No details given in treaty of number of troops to remain, covered by a separate secret agreement, but press reports from Prague give a figure of about 100,000. Kosygin states that the 'temporary' stay of

Soviet troops was intended to 'create solid guarantees of Czechoslovakia's security and of its socialist gains (and) to safeguard reliably the interests of the whole Socialist community from encroachments by the forces of imperialism and reaction'.

Announcement in Switzerland states that Professor Ota Sik had entered the country with his family. (On September 18 it had been reported that he had been appointed special economic adviser at the Czechoslovak Embassy in Belgrade.)

27 October. National Assembly passes unanimously legislation establishing a federal structure for Czechoslovakia, to take effect as from 1 January 1969. National Assembly to be replaced by a bicameral Federal Assembly consisting of a directly elected national Chamber of the People, whose composition would reflect the proportions of the various population groups, and a Chamber of Nations, with 150 deputies, half chosen by the Czech National Council and half by the Slovak National Council. Safeguards included to prevent domination by either nationality; each Chamber would have equal status to ensure, in Cernik's words, that 'no nation will be able to force its will on the other and no measure can be adopted against the will of the majority.' Bill was signed by Svoboda on 30 October at Bratislava Castle.

28–30 October. Meeting at Moscow of Defence Ministers of East European communist countries, attended by General Rusov (Czechoslovak Acting Defence Chief) and Marshal Yakubovsky, to discuss Warsaw Pact matters, and the need to strengthen the Pact.

3 November. US Defence Department report claims that military balance in Europe has not been upset by the Czechoslovak invasion. Pointed out that NATO defence budgets in 1968 totalled $75,000 millions compared with $50,000 for the Warsaw

	Pact countries, and that NATO manpower in Europe was 389,000 as opposed to 360,000 Warsaw Pact troops. Claimed that NATO was qualitatively better prepared than Pact powers in most fields.
4 November.	*Pravda* attacks critics of Moscow Agreement in Czechoslovakia. 'Instead of listening to sober voices and using healthy criticism to improve things, certain officials of the Czechoslovak party are encouraging those forces which used inner party democracy for brazen attacks against party principles.'
7 November.	Anti-Russian demonstrations take place in Prague after Dubcek and Cernik are abused by a pro-Russian crowd at memorial service for Russian soldiers who died in the liberation of Czechoslovakia from the Germans.
12 November.	Brezhnev, in a speech to fifth congress of Polish Communist Party, describes invasion as an 'extraordinary step dictated by necessity', and referred to 'recent activation of forces hostile to Socialism in Czechoslovakia'. Declares that 'when internal and external forces that are hostile to Socialism try to turn the development of some Socialist country towards the restoration of a capitalist régime . . . it becomes not only a problem of the people of the country concerned, but a common problem and concern of all Socialist countries'. Seven Western journalists and photographers expelled from Czechoslovakia.
14–17 November.	Plenary session of Central Committee of Czechoslovak Communist Party. Announcement made of formation of a new eight-man executive committee responsible for 'collective evaluation of urgent political problems' and for co-ordinating the 'procedure and work of Communists in Party, State and Social organs'. Members would be Cernik, Dubcek, Svoboda, Erban, Husak, Sadovsky, Smrkovsky and Dr Strovgal. (Dr Strovgal, Minister of the Interior 1961–5, also

replaced Meynav on the Praesidium.) Dubcek gave assurances that civil liberties and fundamental rights would be upheld.

Resolution passed on 17 November (published following day) condemned right-wing and opportunistic forces for failure in policy that had resulted in the invasion, and criticized the Press for fostering 'anti-Socialist and liberalistic' tendencies; emphasizes that the mass media were responsible for carrying out the policy of the Party and the State. But resolution also stated that Czechoslovakia would be converted into a Federal State, with no return to the pre-January situation.

Some 60,000 students in Bohemia and Moravia start three day sit-in strike at erosion of the Action Programme.

25 November. Severe restriction on travel, particularly to Western Europe, announced in Prague. Permanent exit visas for Czechoslovak citizens abolished. Announced by Deputy Minister of the Interior (Dr Rybar) that 2,067,200 Czechoslovak citizens had been abroad in first ten months of 1968, of whom about 5,000 had applied for asylum. Stated in *The Times* that between January and October 336,000 citizens had made journeys to Western Countries, of which 92,000 were in September and October, as opposed to 26,000 in same months in 1967.

A delegation of artists, writers, and scientists expressed to Dubcek their concern over erosion of reforms.

28 November. *Izvestia* expresses approval of developments in Czechoslovakia, and states that there are 'more and more people facing up to the reality of today'.

Poll published in Catholic People's Party newspaper *Lidova Demokracie* states that public confidence in the Dubcek régime had risen from 55 per cent in February to 85 per cent in November; review also showed concern at failure of Czech leaders to fulfil the democratization policies.

SELECTED CHRONOLOGY

6 December. USA announces it has advanced the timing of its annual military exercises in Europe to January, will delay the planned return of some units to America, and that 15,500 men will be flown to Germany to take part in the exercises, to be held some 30 miles from the Czechoslovak frontier. In addition, it was stated that 100 Phantom aircraft would be sent to Europe to take part in the exercises, and that a brigade of the 24th Infantry Division, due to return to the United States, would remain in Europe indefinitely.

Appointment of Mr Smidmajer as new director of Czechoslovak state television, in succession to Mr Pelikan, announced.

6–8 December. Czech–Soviet meeting at Kiev to discuss, according to *Tass*, 'co-operation' between the two governments and parties. Main topic of the talks was economic planning and links between the two countries, and, in particular, the extent of Soviet economic aid. *Rude Pravo* (10 December) describes the 'deepening of co-operation within the framework of COMECON' as the principal subject.

12 December. Central Committee of Czechoslovak Communist Party begins its plenary session. Dr Sik announces in Geneva that he will not attend the meeting on advice from the Czechoslovak Embassy in Berne.

Prace gives prominence to open letters expressing support for Smrkovsky, questioning his absence from Kiev talks, and a telegram from 42,000 miners in North Bohemia, praising his 'openness, honour, civic pride, and resistance'.

16 December. Indra and Bilak reported to have been confirmed as members of the party Secretariat. *Prace* publishes an open letter urging Sik to return to Czechoslovakia to 'explain to the group of comrades dealing with your case all the circumstances which are not clear'.

THE CZECHOSLOVAK CRISIS 1968

17 December. Nikolai Baibakov, Soviet chief economic planner, arrives in Prague at head of economic delegation. Reports circulating in Vienna that on 1 January Cernik will become Prime Minister of the Federal Government and to replace Dubcek as First Secretary; Dubcek would then become chairman (source, Annelise Schulz, Vienna: *Daily Telegraph*, 18 December). Suggested that these and other leadership changes were discussed at Kiev meeting.

Reports from Prague in *Mlada Fronta* state that Soviet Government has not granted the loan, said to be £167 millions, urgently needed by Czechoslovakia to modernize its consumer goods industries. Deputy Minister of National Planning, said that exports to capitalist countries 'are getting smaller and smaller while our imports increase'. Output increase of 12% in 1968 largely overtaken by higher wages.

Appendix 1

Warsaw Pact and Unified Command Accord, 14 May 1955

The Communiqué
In accordance with the pact of friendship, co-operation and mutual assistance between the People's Republic of Albania, the People's Republic of Bulgaria, the Hungarian People's Republic, the German Democratic Republic, the Polish People's Republic, the Rumanian People's Republic, the Union of Soviet Socialist Republics and the Czechoslovak Republic, the signatory States have decided to set up a unified command of Armed Forces.

This decision provides that general questions relating to the strengthening of the defence capacity and the organization of united Armed Forces of the participating countries are to be examined by the political and consultative communities, which will take appropriate decisions.

The Commander-in-Chief of the united Armed Forces contributed by the participating States is appointed in the person of Marshal of the Soviet Union Konev.

The deputies to the Commander-in-Chief of the united Armed Forces are appointed in the persons of the ministers of defence and military leaders of the participating States, who are to command the Armed Forces of each participating country contributing to the strength of the unified Armed Forces.

The question of the participation of the German Democratic Republic in measures regarding the Armed Forces of the unified command is to be examined later.

The Commander-in-Chief of the united Armed Forces is to set up a headquarters of the unified command of the participating countries, which is to include the permanent representatives of the general staffs of the participating countries.

The headquarters is to be located in Moscow.

APPENDIX 1

The location of the united Armed Forces on the territories of the participating States is to be decided in accordance with the needs of mutual defence by agreement between these States.

The Treaty
The contracting parties

Confirm once again their striving for the creation of a system of collective security in Europe based on the participation of all European States, irrespective of their social or state structure, which would make it possible to unite their efforts in the interest of ensuring peace in Europe.

Taking into consideration at the same time the situation which has arisen in Europe as the result of the ratification of the Paris agreements envisaging the formation of a new military alignment in the form of the West European Union with the participation of Western Germany, which is being remilitarized, and her inclusion in the North Atlantic bloc, which increases the danger of a new war and creates a threat to the national security of peace-loving States;

Being convinced of the fact that in these circumstances peace-loving States in Europe must take measures necessary to safeguard their security and in the interests of preserving peace in Europe;

Guided by the aims and principles of the United Nations Charter, in the interests of the further strengthening and developing of friendship, collaboration and mutual assistance in accordance with the principles of respecting the independence and sovereignty of the States and non-interference in their internal affairs;

Have decided to conclude the present treaty of friendship, collaboration and mutual assistance, and have appointed as their representatives: (Names follow)

Who, representing their countries, agreed to the following:

Article 1
The high contracting parties undertake, in accordance with the United Nations Charter, to abstain in their international relations from threats of violence or its use and to settle international disputes by peaceful means, so as not to put each other or international peace in danger.

Article 2
The contracting parties declare their readiness to co-operate in all international actions with the purpose of ensuring international peace and security.

With that, the contracting parties will strive to reach agreement with States desiring to co-operate in that cause and take measures to reduce armaments and the ban of atomic, hydrogen and other weapons of mass destruction.

Article 3
The contracting parties will consult mutually on all important international problems affecting their common interests, taking as their guide the interests of strengthening international peace and security.

Article 4
In case of armed aggression in Europe against one or several states party to the pact by a State or group of States, each state member of the pact, in order to put into practice the right of individual or collective self-defence, in accordance with Article 51 of the United Nations Charter, will afford to the State or States which are the objects of such an aggression immediate assistance, individually and in agreement with other States, party to the pact, with all means which appear necessary, including the use of armed force.

The parties to the pact will immediately take joint measures necessary to establish and preserve international peace and security.

Measures taken on the basis of this article will assist security in accordance with the United Nations Charter.

These measures will be stopped as soon as the Security Council takes measures necessary for establishing and preserving international peace and security.

Article 5
The contracting powers agree to set up a joint command of their Armed Forces to be allotted by agreement between the powers, at the disposal of this command and used on the basis of jointly established principles.

They will also take other agreed measures necessary to strengthen their defences in order to protect the peaceful toil of their peoples, guarantee the integrity of their frontiers and territories and ensure their defence against possible aggression.

Article 6
With the object of carrying out consultations provided by the present treaty between the States participating in the treaty examination of questions arising in connection with the fulfilment of this treaty, a political consultative committee is being set up in which each State

APPENDIX 1

participating in the treaty will be represented by a member of its Government or another specially appointed representative.

The committee may set up any auxiliary organs it considers necessary.

Article 7
The contracting parties undertake not to enter into any coalitions or unions and not to enter into any agreements whose aims are contrary to the terms of this treaty.

The contracting parties declare that their obligations under existing international agreements are not contrary to the terms of the present treaty.

Article 8
The contracting parties declare that they will act in a spirit of friendship and co-operation in order further to develop the economic and cultural ties between them, and will be guided by principles of mutual respect and will not interfere in the internal affairs of each other.

Article 9
The present treaty is open to other States, irrespective of their social or Government régime, who declare their readiness to abide by the terms of this treaty in order to safeguard peace and security of the peoples.

The joining of this treaty by such countries will come into force in agreement with the States party to the treaty, after it has been handed over to the Government of Poland for safekeeping.

Article 10
The present treaty is subject to ratification, and the ratification instruments will be handed to Poland for safekeeping. It will come into force on the day the instruments are handed over to the Polish Government.

The Government of the Polish People's Republic will inform the other State signatories of the treaty when each ratification instrument is handed over.

Article 11
The present treaty will remain in force for twenty years. Those States which do not give notice of abrogation one year before the treaty expires will remain bound by it for a further ten years.

In the event of a system of collective security being set up in

THE WARSAW PACT

Europe and a pact to this effect being signed – to which each party to this treaty will direct its efforts – the present treaty will lapse from the day such a collective security treaty comes into force.

Drawn up in Warsaw, 14 May 1955, in one copy each in Russian, Polish, Czech and German, each text being equally valid.

Attested copies of this treaty will be sent to the Governments of each party to the treaty by the Government of the Polish People's Republic.

In witness whereof the plenipotentiary representatives affixed their signatures and seal.

Bilateral Treaties of Friendship, Co-operation and Mutal Assistance signed by Warsaw Pact Members

	USSR	Poland	Czech.	Hung.	Rum.	Bulg.	Soviet Occupied Zone of Germany
USSR							
Poland	FCMA 4-45 r. 4–65						
Czecho-slovakia	FCMA 13–43 r. 12–63	FCMA 3–47 r. 3–67					
Hungary	FCMA 2–48 r. 9–67	FCMA 6–48 r. 5–68	FCMA 4–49 r. 6–68				
Rumania	FCMA* 2–48	FCMA 1–49	FCMA 7–48	FCMA 1–48			
Bulgaria	FCMA 3–48 r. 5–67	FCMA 5–48 r. 4–57	FCMA 4–48 r. 6–68	FCMA 7–48	FCMA 1–48		
Soviet Occupied Zone of Germany	FMA 6–64	F 7–50 FCMA 3–67	F 6–50 FCMA 3–67	F 6–50 FMCA 5–67	F 8–50	F 8–50 FCMA 9–67	

FCMA – Friendship, Co-operation, and Mutual Assistance Treaty
F   – Friendship Treaty
r.   – replaced

APPENDIX 1

Twenty-one treaties are currently in force. The treaties are valid for a period of twenty years and commit the co-signatories to mutual defence against aggression, particularly aggression by a re-armed German state. In this regard the initial treaties concluded with the Soviet-Occupied Zone of Germany were called only Friendship Treaties.

It was not until June 1964 that the agreement between the Soviet-Occupied Zone of Germany and the USSR was upgraded to the level of a Treaty of Friendship, Co-operation and Mutual Assistance. In 1967, Bulgaria, Czechoslovakia, Hungary and Poland also signed Treaties of Friendship, Co-operation and Mutual Assistance with the Soviet Zone. In ten cases new treaties have replaced the original agreements (between the USSR and Czechoslovakia, USSR and Poland, Poland and Bulgaria, Poland and Czechoslovakia, USSR and Bulgaria, USSR and Hungary, Czechoslovakia and Bulgaria, Poland and Hungary, Hungary and Czechoslovakia and Czechoslovakia and Rumania). Albania has not been included in the table since it has signed a Treaty of Friendship, Co-operation and Mutual Assistance only with Bulgaria, in December, 1947.

Treaties signed during 1967 and 1968 among Warsaw Pact Members

A. *New FCMA Treaties*
Poland–Soviet-Occupied Zone of Germany – 15 March 1967
Czechoslovakia–Soviet-Occupied Zone of Germany – 18 May 1967
Hungary–Soviet-Occupied Zone of Germany – 18 May 1967
Bulgaria–Soviet-Occupied Zone of Germany – 7 September 1967
B. *Replacement of FCMA Treaties*
Poland-Bulgaria – 6 April 1967
Poland-Czechoslovakia – 10 March 1967
USSR-Bulgaria – 12 May 1967
USSR-Hungary – 7 September 1967
Czechoslovakia-Bulgaria 26 April 1968
Poland-Hungary – 16 May 1968
Czechoslovakia-Hungary – 14 June 1968
Czechoslovakia-Rumania – 16 August 1968

---

* According to Soviet Foreign Minister Gromyko's speech of 27th June, 1968, work has been completed on the drafting of a new USSR – Rumanian Treaty, and this has been initiated.

Joint Manoeuvres of Warsaw Pact Forces

Date	Location	Bulg.	Cz.	E. Ger.	Hung.	Pol.	Rum.	Soviet
1961								
June	East Germany			×				×
Oct-Nov	*W. Poland		×	×		×		×
1962								
April	Hungary				×	×		×
July	Bulgaria	×				×		×
Sept.	Czechoslovakia		×	×				×
Oct.	Poland } East Germany			×		×		×
Oct.	Rumania	×					×	×
1963								
Sept.	East Germany		×	×		×		×
Oct.	Hungary				×			×
1964								
July	Czechoslovakia		×					×
July	East Germany			×				×
Sept.	Bulgaria	×					×	×
1965								
Oct.			×	×		×		×
1966								
July	Baltic			×		×		×
Sept.	Czechoslovakia ('VLATAVA")		×	×	×			×
1967								
May June	Poland } East Germany			×		×		×
August	Poland			×		×		×

× indicates nationality of forces taking part.

* First multilateral manoeuvres held.

Appendix 2

The Warsaw Letter and the Czechoslovak Reply

The five-power letter to the Czechoslovak Communist Party Central Committee read:

Dear Comrades,
On behalf of the Central Committees of the Communist and workers' parties of Bulgaria, the German Democratic Republic, Hungary, Poland and the Soviet Union, we are approaching you with this letter, dictated by sincere friendship based on the principles of Marxism-Leninism and proletarian internationalism, as well as by concern for our common matters for the strengthening of the positions of socialism and of the security of the socialist community of nations.

We are deeply disturbed by the course of events in your country. The offensive of reaction, backed by imperialism, against your party and the foundations of the social system of the Czechoslovak Socialist Republic, threatens in our deepest conviction to push your country from the road of socialism, and thereby threatens the interests of the entire socialist system.

We expressed these misgivings at the meeting in Dresden, during a number of bilateral meetings, and also in letters which our parties have recently addressed to the Praesidium of the Central Committee of the Communist Party of Czechoslovakia.

Recently we proposed to the Praesidium of the Central Committee of the CPC to hold a new joint meeting on 14 July 1968, in order to exchange information and views on the situation in our countries, including the development of events in Czechoslovakia.

Alas, the Praesidium did NOT take part in this meeting and did NOT avail itself of the possibility of a collective comradely discussion on the situation that has been created.

THE WARSAW LETTER

It was NOT and is NOT our intention to interfere in such matters which are an internal matter of your party and your Government, to infringe on the relations between Communist Parties and socialist countries.

We are NOT approaching you as representatives of yesterday who would wish to hinder you in correcting errors and shortcomings, including the infringements of socialist legality that had taken place.

We do NOT interfere in the methods of planning and management of the socialist national economy of Czechoslovakia, in your measures aimed at the perfecting of the structure of the economy, at the development of socialist democracy.

We shall welcome the settlement of relations between Czechs and Slovaks on the sound foundations of fraternal co-operation within the framework of the Czechoslovak Socialist Republic.

We cannot reconcile ourselves, however, with the fact of hostile forces pushing your country off the road of socialism and creating a threat of tearing away Czechoslovakia from the socialist community.

This is NO longer only your concern. This is a common concern of all communist and workers' parties and of states united by alliance, co-operation and friendship.

The strength and lasting character of our alliances depends on the internal strength of the socialist system in each of our fraternal countries, on the Marxist-Leninist policy of our parties which are fulfilling the leading role in the political and social life of their respective nations and states.

The undermining of the leading role of the Communist Parties leads to the liquidation of socialist democracy and of the socialist system. Thereby a threat is created to the foundations of our alliance and the security of the community of our countries.

You know that the fraternal parties treated with understanding the decisions of the January plenum of the Central Committee of the CPC, bearing in mind that your party, firmly holding in its hands the levers of power, would direct the entire process in the interest of socialism, and would not allow anti-Communist reaction to utilize it for its aims.

We were convinced that you were going to defend as the apple of your eye the Leninist principle of democratic centralism. To ignore any of the sides of this principle, both democracy and centralism, leads inevitably to the weakening of the party and its leading role, to the transformation of the party either into a bureaucratic organization, or a discussion club.

We have spoken of these matters more than once during our meetings and received assurances on your part that you were aware of all dangers and that you were fully determined to rebut them. Alas events have taken a different course.

The forces of reaction, taking advantage of the weakening of the party leadership of the country, abusing demagogically the slogan of democratization, unleashed a campaign against the CPC and its honest and devoted cadres, with the open intention to liquidate the leading role of the party, to undermine the socialist system, to set Czechoslovakia against the other socialist countries.

Political organizations and clubs formed recently outside the framework of the National Front have in fact become headquarters of the forces of reaction. The social democrats stubbornly demand the creation of their own party, organize under-ground committees, strive to split the working-class movement in Czechoslovakia, to reach out for the leadership of the country with the aim of restoring the bourgeois system.

Anti-socialist and revisionist forces have gained control over the press, radio and television and transformed them into a tribune for attacks on the Communist Party, for the disorientation of the working class and all working people, for an unbridled anti-socialist demagogy, for the undermining of friendly relations between the Czechoslovak Socialist Republic and other socialist countries.

A number of organs of mass information is systematically using moral terror with regard to people who are coming out against the forces of reaction or express their misgivings at the course of events.

Despite the decisions of the May plenum of the Central Committee of the CPC, which pointed to the threat on the part of right-wing and anti-communist forces as the main danger, the intensified attacks of reaction met with NO resistance. This is precisely why reaction obtained the possibility publicly to appear before the country, to publish its political platform under the name of 'Two-thousand words', which contains an open appeal to a struggle against the Communist Party and against the constitutional authority, an appeal to strikes and disturbances. This appeal constitutes a serious threat to the party, the National Front, the socialist state; constitutes an attempt to implant anarchy.

In fact, this statement constitutes an organizational political platform of counter-revolution. No one should be deceived by the assurances of its authors that they do NOT want to overthrow the socialist system, that they do NOT want to act without the communists, that they do NOT want to break the alliances with the socialists countries. Those are empty phrases aimed at legalizing the platform of counter-revolution, to deceive the vigilance of the party of the working class and all working people.

This platform widely circulated in the crucial period preceding the extraordinary congress of the CPC, NOT only was NOT rejected, but even found open supporters within the ranks of the party and its leadership, who support the anti-socialist appeals.

In this atmosphere attacks are being also made on the socialist external policy of the Czechoslovak Socialist Republic, against the alliance and friendship with socialist countries. Voices are heard demanding a revision of our common and agreed-upon policy with regard to the German Federal Republic in spite of the fact that the West German Government conducts immutably a course hostile to the interests of the security of our countries. Attempts at flirtation on the part of the GFR authorities and West German revanchists are finding a response in the leading circles of your country.

The bourgeois press, under the pretext of praising 'democratization' and 'liberalization' in the Czechoslovak Socialist Republic, conducts an incitement campaign against the fraternal socialist countries. A particular activity is shown by the governing circles in the GFR, which attempt to utilize the events in Czechoslovakia to sow discord between socialist countries, to isolate the German Democratic Republic, to carry out their revanchist schemes.

Is it not with the purpose of sowing suspicion and hostility towards the Soviet Union and other socialist countries that the press, radio and television of your country unleashed a campaign in connection with the staff exercises of the armed forces of the Warsaw Treaty? It came to a point that joint staff exercises of troops, customary for military co-operation, with the participation of several units of the Soviet Army are being utilized for groundless accusations of violation of the sovereignty of the Czechoslovak Socialist Republic.

In our conviction a situation has arisen, in which the threat to the foundations of socialism in Czechoslovakia endangers common vital interests of the remaining socialist countries. The peoples of our countries would never forgive us indifference and carelessness in the face of such a danger.

We live in a time when peace, security and the freedom of nations calls more than ever before for the unity of the forces of socialism. International tension is not slackening. American imperialism has NOT renounced its policy of strength and open intervention against nations fighting for freedom. As previously it is engaged in a criminal war in Vietnam, supports the Israel aggressors in the Middle East, impedes the peaceful settlement of the conflict.

The arms race has NOT been checked in the least. The German Federal Republic in which the forces of neo-fascism are growing is attacking the status quo, demanding revisions of frontiers, and does

NOT want to renounce either the striving to annex the German Democratic Republic or to gain access to nuclear weapons, and comes out against disarmament proposals. In Europe, where tremendous means of mass destruction have been accumulated, peace and the security of nations are maintained above all owing to the strength, cohesion and unity of socialist countries. We are all responsible for this strength and unity of socialist countries, for the destinies of peace.

Our countries are linked with one another by treaties and agreements. These important mutual obligations of states and nations are based on the common striving to defend socialism and ensure the collective security of socialist countries. Our parties and nations bear the historical responsibility of seeing to it that the achieved revolutionary conquests should NOT be lost.

Each of our parties bears responsibility not only before its working class and before its nation, but also before the international working class, the world communist movement, and cannot evade the obligations arising therefrom. This is why we should show solidarity and be united in the defence of the conquest of socialism, of our security and of the international positions of the entire socialist community.

This is why we consider that a decisive rebuff to the anti-communist forces and a determined struggle for the preservation of the socialist system in Czechoslovakia is NOT only your task, but ours as well.

The cause of the defence of the power of the working class and all working people, of the socialist conquest in Czechoslovakia demands:

A determined and bold offensive against the right-wing and anti-socialist forces, a mobilization of means of defence created by the socialist state;

A cessation of the activity of all political organizations coming out against socialism;

Seizure by the party of media of mass information – the press, radio and television, and their utilization in the interests of the working class, all working people, socialism; and

Cohesion of the ranks of the party itself on the basis of the principles of Marxism-Leninism, close observance of the principle of democratic centralism struggle against those who abet by their activity hostile forces.

We know that there exist forces in Czechoslovakia, capable of defending successfully the socialist system and of defeating the anti-socialist elements.

The working class, the working peasants, the progressive intelligentsia – the overwhelming majority of the working people of the republic are ready to do everything necessary in the name of the further development of the socialist society. Today's task is to give these sound forces a clear perspective, to rouse them to action, to mobilize their energy for the struggle against the counter-revolutionary forces in order to preserve and consolidate socialism in Czechoslovakia.

In the face of the threat of counter-revolution, the voice of the working class should resound with full strength at the appeal of the Communist Party. The working class together with the working peasants made the greatest efforts in the name of the triumph of the socialist revolution. The preservation of the conquests of socialism is dearest precisely to them.

The following is the reply sent by the Praesidium of the Central Committee of the Czechoslovak Communist Party:

The Praesidium of the Central Committee of the Communist Party of Czechoslovakia has thoroughly studied the letter it received addressed to the Central Committee of our Party from the meeting of the representatives of the parties of five socialist countries in Warsaw.

We are at the same time fully aware that an exchange of letters cannot fully explain such a complex problem which is the subject of attention, and our attitude does not aim at such ends but on the contrary presumes direct mutual talks between parties.

The number of fears explained in the letter were also expressed in the resolution of our May plenary session of the Central Committee of the Communist Party of Czechoslovakia. However, we see the causes of the conflicting situation mainly in the fact that these conflicts accumulated over the years preceding the January plenary session of the Central Committee of the Communist Party of Czechoslovakia.

These conflicts cannot be satisfactorily solved suddenly in a short time. In the process of the realization of the political line of the action programme of our party it is therefore unavoidable that the wide mass stream of healthy socialist activities is accompanied by extremist tendencies, that the remnants of anti-socialist forces in our society are also trying to go along and that at the same time the dogmatic-sectarian forces connected with the faulty policy of the pre-January period are also spreading their activities.

All these things prevent us from achieving only those results in our political work which we ourselves wish.

We do not wish to hide these facts and we do not hide them either from our own party and people.

APPENDIX 2

For this reason also the May plenum of the Central Committee stated clearly that it is necessary to mobilize all forces to prevent a conflict situation in the country and the endangering of socialist power in the Czechoslovak Socialist Republic. Our party has also unequivocally stated that if any such danger occurred that we should use all means to protect the socialist system.

The basic orientation of Czechoslovakia's foreign policy was born and confirmed at the time of the national liberation fight and in the process of the socialist reconstruction of our country – it is the alliance and co-operation with the Soviet Union and the other socialist countries. We shall strive for the friendly relations between our allies – the countries of the world socialist system – to deepen on the basis of mutual respect, sovereignty and equality, mutual esteem and international solidarity. In this sense we shall contribute more actively and with a worked out concept to the common activities of the council of Mutual Economic Assistance and the Warsaw Treaty.

In the letter there is a mention of the attacks against the socialist foreign policy, of assaults against the alliance and friendship with socialist countries, about voices calling for the revision of our common and co-ordinated policy against the GFR (West Germany) and it is even stated that attempts at making advances on the part of the authorities of the GFR and revanchists are finding response in the leading circles of our country.

We are surprised at such statements because it is well known that the Czechoslovak Socialist Republic is applying a thorough socialist foreign policy the principles of which were formulated in the action programme of the Communist Party of Czechoslovakia and the programme statement of the Government. These documents and the statements made by leading Czechoslovak representatives and also our further actions are consistently based on the principles of socialist internationalism, alliance and the development of friendly relations with the Soviet Union and the other socialist states.

We are of the opinion that these facts are decisive and not the irresponsible voices of the individuals which are sometimes heard.

With regard to the bitter historical experiences of our nations with German imperialism and militarism it is inconceivable that any Czechoslovak Government could ignore these experiences and fool-hardily hazard the fate of our country, even less a socialist government, and we must refute any suspicion in this direction.

As regards our relations with the GFR, it is universally known that although Czechoslovakia is the immediate neighbour of the GFR, it was the last to take definite steps towards the partial regulation of mutual relations, particularly in the economic field, while other socialist countries adapted their relations to one or another extent much earlier without it causing any fears.

At the same time we thoroughly respect and protect the interests of the GDR (East Germany), our socialist ally, and do all in our power to strengthen its international position and authority. This is definitely proved by all the speeches of the leading representatives of our party and state in the entire period after January 1948.

The staff exercise of the allied forces of the Warsaw Treaty on the territory of Czechoslovakia are a concrete proof of our faithful fulfilment of our alliance commitments. In order to ensure its smooth course, we took the necessary measures on our side. Our people and the members of the Army gave a friendly welcome to the Soviet and other allied soldiers on the territory of Czechoslovakia. The top representatives of the Party and Government by their participation, proved what importance we attach to it and the interest we have in it. The obscurities and doubts in the minds of our public occurred only after the repeated changes of the time of the departure of the allied armies from the territory of Czechoslovakia at the end of the exercise.

In the action programme of our party we set down the following on the basis of our previous experience:

'In the present time it is especially essential for the party to carry out such a policy that could fully merit it the leading role in our society. We are convinced that under the present circumstances it is a condition for the socialist development of the country. . . .

'The Communist Party depends on the voluntary support of the people. It is not implementing its leading role by ruling over the society but by faithfully serving its free, progressive socialist development. It cannot impel its authority, but must constantly acquire it by its actions. It cannot force its line by orders, but by the work of its members and the veracity of its ideals.

'We do not hide the fact – and we stated this plainly at the May plenum of the Central Committee – that there exist today also tendencies aimed at discrediting the party, attempts to deny it its moral and political right to lead the society. But if we ask the question whether similar phenomena can be correctly judged as a threat to the socialist system as a decline of the political role of the Communist Party of Czechoslovakia, under the pressure of reactionary, counter-revolutionary forces, then we come to the conclusion that this is not so.'

The leading role of our party gravely suffered in the past by the distortions of the fifties and the policy of their inconsistent removal by the leadership headed by A. Novotny. He is even more responsible

APPENDIX 2

for the deepening of the social conflicts; between the Czechs and Slovaks, between the intelligentsia and workers, between the young generation and the older generations. The inconsistent solution of the economic problems has left us in a condition in which we cannot solve a series of justified economic demands of the workers and when the effectiveness of the entire national economy is gravely disrupted. Under that leadership, the confidence of the masses in the party dropped and there were expressions of criticism and resistance, but all this was 'solved' by interference from a position of power against justified dissatisfaction, against criticism and against attempts to consistently solve the social problems in the interests of the party, and in the interests of its leading role.

Instead of the gradual and well considered removal of errors, further mistakes and conflicts accumulated as a result of subjective decision making. In the years when socialist democracy could objectively be developed gradually and scientific management could have been applied, the subjective deficiencies sharpened the social conflicts and difficulties.

On the outside it seemed that everything was in order in Czechoslovakia and it was made to appear that developments were without conflict. In actual fact, the decline in confidence in the party was masked by exterior forms of direct party control. Although this régime was given out as being the firm guarantee of the interests of the entire socialist camp, inside problems were growing, the real solution of which was suppressed by forceful means against those advocates of new and creative approaches.

Any indication of a return to these methods would evoke the resistance of the overwhelming majority of party members, the resistance of the working class, the workers, co-operative farmers, and intelligentsia. The Party would, by such a step, imperil its political leading role and would create a situation in which a power conflict would really arise. This would truly threaten the socialist advantages of the people and also our common interests in the anti-imperialist front of the socialist community.

Our party has laid down the following main aims and stages of political work: (1) To consistently separate the party as a whole from the distortions of the past for which specific persons of the old party leadership are responsible; these specific people are justifiably being called to task. (2) To prepare the fourteenth extraordinary congress of the party which will evaluate the development and political situation after the January plenum and in accordance with the principles of democratic centralism will lay down the compulsory line for the entire party, will adopt an attitude to the federal arrangement of Czechoslovakia, will approve the new party statute and elect a new central committee so that it has the full authority and confidence of the Party and the entire society.

(3) After the 14th Congress, to launch the offensive for the solution of all the fundamental internal political questions, towards the construction of a political system based on the socialist platform of the national front and social self-government, the solution of the federal constitutional arrangement the elections to the representative bodies of the state (federal, national and local) and the preparation of a new constitution.

At present, we are at the stage of the political fight to implement the line of the May plenum of the Central Committee of the Communist Party of Czechoslovakia. It is a real fight and therefore we both win but also suffer drawbacks; according to the results of the individual battles, however, it would not be correct to judge the outcome of the whole war. In spite of this we think that we have managed to consolidate the political situation since the May plenum.

In the past days, the extraordinary district and regional conferences have plainly shown that the Party is becoming unified on the line of the action programme. Delegates have been elected to the Congress and their composition is a guarantee that the future fate of the party will not be decided on by representatives of extremist opinions, but the democratically appointed progressive core of our party. The representatives of the new leadership of the Communist Party of Czechoslovakia, who are associated with the line of the action programme and the May plenum of the central committee, were all proposed by the regional conferences into the new central committee. Therefore a certain stabilization is going on in the Party and the basic steps for the preparations of the Congress took place with success.

In September immediately after the party congress other new important laws will be discussed: the constitutional law on the national front which is to confirm the permanent existence of the system of political parties on the ground of the national front and, further, a law on the right for assembly and association which lay down the legal regulations for the birth and activities of various voluntary organizations, associations, clubs, etc. This will give the opportunity to effectively face attempts of anti-communist forces to gain an organizational basis for public activities.

The communists have also taken the initiative, according to the resolution of the May plenary session of the central committee to solve the important questions of the work of the trade unions and enterprise workers' councils. In general, the Party has been able to

APPENDIX 2

overcome political demagogy in these questions which attempted to utilize the justified demands of the workers to disorganize our system and which fanned an impromptu movement in the name of 'workers' demands' in order to make the economic and political situation in the country more difficult. At the same time, however, according to the means at our disposal we are solving some urgent social and political problems such as the increase of low pensions and urgent wage increases. The Government is gradually dealing with the fundamental economic problems of the country in order to give the impulse for the new development of production and in order to be able to move over to the further improvement of the living standard of our people.

We have taken the necessary measures to ensure the safety of our state borders. The Party fully supports the consolidation of the Army, security forces, prosecutors and judiciary, of the workers' militia whose statewide meeting gave full support to the new leadership of the Party and the action programme. The importance of this step, as is known, was welcomed by the workers not only in this country, but also in the USSR.

We consider all these steps to be important results arising from the fulfilment of the line adopted at the plenary session of the Central Committee of the Communist Party of Czechoslovakia to be important features of the consolidation of political conditions and the strengthening not only of the declared but the genuinely leading influence of the Party in our Country.

In spite of this we see and do not want to conceal the fact that not all conclusions drawn at the May plenary session of the Central Committee of the Communist Party of Czechoslovakia have been carried out satisfactorily. Now too it happens that voices and tendencies appear in the press and the radio and in public meetings which are outside the positive endeavours of the Party, the State bodies and the national front. We consider the solution of these questions to be a long-term task and are guided by the resolutions of the May plenary session of the central committee according to which 'political leadership cannot be imposed by the old administrative and power structures'.

The Praesidium of the Central Committee of the Communist Party of Czechoslovakia, the Government and the national front clearly rejected the appeal of the statement of 'two-thousand words', which urge people to engage in anarchist acts, and to violation of the constitutional character of our political reform. It should be noted that, following these negative positions, similar campaigns did not in fact occur in our country and that the consequences of the appeal 'two-thousand words' did not threaten the Party, the national front and the socialist state.

The campaigns and unjustified slanders against various functionaries and public officials – including members of the new leadership of the Communist party of Czechoslovakia – which are conducted from extremist positions both left and right, are still a negative aspect of our situation.

The secretariat of the Communist Party Central Committee and leading officials have unequivocally come out against these methods in specific cases. We know that this situation is facilitated by the abolition of censorship in our country and the enactment of freedom of expression and of the press. What had been spread in the form of 'whispered propaganda', etc. before can now be expressed openly.

If we ask ourselves whether it is correct to consider such phenomena as forfeiture of the leading political role of the Communist Party of Czechoslovakia under pressure of reactionary, counter-revolutionary, forces, we reach the conclusion that this is not so. For all this is only part of our present political situation.

There is also another and in our opinion decisive aspect to this situation. The rise of the authority of the new, democratic policy of the Party in the eyes of the broadest masses of the workers, the growth of the activity of the overwhelming majority of the people. The overwhelming majority of the people of all classes and sectors of our society favour the abolition of censorship and are for freedom of expression. The Communist Party of Czechoslovakia is trying to show that it is capable of a different political leadership and management than the discredited bureaucratic-police methods, mainly by the strength of its Marxist-Leninist ideas, by the strength of its programme, its just policy supported by all the people.

Our party can prevail in the difficult political struggle only if it has an opportunity to implement the tactical line of the May plenary meeting of the Central Committee and settle basic political questions at the extraordinary 14th Congress in the spirit of the action programme. We therefore consider all pressure directed at forcing the party on to another path, that is to settle basic questions of its policy elsewhere and at another time than at the 14th Congress, the principal danger to the successful consolidation of the leading role of the Party in the Czechoslovak Socialist Republic. Pressure of this sort is being brought to bear by domestic extremist forces.

At the given time the interests of socialism in our country can be served best by a ration of confidence in the leadership of the Communist Party of Czechoslovakia and of full support of its policy by our fraternal parties. For this reason we have proposed, as a prerequisite of successful joint discussions, bilateral meetings of the representatives of our parties so that the joint talks may proceed from deep mutual consultations and factual information.

We sincerely regret that these proposals put forward by us were not implemented. It is not our fault that the meeting in Warsaw was held without us.

We think that the common cause of socialism is not advanced by the holding of conferences at which the policy and activity of one of the fraternal parties is judged without the presence of their representatives. We consider the principle expressed in the declaration of the Soviet Union of 30 October 1956, and which says: 'The countries of the great community of socialist nations united by the common ideals of the building of a socialist society and the principles of proletarian internationalism, can build their mutual relations only on the basis of complete equality, respect of territorial integrity, national independence and sovereignty and mutual non-interference in their internal affairs', to be still valid. This principle, as is generally known, was confirmed at the conference of the representatives of communist parties in Moscow in November 1957 and generally adopted. In our activity we wish to continue to strengthen and promote the deep internationalist tradition which, according to our conception, must include an understanding of the common interests and goals of the progressive forces of the world as well as an understanding of each nation's specific requirements.

Appendix 3

Security Council Resolutions on Czechoslovakia, 22 and 23 August 1968
(S/8761 and S/8767)

The Draft Resolution was sponsored by Brazil, Canada, Denmark, France, Paraguay, Senegal, the United Kingdom and the United States, and introduced by Denmark on 22 August.

The Security Council,
Recalling that the United Nations is based on the principle of the sovereign equality of all its members,
  Gravely concerned that, as announced by the Praesidium of the Central Committee of the Communist Party of Czechoslovakia, troops of the Soviet Union and other members of the Warsaw Pact have entered their country without the knowledge and against the wishes of the Czechoslovakian Government,
  Considering that the action taken by the Government of the USSR and other members of the Warsaw Pact in invading the Czechoslovak Socialist Republic is a violation of the United Nations Charter and, in particular, of the principle that all members shall refrain in their international relations from the threat or use of force against the territorial integrity or political independence of any State,
  Gravely concerned also by risks of violence and reprisals as well as by threats to individual liberty and human rights which cannot fail to result from imposed military occupation,
  Considering that the people of the sovereign State of the Czechoslovak Socialist Republic have the right in accordance with the Charter freely to exercise their own self-determination and to arrange their own affairs without external intervention,
  1. Affirms that the sovereign, political independence and territorial integrity of the Czechoslovak Socialist Republic must be fully respected,
  2. Condemns the armed intervention of the USSR and other

APPENDIX 3

members of the Warsaw Pact in the internal affairs of the Czechoslovak Socialist Republic and calls upon them to take no action of violence or reprisal that could result in further suffering or loss of life, forthwith to withdraw their forces, and to cease all other forms of intervention in Czechoslovakia's internal affairs,

3. Calls upon member States of the United Nations to exercise their diplomatic influence upon the USSR and the other countries concerned with a view to bringing about prompt implementation of this resolution,

4. Requests the Secretary-General to transmit this resolution to the countries concerned, to keep the situation under constant review, and to report to the Council on compliance with this resolution.

The following Draft Resolution was sponsored by the same members and introduced by Canada on 23 August.

The Security Council,
Concerned at reports about the current developments in Czechoslovakia including the arrest of Czechoslovak leaders,
Requests the Secretary-General to appoint and dispatch immediately to Prague a special representative who shall seek the release and ensure the personal safety of the Czechoslovak leaders under detention and who shall report back urgently.

Appendix 4

Text of the Substantive Part of the Communiqué Issued on 27 August after the Moscow Talks

During the talks in a free comradely discussion the two sides considered questions relating to the present development of the international situation, the activization of imperialism's machinations against the Socialist countries, the situation in Czechoslovakia in the recent period and the temporary entry of troops of the five Socialist countries into Czechoslovak territory.

The sides expressed their mutual firm belief that the main thing in the present situation is to carry out the mutual decisions adopted in Cierna-nad-Tisou and the provisions and principles formulated by the Bratislava Conference, as well as to implement consistently the practical steps following from the agreement reached during the talks.

The Soviet side stated its understanding of and support for the position of the leadership of the Czechoslovak Communist Party and the Czechoslovak Socialist Republic which intends to proceed from the decisions passed by the January and May Plenary Meetings of the Central Committee of the Czechoslovak Communist Party with a view to improving the methods of guiding society, developing Socialist democracy and strengthening the Socialist system on the basis of Marxism-Leninism.

Agreement was reached on measures aimed at the speediest normalization of the situation in the Czechoslovak Socialist Republic. Czechoslovak leaders informed the Soviet side on the planned immediate measures they are carrying out with these aims in view.

It was stated by the Czechoslovak side that all the work of party and state bodies through all media would be directed at ensuring effective measures serving the Socialist power, the guiding-role of the working class and the Communist Party, the interests of developing

APPENDIX 4

and strengthening friendly relations with the peoples of the Soviet Union and the entire Socialist community.

Expressing the unanimous striving of the peoples of the USSR for friendship and brotherhood with the peoples of Socialist Czechoslovakia, the Soviet leaders confirmed their readiness for the broadest sincere co-operation on the basis of mutual respect, equality, territorial integrity, independence and Socialist solidarity.

The troops of the allied countries, that entered temporarily the territory of Czechoslovakia, will not interfere in the internal affairs of the Czechoslovak Socialist Republic. Agreement was reached on the terms of the withdrawal of these troops from its territory as the situation in Czechoslovakia normalizes.

The Czechoslovak side informed the Soviet side that the supreme Commander-in-Chief of the Czechoslovak armed forces had given the latter appropriate orders with the aim of preventing incidents and conflicts capable of violating the peace and public order. He had also instructed the Military Command of the Czechoslovak Socialist Republic to be in contact with the Command of the allied troops.

In connection with the discussion in the United Nations Security Council of the so-called question on the situation in Czechoslovakia, the representatives of the Czechoslovak Socialist Republic stated that the Czechoslovak side had not repeat not requested the submission of this question for consideration by the Security Council and demanded its removal from the agenda. The leaders of the CPSU and the leaders of the Communist Party of Czechoslovakia confirmed their determination to unswervingly promote in the international arena a policy meeting in the interests of strengthening the solidarity of the Socialist community, upholding the cause of peace and international security.

As before, the Soviet Union and Czechoslovakia will administer a resolute rebuff to militaristic, revanchist and neo-Nazi forces that want to recise the results of the Second World War, to encroach on the inviolability of the existing borders in Europe. They confirmed again the determination to fulfil unswervingly all commitments undertaken by them under multilateral and bilateral agreements concluded between Socialist states, to strengthen the defensive might of the Socialist community, to raise the effectivity of the defensive Warsaw Treaty Organization.

The talks passed in an atmosphere of frankness, comradeship and friendship.

Appendix 5

Legal Aspects of the Invasion of Czechoslovakia

The entry of Soviet, Polish, Hungarian, East German and Bulgarian forces into Czechoslovak territory on the night of 20–21 August was *prima facie* a breach of international law. It appears to be, *inter alia*, a breach of the rule which finds expression in Article 2 (4) of the United Nations Charter:

> All Members shall refrain in their international relations from the threat or use of force against the territorial integrity or political independence of any state, or in any other manner inconsistent with the Purposes of the United Nations.

A number of justifications for the invasion were advanced in the Security Council debates, and later elaborated in the General Assembly and in various publications. The justifications would seem to fall into four interrelated categories: (1) that the movement of troops was at the invitation of the Czechoslovak Government or some other Czechoslovak group; (2) that the movement of troops was in accordance with bilateral or multilateral treaty provisions; (3) that the invasion was an act of self-defence in the face of threats to the statehood of Czechoslovakia and its socialist system; (4) that the invasion was a protection of the 'Socialist Commonwealth' which was in the interests of European security.

The assertion that the troops were invited to enter Czechoslovakia does not re-appear after the Security Council debate ended on 24 August. During the course of that debate, the Czechoslovak representative stated that there had been no such invitation and read a series of official statements to that effect. It is doubtful whether an invitation from a private source would provide a legal justification for the invasion. Certainly, no invitation from either a public or private source has yet been published.

APPENDIX 5

Similarly, the assertion that the movement of troops accorded with treaty provisions seems difficult to sustain. The bilateral treaties of friendship, co-operation and mutual assistance between Czechoslovakia and the invading countries do not contain a provision for uninvited entry into Czechoslovakia. However, the treaties do express respect for the principle of non-interference in internal affairs.[1]

It is possible that, where there is an invitation, a collective self-defence treaty may be relied upon in taking collective action against an internal threat to the political independence of a member state.[2] Without such an invitation the Warsaw Pact permits entry into the territory of a member state only in the exercise of the right of self-defence 'in accordance with Article 51 of the United Nations Charter'.[3]

Article 51 of the United Nations Charter certainly does provide one exception to the general prohibition on the use of force. It reads:

Nothing in the present Charter shall impair the inherent right of individual or collective self-defence if an armed attack occurs against a Member of the United Nations, until the Security Council has taken measures necessary to maintain international peace and security. Measures taken by Members in the exercise of this right of self-defence shall be immediately reported to the Security Council and shall not in any way affect the authority and responsibility of the Security Council under the present Charter to take at any time such action as it deems necessary in order to maintain or restore international peace and security.

It should be noted in passing that while the countries concerned asserted the right of self-defence in accordance with Article 51, they did not report the action to the Security Council, and, in fact, consistently denied that it had jurisdiction to consider the matter.

The extent of the right of self-defence now permitted by international law is much disputed.[4] The implications of the juxtaposition

[1] See Czechoslovak–Soviet Treaty of Friendship, Mutual Aid and Post-War Collaboration 1943, Article IV, and the Protocol of Prolongation 1963; Czechoslovak–Polish Treaty of Friendship, Co-operation and Mutual Assistance 1967, Article I; Czechoslovak–German Democratic Republic Treaty of Friendship, Co-operation and Mutual Assistance 1967, Article I; Czechoslovak–Hungarian Treaty of Friendship, Co-operation and Mutual Aid 1968, Article I; Czechoslovak–Bulgarian Treaty of Friendship, Co-operation and Mutual Assistance 1968, Article I.

[2] For a view on the possible application of the North Atlantic Treaty for this purpose see the press statement of US Secretary of State Acheson cited in Salvin, *The North Atlantic Pact*, Int. Concil. No. 451 (1949), App. E, p. 431 at pp. 432–3.

[3] Warsaw Treaty of Friendship, Co-operation and Mutual Assistance 1955, Article 4.

[4] See H. Kelsen, *The Law of the United Nations* (1951); L. M. Goodrich and E. Hambro, *Charter of the United Nations* (1949); J. Stone, *Aggression and World*

of Article 2 (4) and Article 51 of the Charter, and the legitimacy of the concept of collective self-defence, are two of the important areas of disagreement. However, there is general agreement that the legal use of force in self-defence is dependent on the fulfilment of certain conditions. These conditions were well expressed by Secretary of State Webster in the *Caroline* incident as 'a necessity of self-defence, instant, overwhelming, leaving no choice of means, and no moment for deliberation'.[1] Furthermore, the force employed must be neither unreasonable nor excessive. There seems to be no reason to suppose that similar conditions do not apply to collective defence actions. Indeed, some advocates of collective defence as a part of a developed right of self-defence argue that collective action demands even stricter compliance with such conditions.[2]

Prior to the invasion of Czechoslovakia, Warsaw Pact forces had been engaged in manoeuvres and later events showed these forces to be at a high state of preparedness. The external threat to the independence of Czechoslovakia was based in the main on the alleged discovery of caches of foreign arms in the country. The facts of such a situation hardly fall within the terms of the *Caroline* doctrine. And while it may be considered that the exigencies of modern warfare leave it difficult to comply with such conditions, yet a broad definition of the right of self-defence invites abuse.

The fourth category of justification was that the invasion was in defence of the 'Socialist Commonwealth'. This concept was used in the Security Council debate. It was later given a much broader base in a significant *Pravda* article on sovereignty and the international duties of socialist countries.[3] The article included the following observations. 'However, from a Marxist point of view, the norms of law, including the norms of mutual relations of the socialist countries, cannot be interpreted narrowly, formally, and in isolation from the general context of class struggle in the modern world.' A later passage reads:

Those who speak about the 'illegal actions' of the allied socialist countries in Czechoslovakia forget that in a class society there is not and there cannot be non-class laws. Laws and legal norms are subjected to the laws

[1] Webster to Fox, 24 April 1841, 29 B & F S P 1138.
[2] See M. S. McDougal and F. Feliciano *Law and Minimum World Public Order* (1961) Yale U.P., pp. 244–251.
[3] *Pravda*, 25 September 1968.

Order (1958); D. W. Bowett, *Self-Defence in International Law* (1958); I. Brownlie, *International Law and the Use of Force by States* (1963); J. L. Brierly, *The Law of Nations* (1963) (ed. Sir Humphrey Waldock).

APPENDIX 5

of the class struggle, the laws of social development . . . Formally juridical reasoning must not overshadow a class approach to the matter.

This concept, which places the furtherance of political ideology beyond the law, must be repugnant to the lawyer. It is more than any envisaged doctrine of self-defence. It implies the right of a state, without invitation, to maintain by force a political system in another state which it considers within its sphere of influence. No principle of international law can yet be said to permit such an interpretation.

The conclusion which must be drawn is that the invasion was without invitation and unjustified by treaty. Nor would it seem to fulfil the basic conditions necessary to exercise the right of self-defence, whatever the present scope of that right may be. Consequently, while this brief analysis, restricted by considerations of space, may beg more questions than it answers, it seems clear that the justifications presented by the Soviet Union and her allies for the invasion of Czechoslovakia are unconvincing as legal arguments.

Select Bibliography

V. Benes, A. Gyorgy and G. Stambuk, *Eastern European Government and Politics* (Harper Row, 1967)

A. Bromke, *Poland's Politics* (Harvard, 1967)

J. F. Brown, *The New Eastern Europe: The Khruschev Era and After* (Praeger, 1966)

R. V. Bruks, *The Dynamics of Communism in Eastern Europe* (Princeton, 1961)

Z. K. Brezezinski, *The Soviet Bloc – Unity and Conflict* (Harvard, revised and enlarged edition, 1967)

'Peace and Power', (*Encounter*, November 1969)

C. Chapman, *August 21st, The Rape of Czechoslovakia* (Cassell, 1968)

S. Fischer-Galati (ed.), *Eastern Europe in the Sixties* (Praeger, 1963)

Raymond L. Garthoff, 'The Military Establishment' (*Eastern Europe*, September 1965)

Thomson S. Harrison, *Czechoslovakia in European History* (Archon, 1965)

Herman Kahn, 'How to think about the Russians' (*Fortune* Magazine, November 1968)

M. Kaser, *COMECON – Integration Problems of the Planned Economies* (Oxford, 2nd edition, 1967)

Kurt L. London (ed.), *Eastern Europe in Transition* (John Hopkins, 1966)

R. Lowenthal, 'Why Prague is Occupied' (*Encounter*, January and February 1969)

Gordon Schilling, *The Governments of Communist East Europe* (Crowell, 1966)

H. Seton-Watson, *The East European Revolution* (3rd edition, Praeger, 1956)

Marshal V. D. Sokolovsky (ed.), *Military Strategy; Soviet Doctrine and Concepts* (Praeger, 1963)

R. F. Staar, *The Communist Regimes of Eastern Europe* (Stanford, Hoover Institution, 1967)

E. Tabarsky, *Communism in Czechoslovakia 1948–60* (Princeton, 1961)

P. Windsor and A. Roberts, *Czechoslovakia 1968. Reform, Repression and Resistence* (Chatto & Windus for the Institute for Strategic Studies, 1969)
T. W. Wolfe, *Soviet Strategy at the Crossroads* (Harvard, 1964)
The Evolving Nature of the Warsaw Pact (Rand Corporation, December 1965)
Z. A. B. Zeman, *Prague Spring, A Report of Czechoslovakia 1968* (Penguin, 1969)
Paul Zinner, *Communist Strategy and Tactics in Czechoslovakia 1918–48* (Praeger, 1963)
'Press Group of Soviet Journalists', *On Events in Czechoslovakia* (Moscow, 1968)

Index

Acheson, Dean, 184 n. 2
Action Programme, *see* Czechoslovakia
African states, voting at UN, 93, 103, 108
Agence France Presse (AFP), on Rumania, 45; on crisis, 146
Aggression and World Order, 184 n. 4
Albania, and Warsaw Pact, 32 n. 2, 151, 161; attacks invasion, 145
Aleksandrov, Mr, 141
Algeria, relations with Soviet Union, 75 n. 3, 88, 135; voting in Security Council, 93–102, 106, 143, 144, 146
Amsterdam, 143
Arabs, 13, 14, 74, 75, *see also* Middle East
Asian states, voting at UN, 103, 108
Austria, and Austrian State Treaty, 1955, 35; border with Czechoslovakia, 53; in relation to NATO; press in, 112 n. 3

Babistsky, Konstantier, 155
Bacilek, 4 n. 2, 5
Baibakov, Nikolai, 116, 160
Baldwin, Stanley, 81 n. 1
Ball, Mr, 95–9, 101
Baranski, Brigadier-General, 141
Batov, General, 50 n. 1
Beaufre, A., 66 and n. 1
Belgium, and NATO, 60, 84; and Brussels Treaty, 61 n. 2; and EURATOM, 73; reaction to invasion, 145
Belgrade, 138, 146, 156
Berlin, Conference of Foreign Ministers at, 1954, 32; Soviet moves over, 39, 71; and Berlin Wall, 39; President Johnson on, 151
Berliner Zeitung, on crisis, 130, 137
Berne, 159
Bilak, visits Moscow, May 1968, 22,
129; visits Moscow, August 1968, 145; replaced by Husak, 147; member of party Secretariat, 159
Black Sea, 75
Bohemia, 53, 158, 159
Bonn, 15, 135, 147, 149
Borba, reports Action Programme, 21 n. 3; reports Warsaw Pact meetings, 1966, 47 n. 1
Bouattoura, Mr, 98
Bowett, D. W., 184 n. 4
Brandt, Willi, 149
Bratislava, 5, 156, *for* Bratislava Declaration *see* Czechoslovakia
Brazil, voting in Security Council, 96–102, 106, 143, 145, 146, 179
Brezhnev, Mr, visits Bratislava, June 1966, 5; visits Prague, December 1968, 11, 137; foreign policy of, 12, 15; on Dubcek, 21–2, 129; on Warsaw Pact, 45, 46; visits Bucharest, May 1966, 45, 46; and 'Brezhnev doctrine', 87; at Moscow meeting, August 1968, 145; at Moscow meetting, October 1968, 154; visits Poland, November 1968, 157
Brierly, J. L., 184 n. 4
Britain, and Brussels Treaty, 61 n. 2; and NATO, 63, 66, 76, 85 and n. 1; missile bases in, 64; proposals for ANF, 67–8; and Berlin, 71 and n. 1; and non-proliferation treaty, 73–5; and Second World War, 79; and debates on 'military balance', 81 n. 1; at United Nations, 94–104, 143–6, 179; free press in, 119 n. 2; reaction to invasion, 142, 145
Brno, 21 n. 2, 127, 130
Brown, J. F., 3 n. 3, 6 n. 3, 8 n. 2
Brownlie, I., 184 n. 4
Brussels, 83, 134, 154; and Brussels Treaty, 61 and n. 2

191

INDEX

Brzezinski, B. Z., 16 n. 2
BTA, 138
Buchan, Alastair, 63 and n. 1
Bucharest, 45, 46, 142, 146; and Bucharest Declaration, 15, 33, 47, 49
Bucharest Radio, on Yakubovsky's visit to Prague, September 1968, 153
Budapest, 117, 131, 145
Budapest Radio, on Bratislava talks, 140
Bulganin, Mr, 33
Bulgaria, represented at Dresden 'confrontation', 21, 127; represented at Moscow meeting, May, 1968, 22, 129; represented at Warsaw meeting, July, 1968, 25, 133, 166; and invasion of Czechoslovakia, 30, 86, 142, 145, 183; at United Nations, 99–102; and Czech-Bulgarian Treaty of Friendship, 129, 184 n. 1; *Le Monde* on, 129; visited by Hajek, 132; hostility towards Czechoslovakia, 134, 137; relations with Rumania, 146; represented in Moscow, August 1968, 147; and Warsaw Pact, 161

Canada, 58 n. 1, 84 and n. 1, 142; voting in Security Council, 94–104, 143–6, 179
Caradon, Lord, 102, 106
Carpathia, 45
Ceausescu, President Nicolae, visits Czechoslovakia, 1968, 28, 29, 141; on Warsaw Pact, 45, 46, 54, 134; supports Czechoslovakia, 133, 142, 148; meets Tito, August, 1968, 146
Cepicka, Alexei, 4 n. 2
Cernik, Oldrich, replaces Lenart as Prime Minister, 18, 128; and Action Programme, 21 n. 2; visits Moscow, May 1968, 22, 129; returns to Prague, August 1968, 113; on Warsaw Pact, 128; on World Bank loan, 141; visits Moscow, August 1968, 145; visits Moscow, September 1968, 151; statement of 10th September 1968, 151; receives Yakubovsky, September 1968, 153; visits Moscow, October 1968, 154, 155; signs Treaty, 16th October 1968, 155; and federal legislation, 156, 160; abused by pro-Russians, 157;
on new executive committee, November 1968, 157
China, and relations with United States, 14; observes Conference on Collective Security, 1954, 32; and Warsaw Pact, 32 and n. 2; relations with Rumania, 47; *Tass* comments on, 146; and Sino-Soviet relations, *see* Soviet Union
China (Formosa), voting in Security Council, 96–102, 143, 144, 146
Chita, 155
Chou-en-lai, Mr, 46
Chudik, Mr, 4 n. 3
Churchill, Winston, 81 n. 1
Cierna-nad-Tisou meeting, *see* Czechoslovakia
Cisar, Dr Cestmir, 9, 18
Clementis trials, 3
Clifford, Mr, 149, 150, 152
Club, K–231, 22
Cluj, 148
coexistence, 13, 89, *see also* détente
Colotka, Deputy Prime Minister, 119
COMECON, 2, 19, 21, 25, 42, 46, 51, 115, 116, 159
COMECON – Integration Problems of the Planned Economies, 2 n. 1, 46 n. 1
Cominform, 48
'Committed Non-Party Persons' (KAN), 22
'Committee on Non-Military Cooperation', *see* NATO
Conference on Collective Security, 1954, 32
Congo, the, 109 n. 1
Cooper, Senator, 82, 86
CTK, 23 n. 1, 130, 135, 137, 138, 139, 141
Cuba crisis, 41, 77
Czechoslovak Communist Party, liberal-conservative struggle within, 1, 3–10, 23, 118, 129, 131; and 12th Party Congress, 4, 5, 9; and 13th Party Congress, 4 n. 3, 5, 6, 7; its supremacy questioned, 16, 17, 21, 22, 25, 120; 'democratization' of, 18 and n. 1, 22, 23, 24, 118; and 14th Party Congress, 23, 27–8, 110, 113, 139, 149, 174–5, 177; quoted at UN, 96, 99; unity during crisis,

INDEX

110, 112–13, 117, 133–4, 144, 181–2; and Central Committee Resolution, November 1968, 118, 120 and n. 1, 158; *for* Action Programme and Draft Party Statutes *see* Czechoslovakia, *see also* Czechoslovak Party Praesidium

Czechoslovak News Agency, *see CTK*

Czechoslovak Party Praesidium, members of, 4, 10, 18, 158; and disavowal of '2,000 words' manifesto, 24, 131, 176; in favour of bilateral talks, 25 and n. 2, 132, 178; criticized by Soviet Union, 26, 112, 144; conservative faction in, 29, 112 and n. 3, 127; delegation visits Moscow, October 1968, 117 n. 3; elections of, 128, 148; *Literarni Listy* appeal to, 137; *for* its reply to Warsaw Letter *see* Czechoslovakia

Czechoslovakia, position of Slovaks in, 1, 4–5, 8, 19, 122, 127, 145, 147, 156, 174; economy of, 1–8, 19, 20, 116, 121–2, 160, 174, 176; and events 1963–7, 1–11; censorship in, 4, 7, 116, 119, 149; lifting of censorship in, 7 n. 1, 18–23, 119, 129, 131, 137, 169, 176–7; mass media in, 9, 119–20, 138, 149, 153, 158, 170; view of 'democratic centralism', 10, 20, 28, 174, 177; and events January–mid-April 1968, 16–21, 127–8; and Action Programme, 18–25, 28, 48, 53, 110, 128–9, 172–3, 175–6; allegiance to Warsaw Pact, 19, 21, 23, 31, 94, 102, 115, 128, 134–5, 172; and National Assembly, 19–22, 97, 113 and n. 2, 116, 128–32, 144, 151, 155–6; and Dresden 'confrontation', 21–2, 31, 52, 127–8, 166; and May plenum, 22–3, 168, 171–7, 181; and '2,000 words' manifesto, 24, 131–3, 168, 176–7; and conflict within Warsaw Pact, 25, 31, 133, 136; and reply to Warsaw Letter, 25, 40, 134, 135, 166, 171–8; and Bratislava Declaration, 26–7, 52, 68, 80, 112, 139–41, 144, 181; and Cierna-nad-Tisou meeting, 26–9, 52, 80, 112, 137, 139–41, 144, 181; and Draft Party Statutes, 28–9, 110, 140; invasion of, 30–1, 53–5, 80, 86, 110–14, 116, 142; at Security Council, 94–9, 102–3, 106, 144–7, 182–3; and Moscow Agreement, 106, 108, 113, 150–2, 157, 181–2; at General Assembly, 107–8, 136, 152–3, 154; and erosion of Action Programme, 116, 118, 158; and events, August – December 1968, 116–20, 139–60; and trade unions, 120, 129, 175; and Treaties of Friendship, 129, 131, 141, 184 n. 1; and Czech-Soviet economic agreement, 131, 151, 159; and Treaty, 16 October 1968, 155–6; and federal legislation, 153, 156, 158, 160; and legal aspects of invasion, 183–6, *see also* Czechoslovak Communist Party

Daily Telegraph, on Warsaw Pact, 48 n. 3; on Kiev meeting, 160
Daniel, Mrs Larissa, 155
de Arechaga, Jimenez, 95 n. 1
de Gaulle, General, 70, 142, 150
de Jong, Piet, 143
'Defence of the Mediterranean and the NATO southern flank', 75 n. 2
'democratic centralism', *see* Soviet Union *and* Czechoslovakia
Denmark, voting in Security Council, 94–102, 143–6, 179
détente, 13, 61, 67–8, 70, 78–9, 88, 109, 126, 142; *see also* coexistence
Die Presse, reports Praesidium meeting, August 1968, 112
Dille, John, 37 n. 4
Dobrynin, Ambassador, 148
Documents on Disarmament, 73 n. 1
Dokumente zum Ostrecht, 36 ns. 1 and 2
Draft Party Statutes, *see* Czechoslovakia
Draper, Colonel G., vii
Dresden 'confrontation' *see* Czechoslovakia
Dubcek, Alexander, replaces Novotny as First Secretary of Czechoslovak Party, 1, 10, 127; as First Secretary of Slovak Party, 1, 48 and n. 3, 5; position in Praesidium, 4, 112 and n. 3; and Action Programme, 18, 21 and n. 2, 134; visits Moscow, January 1968, 21, 52, 127; visits Moscow, May 1968, 22, 52, 129,

193

INDEX

130; pressured to compromise, 23; disavowal of '2,000 words' manifesto by, 24, 131; and apparent defiance of Soviet threats, 26 n. 3; meets Ulbricht, August 1968, 29, 140; and NATO, 79; returns to Prague, August 1968, 113; attitude to press of, 119 n. 1; speech at Brno, March 1968, 127; speech, April 1 1968, 128; speech at Brno, June 1968, 130; broadcasts to nation, July 1968, 134; on Rochet's visit, 135; on Cierna talks, 139–40; on Bratislava talks, 139–40; attacked by *Pravda*, 144; in Moscow, August 1968, 145; speech, 28 August 1968, 147; speech, 31 August 1968, 148; speech, 1 September 1968, 149; statement of 10 September 1968, 151; on Moscow Agreement, 151; receives Yakubovsky, September 1968, 153; visits Moscow, October 1968, 154; speech 11 October 1968, 155; abused by pro-Russians, 157; on new executive committee, November 1968, 157–8; and Kiev meeting, 160

Dublin, Easter Rising in, 1

Dulles, J. Foster, 62

Dzur, General, as Minister of Defence, 49, 132, 133; visits Moscow, August 1968, 145; receives Yakubovsky, September 1968, 153; on occupation troops, 154

East German Radio, 43 n. 5

East Germany, economy of, 2; represented at Dresden, 21, 127; represented at Moscow meeting, May 1968, 22, 129; criticism of Czechoslovakia, 24, 26, 30, 128, 130, 133; represented at Warsaw meeting, July 1968, 25, 133, 166; and Warsaw Pact, 27, 32, 36, 43–4, 48, 55, 141, 149, 161, 173; and invasion, 30, 86, 142, 144, 145, 183; Friendship treaty with Soviet Union, 34; and proposals for German Confederation, 36; and Berlin Wall, 39; participation in 'Vltava' manoeuvres, 43; relations with West Germany, 71, 169, 170; at UN, 101, 102, 146; decentralization in, 121; visited by Hajek, June 1968, 131; and NATO, 134; represented at Moscow, August 1968, 147; and Czech-GDR Treaty of Friendship, 184 n. 1

Easter Rising, *see* Dublin

Eastern Europe, 37 n. 3, 50 n. 1

EEC, 72–3

Eighteen National Disarmament Committee, *see* ENDC

Eisenhower, President, 62, 64

Encounter, 16 n. 2

ENDC, 72 and n. 2, 74

Epishev, General, 22, 129, 130

Erban, Mr, 157

Ethiopia, voting in Security Council, 96–103, 106, 109, 143–4, 146

EURATOM, 73

'European Security System', 14–15, 47, 69

Evening Standard, reports on NATO and Czech crisis, 56 n. 2

Evolving Nature of the Warsaw Pact, The, 37 n. 4, 38 n. 2

Feliciano, F., 185 n. 2

'Fifty Years in Defence of Peace', 43 n. 3

'Fighting Alliance of Fraternal Peoples', 43 n. 3.

Financial Times, on Czech economy, 3 n. 1

Finland, 154

Foreign Affairs, 75 n. 2

Fortune, 17 n. 1

Fox, Mr, 185 n. 1

France, position in NATO, 15, 47, 60, 67–9, 74 n. 1, 88, 149–50, 152; and reports on crisis, 21; against European Defence Community, 61; and Brussels Treaty, 61 n. 2; against US hegemony, 66 and n. 1; relations with West Germany, 70, 136; and Berlin, 71 and n. 1; voting in Security Council, 94–102, 143–6, 179; and French Communist Party, 135; comments on invasion, 142

Franco – Prussian War, The, 81 n. 2

'Future of NATO, The', 63 n. 1

Galati, 133

Garthoff, Raymond L., 37 n. 3, 50 n. 1

Gasteyger, C., 75 n. 2

INDEX

General Assembly, reaction to Czech crisis, 92, 103–4, 107–8, 153, 154, 183; first Session, 1946, 93; and UN expenses crisis, 94 n. 1; Gromyko's address to, 3 October 1968, 96 n. 1, 103, 114, 153; and Third Committee, 103 n. 3, 104; and Committee on Friendly Relations, 104; and Special Committee on the Question of Defining Aggression, 104; and Legal Committee, 104; and 'Uniting for Peace' procedure, 107 and n. 1; *see also* United Nations
Geneva, 33, 73, 74, 159
Germany, *see* East Germany, West Germany
Germany and the Atlantic Alliance, 66 n. 2
Gierek, Edward, 123
Goldstücker, Professor, 7 n. 1
Gomulka, Mr, 15, 48, 123, 150
Goodhart, F. J., 75 n. 2
Goodrich, L. M., 184 n. 4
Grechko, Marshal, visits Czechoslovakia, May 1968, 22, 52, 130; meets General Hoffmann, 27, 141; as Commander-in-Chief of Pact forces, 37, 38, 43 n. 3; on military strategy, 44 and n. 7; as Minister of Defence, 49; visits Algeria, 1968, 135; on 'imperialism', 137; visits Prague, October 1968, 155
Greece, 75, 85
Gromyko, at UN, 96 n. 1, 103–4, 114, 153; visits Prague, October 1968, 155

Hager, Mr, 128
Hague, The, 69
Hajek, Jiri, as Foreign Minister, 97 and n. 1; 152; at Security Council, 102–3, 144, 146–7; visits Soviet Union, May 1968, 129; visits East Germany, June 1968, 131; visits Bulgaria, July 1968, 132
Hambro, E., 184 n. 4
Hammarskjold, Dag, 109 n. 1
Hamouz, Mr, 18, 151
Harmel, Pierre, *see* NATO
Harrison, Sir Geoffrey, viii
Havel, Vaclac, 18 n. 1
Havelka, Mr, 119–20
Healey, Dennis, 85 n. 1, 123 n. 3

Hejzlar, Mr, 153
Hendrych, Jiri, 7, 18, 127
Higgins, Dr Rosalyn, viii
Hill, Professor R. V., 81 n. 1
Hitler, Adolf, 97
Hoffmann, General, 27, 43, 141
'How to think about the Russians', 17 n. 1
Howard, M. E., 81 n. 2
Humanité, on Rumania, 45 n. 6
Hungary, and events of 1956, 3, 24, 31, 35, 52, 58 and n. 1, 94, 98 and n. 1, 100, 107, 132; represented at Dresden meeting, 21, 127; represented at Moscow meeting, May 1968, 22, 129; represented at Warsaw meeting, July 1968, 25, 133, 166; and invasion, 30, 86, 142, 145, 183; Soviet troops in, 35; participation in 'Vltava' manoeuvres, 43; position in Warsaw Pact, 48, 51, 161; attitude to Czechoslovak crisis, 48 and n. 2, 51, 134–5, 137–8, 140; voting in Security Council, 94–102, 108, 143, 144, 146; economic reforms in, 121; and Czech-Hungarian Treaty of Friendship, 131, 184 n. 1; relations with Britain, 145; represented in Moscow, August 1968, 147
Hunt, Brigadier Kenneth, viii
Husak, Mr, trial of, 5; visits Moscow, August 1968, 145; as First Secretary of Slovak Party, 147; and statement of 10th September 1968, 151; on mass media, 153; visits Moscow, October 1968, 154; on new executive committee, November 1968, 157

IAEA, *see* International Atomic Energy Agency
India, 33; voting in Security Council, 93–102, 106, 143, 144, 146
Indra, Mr, 145, 159
International Atomic Energy Agency, 73
International Conciliation, 63 n. 1
International Court of Justice, *see* General Assembly
International Law and the Use of Force by States, 184 n. 4
'International Year for Human Rights' *see* United Nations

195

INDEX

Israel, 74, 75, 169
Italy, and NATO, 58 n. 1, 85, 144; accedes to Brussels Treaty, 61; missile bases in, 64; and EURATOM, 73; maritime supply lines to, 75; reaction to invasion, 144, 145
Izvestia, reports on Warsaw Pact meeting, March 1961, 39 n. 1; and 'Fifty Years in Defence of Peace', 43 n. 3; attacks Pavel, 136; announces military exercises, July 1968, 136; attacks Ceausescu, 146; announces postponement of 14th Party Congress, 149; attacks Dr Sik, 152; approves developments, November 1968, 158

Japan, 103 n. 4
Javoruna, 135
Jesenica, Zora, 18 n. 1
Johnson, President, and non-proliferation treaty, 74; and speech, 30th August 1968, 87, 89, 148; and speech, 11th September 1968, 151
June War, 1967, 14, 75

Kadar, Mr, 139
Kahn, Herman, 17 n. 1
KAN, *see* 'Committed Non-Party Persons'
Karlovy Vary, meeting of Ulbricht and Dubcek at, August 1968, 29, 140; meeting at, April, 1967; Declaration of, 69 and n. 2
Kaser, M., 2 n. 1, 46 n. 1
Kashmir dispute, 93
Kekkonen, President, 154
Kelsen, H., 184 n. 4
Kennedy, President, 40–1, 65, 81 n. 3
Kiesinger, Chancellor, 71, 147, 149, 153
Kiev, 134; meeting at, December 1968, 116, 159, 160
Kissinger, Dr, ix, 64 n. 2, 65 and n. 1
Kohler, Mr, 4 n. 2
Kolesnichenko, Mr, 141
Komocsin, Zoltan, 140
Konev, Marshal, 37, 161
Kosygin, Mr, foreign policy of, 12, 15; visits Czechoslovakia, May 1968, 22, 52, 130; and non-proliferation treaty, 74; visits Stockholm, July 1968, 133; at Moscow meeting, August 1968, 145; at Moscow meeting, October 1968, 154; visits Finland, 1968, 154; signs Treaty, 16 October 1968, 155
Kouchy, Vladimir, 22, 129
Koivisto, Prime Minister, 154
Krasnaya Zvezda, *see Red Star*
Khruschev, Nikita; and Marxism-Leninism, 12; successors of, 13; and NATO, 15; visits United States, 37; military thinking of, 37–40, 44; and Eastern Europe, 115
Kucera, Mr, 145
Kulturny Zivot, and criticism of Novotny régime, 5; and 'The Rights of the Citizen', 18 n. 1
Kuznetsov, V., 117, 150

Lange, Halvard, 58 n. 1
Latin America, and United Nations, 93, 103
Law and Minimum World Public Order, 185 n. 2
Law of Nations, The, 184 n. 4
Law of the United Nations, The, 184 n. 4
Lederer, Prof. Ivo, viii
Lenart, Mr, 5, 18, 128
Lidova Demokracie, denounced by *Pravda*, 118 n. 2; on support for Dubcek, 158
Lippman, Walter, 68
Lisbon, 64
Literarni Listy, and 'On the Subject of Opposition', 181 n. 1; attacks Soviet Union, 28; publishes '2,000 words', 131; address to Praesidium, 137; and 'From Warsaw to Bratislava', 140
Literarni Noviny, reports 4th Writers' Congress, 7 and n. 2
Literaturnaya Gazeta, attacks '2,000 words', 132; attacks *Literarni Listy*, 141
Litvinov, Pavel, 155
Lomakin, Mr, 152
Lomsky, General Bohumir, 43, 53 and n. 2, 128
London, viii, 74, 142
Luxembourg, and Brussels Treaty, 61 n. 2; and EURATOM, 73
Lvov, 134

INDEX

McDougal, M. S., 185 n. 2
McNamara, Robert S., 63, 64 n. 1, 65 and n. 2, 68, 75 n. 3
Malik, Mr, at United Nations, 94–8, 100, 102, 106
Malinovsky, Marshal, 40, 50 n. 1
Manchester Guardian, reports Brezhnev on Warsaw Pact, 45 n. 2
Mansfield, Senator, 150
Maritime Air Forces Mediterranean (MARAIRMED), *see* NATO
Martino, Dr Gaetano, 58 n. 1
Marxism-Leninism, Czech loyalty to, 8, 10, 11, 154, 177, 181; as interpreted by Soviet Union, 12, 141, 166, 167, 170, 185; and revisionism, 121 n. 1, 138
Masaryk, Jan, 97
Mazyar Hirlap, on Czech situation, July 1968, 138
Meissner, Mr, 36 ns. 1 and 2
Mers-el-Kebir, 88
Middle East, 14, 70, 74, 93, 100, 111, 169
Military Balance, The, 50 n. 2
'Military Establishment, The', 37 n. 3
Military Strategy – Soviet Doctrine and Concepts, 40–2, 54 and n. 2
Mlada Fronta, publishes '2,000 words', 131; on Soviet aid, 160
Moczar, General, 123
Molotov, Mr, 32
Monat, Pavel, 37 n. 4
Monde, Le, reports Brezhnev's concern over Czech developments, 22 n. 1; on Polish riots, March 1968, 122 n. 1; reports CPSU meeting, April 23 1968, 129, 130
Moravia, 158
Morning Star, on invasion, 117 n. 1; on Polish riots, March 1968, 122 n. 2
Moscow, Dubcek's visit, January 1968, 21, 22, 52, 127; Dubcek's visit, May 1968, 22, 52, 129, 130; view of Tito and Ceausescu, 28; Ulbricht's report, August 1968, 29; as seat of Warsaw Pact organizations, 34, 37, 39, 47, 48, 50, 156, 161; 81 – Party meeting, November 1960, 38; Soviet-Czechoslovak friendship rally, September 1965, 45; relations with Rumania, 45–6; non-proliferation treaty signed, 74; Svoboda's visit, August 1968, 103, 106, 108, 113, 145–7; and World Communist Conference, 117, 153; visit of Czech delegation, October 1968, 117 and n. 3; and Aeroflot, 149; economic talks, September 1968, 151; Dubcek's visit, October 1968, 154; Cernik's visit, October 1968, 155; *for* Moscow Agreement *see* Czechoslovakia, *see also* Soviet Union
'Moscow and the Mediterranean', 75 n. 2
Moscow Radio, criticisms of Czechoslovakia, 24 n. 4; and Brezhnev on Warsaw Pact, 45 n. 2; attacks Dr Sik, 118 n. 2
MTI, publishes reply to Warsaw Letter, 135
Mulley, F. W., 63 and n. 3
Muzik, Mr, at United Nations, 96–7, 99

Nagy, Imre, 35, 115
National Democratic Party, *see* NPD
NATO, stresses within, vii, 15, 48; proposal to disband, 15; and Paris Agreements, October 1954, 32, 33, 61, 162; in relation to Warsaw Pact, 33, 39, 49–50, 62, 75, 83, 91, 156–7; military role of, 43, 44, 47, 50, 61–8; view of Soviet Union, 56, 58, 61–7, 70, 77, 87–91; purposes of, 56–7, 184 n. 2; political function of, 57–61; and 'Committee on Non-Military Co-operation', 58; and Harmel Report, 60, 69–70, 126; and 'Report of the Future Tasks of the Alliance', 61 n. 1; and MLF/ANF debate, 67–8; and Nuclear Planning Group (NPG), 68 n. 1; and Nuclear Defence Affairs Committee, 68 n. 1 and Military Committee 68, 82; and SHAPE, 68–9; and Defence College, 69; and SACLANT, 69; during pre-crisis period, 69–76; and MARAIR-MED, 76; and *NATO Letter*, October 1968, 76 n. 1; during Czechoslovak crisis, 76–82, 121, 134, 142, 144, 145, 146, 147; and Political Committee, 77; and 'military balance',

197

INDEX

80–2, 83, 86, 156; and military consequences of crisis, 82–6, 148–53; and political consequences of crisis, 86–91, 116, 125; *see also* North Atlantic Council.
NATO and Europe, 66 n. 1
'NATO Latest No. 4', 86 n. 1
NATO Letter (October 1968), *see* NATO
Nepszabadsag, on Czech Action Programme, 48 n. 1, 51 n. 1; on Czech situation, July 1968, 134, 136
Netherlands, and Brussels Treaty, 61 n. 2; and EURATOM, 73; and NATO, 85; comments on invasion, 143
Neue Zurcher Zeitung, on Warsaw Pact, 37 n. 2; on Rumania, 45 n. 6, 47 n. 3
Neues Deutschland, and 'The Strategy of Imperialism and the Czechoslovak Socialist Republic', 24 n. 3, 133; on Socialist internationalism, 30 n. 2, 142; quotes Bulganin on Warsaw Pact, 33 n. 2; reports E. German Defence Minister on Warsaw Pact, 44 n. 3; and 'Overcome Mistakes so as to strengthen the Socialist worker-peasant power', 138
New Directions in the Soviet Economy, 123 n. 1
New Eastern Europe, The, 3 n. 3, 6 n. 3, 8 n. 2
New York Times, on Rumania, 45 n. 6; on NATO, 150
Nixon, President, 81 n. 3
'Non-Military Co-operation in NATO', *see* North Atlantic Council
North Atlantic Council, procedure of, 50, 59, 60, 80, 85; and 'Non-Military Co-operation in NATO', 58–60; and Defence Planning Committee, 67, 69, 83, 149; action over Berlin, 1968, 71; discusses arms control, 1968, 74; discusses Mediterranean situation,75; discusses Czechoslovak crisis, 77, 142, 145, 154; *see also* NATO
North Atlantic Pact, The, 184 n. 2
North Atlantic Treaty, *see* NATO
Norway, 58 n. 1, 85, 144
Nova Mysl, and writings of Dr Sik, 6

Novomesky, Mr, 5
Novotny, Antonin, downfall of, 1, 10–11, 18, 23, 77, 127, 130; movement against, 2–10, 25, 121, 122, 123, 173; attitude towards Rumania, 48; and trade unions, 120
NPD, *see* West Germany

Observer, on Czech crisis, 56 n. 2; on Polish Party Congress, November 1968, 121 n. 1; on Polish riots, March 1968, 122 n. 1
Omsk, 155
'On the Subject of Opposition', 18 n.1
Ottawa, 67

Pakistan, voting in Security Council, 93–102, 106, 143, 144, 146
PAP, *see* Polish Radio
Paraguay, voting in Security Council, 94–102, 106, 143–6, 179
Paris, 37, 38, 58 n. 1, 70, 142; *for* Paris Agreements *see* NATO
Pavel, Josef, 136
Pavlovski, General, 53
'Peace and Power', 16 n. 2
Pearson, Lester B., 58 n. 1
Pelikan, Jiri, 9, 153, 159
Peprny, General Karel, 136
Pesic, D., viii
Peter, Mr, 144
Piller, Mr, 145
Pleskot, Mr, 107
Podgorny, President, 22, 129, 145, 154
Polacek, Mr, 120
Poland, economy of, 2; events of 1956, 3, 35; represented at Dresden 'confrontation', 21, 127; represented at Moscow meeting, May 1968, 22, 129; criticisms of Czechoslovakia, 24, 129, 133, 137; represented at Warsaw meeting, July 1968, 25, 133, 166; and invasion, 30, 86, 142, 145, 183; and Pact manoeuvres, 43 and n. 4, 44, 131; and Warsaw Pact, 48, 161, 164, 165; at UN, 101; and Party Congress, November 1968, 121 n. 1; comments on Czech economic reforms, 121; recent disturbances in, 121–3; and Writers' Union, 122; restricts travel to

INDEX

Czechoslovakia, 136; represented in Moscow, August 1968, 147; visited by Brezhnev, November 1968, 157; and Czech-Polish Treaty of Friendship, 184 n. 1
Polish Free Press, on invasion, 112 n. 2
Polish Radio (PAP), on Warsaw Pact manoeuvres, October 1962, 43 n. 4; on nuclear sharing, 44 n. 6; on student riots, March 1968, 122 n. 1; on Polish economy, 122 n. 3; on Czech crisis
Political Consultative Committee (Warsaw Pact), meets, March 1968, 31, 49, 52, 127; meets, January 1956, 32, 34, 36; function of, 33–4, 46, 49–50, 51; meets, May 1958, 33, 36, 44; meets, February 1960, 37; meets, March 1961, 39; meets, January, 1965, 44, 45; meets, July 1966, 47; *see also* Warsaw Pact
Politics of Western Defence, The, 63 n. 3
Politika, 119
Politika Express, and 'Support for Prague with heart and mind', 138
Pompidou, Mr, 66 n. 1
Potsdam, Four-Power Agreement, 35
Prace, on Epishev, 129; publishes '2,000 words', 131; on arms cache, 135; on support for Smrkovsky, 159; supports Dr Sik, 159
Prague, City Conference of, 23 n. 1; and publication of '2,000 words', 24; occupation of, 30, 86; Warsaw Pact meeting, January 1956, 32; 14th Party Congress, 113; visited by Baibakov, December 1968, 116, 160; visited by Kuznetsov, 117, 150; journalists meeting, November, 1968, 119 n. 2; visited by Rochet, July 1968, 135; US Embassy in, 147; Treaty signed in, 16th October 1968, 155; demonstrations in, November 1968, 157; *see also* Czechoslovakia
Prague Radio, and Dresden 'confrontation', 21 and n. 4; on '2,000 words', 24 n. 1; on bilateral talks, 25 n. 2; on 'Vltava' manoeuvres, 44 n. 1; reports on Warsaw Pact, 49 ns. 1–3; on 1968 Warsaw Pact manoeuvres, 53 n. 3; on Resolution of November 1968, 118 n. 3; reports on censorship, 119 and n. 2; on situation in Czechoslovakia, July 1968, 132; on occupation troops, 139; on Yakubovsky's arrival, 153
Pravda, on Action Programme, 21 and n. 5; on '2,000 words' manifesto, 24 and n. 2, 132, 133; on 'discovery' of arms cache, 26 and n. 2, 134, 135; on 'democratic centralism', 28, 140; on Warsaw Pact, 34 n. 3, 55 and n. 2, 115 n. 1; reports Soviet demobilization, 37 n. 1; reports Warsaw Pact moves, 1961, 39 ns. 2–4; and 'Fighting Alliance of Fraternal Peoples', 43 n. 3; reports Khruschev on West Germany, 44 n. 4; reports Marshal Grechko on defence, 44 n. 7; reports Brezhnev on Warsaw Pact, 45 n. 3; and 'Unity – the source of our strength', 49; on 'Socialist Commonwealth', 96 n. 1, 185 and n. 3; on invasion, 112, 113 n. 2, 114 and n. 1, 115, 144, 147, 149; criticisms of Czech press, 117 n. 2, 118 n. 2, 129, 141, 151; criticisms of Czech party leaders, 136, 157; attacks Dr Sik, 137; on 'revisionism', 138, 144, 152; suspends attacks, 1st August 1968, 139; on Bratislava talks, 140, 144; and 'Loyalty to international duty', 141; and 'Blatant outbursts of reaction', 141; on Cierna talks, 144; on Yugoslavia, 152; on world Communist movement, 153
Prchlik, General Vaclav, 48, 132; and criticism of Warsaw Meeting, July 1968, 26, 53, 133, 136, 137

Rabotnichesko Delo, and 'The counter-revolution should be routed', 134; on Czechoslovak crisis, 138; on Bratislava talks, 140
Radio Free Europe, and Ermath Research Report, 44 n. 5; and 'New Warsaw Pact Commander likely to be Soviet', 49 n. 4
Radio Free Slovakia, on collaborators, 147
Rapacki plan, 36
realpolitik, 126

199

INDEX

Red Star, on Czechoslovak crisis, 30 and n. 1, 135; on Warsaw Pact, 43, 53 n. 2, 132; attacks Prchlik, 136; and 'Our common concern and common responsibility', 141

'Remnants of Dogmatism in Political Economy must be overcome, The', 6

Report of the Czechoslovak Central Authority State Control and Statistics on the Development of the Czechoslovak National Economy for the First Half of 1962, 3 and n. 1

Reporter, 119

Reykjavik, 75, 83

Richardson, J. L., 66 n. 2

'Rights of the Citizen, The', 18 n. 1

Rochet, Waldeck, 135

Roshchin, Mr, 73

Rude Pravo, on Czech economy, 3 n. 1, 6 n. 3; on bilateral talks, 25 n. 2; on 1968 Warsaw Pact manoeuvres, 53 n. 3; reports Praesidium meeting, 20th August 1968, 112 n. 3; reports Kiev meeting, December 1968, 116 n. 2 159; on reform of Warsaw Pact command, 133; reports Dr Sik on Brezhnev, 137, reports Dr Sik on *Pravda*, 137; on relations between Communist parties, 138; reports Draft Party Statutes, 140; on invasion, 150; defends Dr Sik, 152

Rumania, and COMECON, 2, 42, 46; and relations with West Germany, 15, 48; comments on Action Programme, 21; ommission from meeting of party leaders of invading states, 22 and n. 2, 52, 128; Soviet troops in, 35; Party Congress of June, 1960, 38; moves towards autonomy, 42–3, 115; and Warsaw Pact, 44, 45–9, 51, 52, 54, 161; National Assembly of, 45 n. 4; and Declaration of April, 1964, 46 n. 1; and relations with China, 47, 146; in relation to NATO, 87, 146; decentralization in, 121; support for Czechoslovakia, 133, 141, 145, 146, 148; and Czech-Rumanian Treaty of Friendship, 141; attacked by *Tass*, 146; and relations with Yugoslavia, 146

Rusk, Dean, 134, 148; at UN, 104

Rusov, General, 156

Russia, *see* Soviet Union

Rybar, Dr, 158

SACLANT, *see* NATO

Sadovsky, Mr, 157

San Antonio, speech at 30th August 1968, 87, 89, 148

Schapino, Prof. Leonard, viii

Scinteia, reports Ceausescu on Warsaw Pact, 45 n. 5; reports Bucharest Declaration, July 1966, 47 ns. 4 and 5; reports Ceausescu on Czechoslovakia, 133; reports Warsaw Letter and reply, 135; and 'Full Confidence in the Czechoslovak People, in its Communist Party', 135; and 'The road to strengthening the unity of the Socialist countries', 138

Second World War, 43, 53, 72 n. 1, 79, 182

Security Council, function of, 72 n. 1, 105, 163, 184; reaction to Czechoslovak crisis, 80, 92–4, 105–8, 112, 125, 147, 183–5; Draft Resolution of 22 August, 94–101, 143–4, 179–80; Draft Resolution of 23 August, 101–3, 145, 146, 180; Moscow communiqué reference to, 182; *see also* United Nations

Self-Defence in International Law, 184 n. 4

Senegal, voting at Security Council, 96–102, 106, 143–6, 179

Shahi, Mr, 93

SHAPE, *see* NATO

Sharp, Mr, 142

Shtemenko, General, 27, 53

Sik, Dr Ota, as member of Central Committee, 3; proposals for economic reform, 3, 6 and n. 3, 7; as Deputy Prime Minister, 18; resignation of, 116, 149; attacked by *Tass*, 116; attacked by Moscow Radio, 118 n. 2; attacked by *Pravda*, 137; defended in *Rude Pravo*, 152; attacked by *Izvestia*, 152; moves to Switzerland, 156, 159

Siroky, Mr, 4 n. 2, 5

Slansky trials, 3

Slovakia, *see* Czechoslovakia

Smidmajer, Josef, 119–20, 159

INDEX

Smrkovsky, Mr, as chairman of National Assembly, 22, 129; visits Moscow, May 1968, 22, 129; criticized by Hager, 128; visits Soviet Union, June 1968, 130, 131; criticism of '2,000 words', 132; on Cierna talks, 139; on Moscow Agreement, 148, 152; statement of 10 September 1968, 151; speech, 23 September 1968, 152; on new executive committee, November 1968, 157; absent from Kiev talks, 159
'Socialist Commonwealth', see Soviet Union
Sofia, 31, 48 n. 4, 49, 127
Sokolovsky, Marshal, 40 and n. 1, 54 and n. 2
South-East Asia, 14, 100
Soviet News, 43 n. 2, 45 n. 1
Soviet Strategy at the Crossroads, 38 n. 1, 42 n. 1
Soviet Union, economy of, 2, 176; foreign policy of, 12–16, 90–1, and spheres of influence, 13, 125; presence in Mediterranean, 14, 75, 88; and Sino-Soviet relations, 14, 38 and n. 1, 43; dilemma over Czechoslovakia, 16–18, 30, 52–3; view of 'democratic centralism', 20, 25, 140, 167, 170; pre-invasion pressure on Czechoslovakia, 21–2, 23, 24–9, 52, 77; utilization of Warsaw Pact, 31, 42–51, 53–6, 125, 130, 166; and conclusion of Warsaw Pact, 32–5, 161; and Declaration of 30 October 1956, 35, 178; and 20th Party Congress, 35; military presence in Eastern Europe, 35–7, 86, 169; military strategy of, 37–42; and Berlin, 39, 71; and post-invasion policy, 68, 113–14, 116–18, 43–60, 181–2; and disarmament, 72–5, 78–9; and 'Socialist Commonwealth', 87, 95, 96 n. 1, 103–4, 114–16, 121, 124, 183, 185; at Security Council, 93–103, 106–7, 112, 143–4, 146, 179–90; at General Assembly, 103–4; reasons for invasion, 110–13, 114–16; and US cultural agreement, 149; and Czech economic agreement, 151; and Soviet protests against invasion, 155; and Treaty, 16 October 1968, 155–6; and Czech-Soviet Treaty of Friendship, 184 n. 1; and legal aspects of invasion, 183, 186; *for* Moscow Agreement *see* Czechoslovakia
Spacek, Josef, 127
Spy in the US, 37 n. 4
Spychalski, General, 43
Stalin, Josef, death and denunciation of, 3, 33, 115, 123; victims of, 4; interpretation of Marxism-Leninism, 12, 121; and 'democratic centralism', 20; East European defence under, 34
Stephens, James, 1
Stewart, Michael, 104 and n. 2, 145
Stockholm, 133
Stone, J., 184 n. 4
'Strategy of Imperialism and the Czechoslovak Socialist Republic, The', 24
Strougal, Dr, 157
Suez crisis, 58 and n. 1, 107
Supplementary Statement on British Defence Policy (July 1968), 76 n. 2
Supreme Headquarters Allied Powers in Europe, *see* SHAPE
Survival, 69 n. 2
Svoboda, President, replaces Novotny as President, 10, 18; quoted at UN, 96; visits Moscow, August 1968, 103, 113, 145–7; supported by National Assembly, 113, 144; on Czech policy, 118 n. 1, 135, 155; at Cierna talks, 137; on Action Programme, 147; accepts Sik's resignation, 149; statement of 10 September 1968, 151; receives Yakubovsky, September 1968, 153; ratifies Treaty, 16 October 1968, 155, signs federal bill, 27 October 1968, 156; on new executive committee, November 1968, 157
Switzerland, 156
Syria, 75 n. 3

Tanyug, quotes Tito on Czechoslovakia, 132
Tass, on Dubcek's visits to Moscow, 22, 129; on invasion, 95, 103, 142; on Dr Sik, 116, 149; announces July talks, 134; publishes address to

201

INDEX

Czech 'brothers', 145; attacks Rumania, 146; attacks Yugoslavia, 146, 152; attacks Czech press, 151, 152; on 'imperialism', 153; on Kiev meeting, 159

Times, The, reports Warsaw Pact manoeuvres and meetings, 44 n. 2, 45 ns. 1 and 2, 47 n. 2, 48 n. 4, reports on Rumania, 47 n. 3 and 5, reports on Communist Conference, 51 n. 1; on Yakubovsky's tour, 55 n. 1; on invasion, 117 n. 1; on Polish Party Congress, November 1968, 121 n. 1; on Czech refugees, 158

Tito, President, visits Czechoslovakia, 28–9, 140; on Czechoslovakia, 132; meets Ceausescu, August 1968, 146

Treaty of Collective Security (all-European), 32, 33

Troubled Partnership, The, 64 n. 2, 65 n. 1

Trudeau, Pierre, 84 n. 1

Trybuna Ludu, criticizes Czechoslovakia, 133; on Bratislava talks, 140

Trygve Lie, 109 n. 1

Turkey, 64, 75, 85, 145

'Turning-Point in Czechoslovakia', 4 n. 1, 6 n. 1

'2,000 words' manifesto, *see* Czechoslovakia

U Thant, *see* United Nations, Secretary-General of,

UAR, 75 n. 3, 103 n. 4

Ulbricht, Mr, 15, 29, 52, 140

UNESCO, *see* United Nations

L'Unita, interview with Roshchin, 73 and n. 1

United Nations, NATO allegiance to, 57; and Middle East crisis, 70; Charter of, 72 and n. 1, 92–8, 101 n. 2, 104–6, 132, 142, 162–3, 179, 183–5; and Secretary-General, 92, 108–9, 143, 180; function of, 92–3, 105, 124–5; during Czech crisis, vii, 92–105, 125, 143–6, 152, 154, 180; and 'International Year for Human Rights', 103 n. 3, 104; and UNESCO Conference, 1968, 104; verdict on its handling of crisis, 105–9; and conference of nonnuclear states, 149; *see also* Security Council, General Assembly

United States, relations with Soviet Union, 13–15, 79, 89, 111, 134, 149; and Vietnam War, 14, 47, 79, 169; and alleged presence in Czechoslovakia, 22, 26, 130, 134–5; visited by Khruschev, 37; military strategy of, 40–1; and NATO, 41, 50, 61–9, 78, 86, 116–17, 136, 149–52, 184 n. 2; proposals for MLF, 67–8; and Berlin, 71 and n. 1, 151; and nonproliferation treaty, 72–5; in Mediterranean, 75, 87; and 'military balance', 81 n. 3, 82, 156; at United Nations, 93–106, 143–6, 179; and spheres of influence, 13, 125; and CIA, 134; comments on invasion, 142, 147, 148

Urchatz, 146

USSR, *see* Soviet Union

U-2 incident, 38

Vaculik, Ludvik, 24, 131

Valka, Josef, 28, 140

Vecerni Praha, reports on crisis, 131

Vienna, 73, 160

Vietnam, 13–14, 17, 47, 79, 111

Vintera, Mr, 160

'Vltava' manoeuvres, *see* Warsaw Pact

Voting and the Handling of Disputes in the Security Council, 95 n. 1

Waniolka, Mr, 122 n. 3

Warsaw, and Warsaw Letter, 25–7, 48, 52–3, 133–9, 166–71, 178; and conclusion of Warsaw Pact there, 32, 165; Warsaw Pact meeting, January 1965, 44; University of, 122; *for* reply to Warsaw Letter *see* Czechoslovakia

Warsaw Pact, role in Czechoslovak crisis, vii, 29–31, 51–4, 80, 111, 124, 142, 145–54; proposal to disband, 15; manoeuvres in Czechoslovakia, 1968, 22, 24–5, 27, 31, 130–2, 169, 173, 184; Articles of, 26 and n. 1, 161–5, 184 and n. 3; development of, 1955–68, 31–51; and 'Vltava' manoeuvres, 43; immediate future

INDEX

World Bank, 141
World Communist Conference, 16 n. 1, 17, 117, 153
World Today, The, 4 n. 1, 6 n. 1
World Youth Festival, 137

Yakubovsky, Marshal, as Warsaw Pact Commander-in-Chief, 43 n. 3, 49, 54, 156; tour of Warsaw Pact countries, 48, 55, 153
Yalta agreements, 142
Yemen, 75 n. 3
Yugoslavia, interest in Action Programme, 21; and reports on Warsaw Pact meetings, 47; and relations with West Germany, 71; in relation to NATO, 87, 89, 146; at UN, 101, 107; support of Czechoslovakia, 132, 146; Hajek visits, August 1968, 144; and relations with Rumania, 146; attacked by *Tass*, 152; attacked by *Pravda*, 152

Zalyzi, 152
Zaruba, 148
Zednik, Josef, 131
Zemedelske Noviny, publishes '2,000 words' manifesto, 131
Zhivkov, Mr, 144
Zhukov, Yurg, 141
Zolnierz Wolnosci, on Czechoslovak crisis, 137
Zycie Warszawy, on Czechoslovak crisis, 138

Washington, 74, 134, 142, 148, 149
Webster, Mr, 185 and n. 1
West Germany, relations with Eastern Europe, 15, 16, 46-7, 70-2, 123 n. 1, 132, 138, 169, 172; alleged presence in Czechoslovakia, 22, 112, 130, 133, 137; border with Czechoslovakia, 26, 53, 78, 134, 136, 152, 159; and NATO, 32, 44, 61-3, 67-8, 83-5, 152-3, 162; and relations with Rumania, 48, 71; accedes to Brussels Treaty, 61; military strength of, 66 and n. 2, 67-8, 83-4, 150; and the Bundestag, 70, 71, 153; and Declaration of 13 December 1966, 70 n. 1; and relations with Yugoslavia, 71; and relations with East Germany, 71, 169; and West Berlin, 71 and n. 1; and NPD, 71; and non-proliferation treaty, 73; and EUR-ATOM, 73; during Czechoslovak crisis, 82, 144, 146; economic and political expansion of, 111; comments on invasion, 143, 147
Western European Union (WEU), 61, 63, 75 n. 2, 162
Winter, Kamil, viii
Winzer, Otto, 131
Wolfe, T., 37 n. 4, 38 ns. 1 and 2, 42 n. 1

of, 54-5, 56, 125, 156; equated with 'Socialist Commonwealth', 115; in relation to NATO, *see* NATO, *see also* Political Consultative Committee

H 80/No EN

WITHDRAWN